Critical Writing for Embodied Approaches

Elizabeth Mackinlay

Critical Writing for Embodied Approaches

Autoethnography, Feminism and Decoloniality

Elizabeth Mackinlay
School of Education
The University of Queensland
St Lucia, QLD, Australia

ISBN 978-3-030-04668-2   ISBN 978-3-030-04669-9   (eBook)
https://doi.org/10.1007/978-3-030-04669-9

Library of Congress Control Number: 2018964565

This Palgrave Macmillan imprint is published by the registered company Springer Nature Switzerland AG
The registered company address is: Gewerbestrasse 11, 6330 Cham, Switzerland

Who are I?
To the others: for you

For Macsen and Hamish and the girls

Acknowledgments

This is the book I did not want to write; it is the book I thought I could not write, that my words and worlds were lost forever, and yet, here it is. There are many words in this book but there is one word as two that needs to be written, a word that once written can but hope to touch the meaning it holds—thank you. Thank you Eleanor Christie, Rebecca Wyde, Natasha Innes and Renee Jarratt for your patience and compassion. Thank you Ailie McDowall, Julie Bower and Linda Willis for your open doors and hearts. Thank you to my comrades in arms Susan Monk, Lachlan Hurse and David Szumer. Thank you to my Yanyuwa family; always already *kundiyarra*. Thank you running babes Claire Backhouse, Janine Roberts and Jane Fisher for making sure I did not record a DNF (did not finish) in words and the world. Thank you Keith Mackinlay, Lyn Mackinlay, John Barlow, Debbie Walsh and Sally Cross, for carrying my words and worlds when I couldn't. Thank you Pamela Burnard, Anne Harris, Stacy Holman Jones, Fetaui Iosefo and Briony Lipton for holding me close even though you are far away. Thank you sister girl Sandra Rennie, simply thank you, and to John Rennie the same. Thank you my BFF Lily Terzo for your beautiful presence and drawing, and your brothers Noah and Finn for making room in your lives for our blend of seven. Thank you Rusty-James Holden, for the lists and the love you bring. Thank you Macsen Douglas and Hamish Alexander, you keep my words and my world still breathing.

Contents

About the Author

Elizabeth (Liz) Mackinlay is an Associate Professor in the School of Education at the University of Queensland where she teaches Research Methods, Gender Studies and Arts Education. She holds a PhD in Ethnomusicology from The University of Adelaide and a PhD in Education from the University of Queensland. Her book, *Teaching and learning like a feminist: Storying our experiences in higher education* was published by Sense Publishers in 2016 and together with Briony Lipton, she co-authored the 2017 Palgrave publication, *We only talk feminist here: Feminist academics, voice and agency in the neo-liberal university*. In 2007 she published her Education PhD as a book, *Disturbances and dislocations: Teaching and learning Aboriginal women's music and dance* with Peter Lang and has co-edited a number of books since then including *Musical islands: Exploring connections between music, place and research* (2009), *Applied ethnomusicology: Historical and contemporary approaches* (2010), *The Routledge international handbook of intercultural arts* (2015).

Liz is currently involved in a number of research projects which include decoloniality and education, critical autoethnography as heartline work, and feminism in higher education. She has professional associations with the Australian Women's and Gender Studies Association, the Australian Association for Research in Education, the Association for Qualitative Research, and Contemporary Ethnography Across the Disciplines.

Liz's passion for her academic work flows into all areas of her life. Alongside reading-writing-thinking-wondering-drawing, she can be found regularly running the streets of her hometown with her girlfriends. Liz is a material girl at heart who enjoys making quilts and all manner of clothing to wrap around those she loves. She enjoys spending long, lazy and lovely weekends with her beautiful and blended family; drinking coffee on the back deck with a crossword, baking anything that has chocolate as a main ingredient, watching her boys play football, binging on the her latest Netflix addiction, and relaxing in the loving arms of her partner in the warmth of their home.

List of Figures

1

A-Way of Writing, the Way it is Written

*How am I to begin it? And what is to be? I feel no great impulse; no fever,
only a great pressure of difficulty. Why write it then? Why write at all? Every
morning I write a little sketch to amuse myself. I am not saying, I might say,
that these sketches have any relevance. I am not trying to tell a story. Yet
perhaps it might done in that way. A mind thinking.*
Woolf ([Diary entry 28 May, 1929], 1980, p. 229)
*Nothing was changed; nothing was different save only—here I listened with
all my ears not entirely to what was being said, but to the murmur or current
behind it. Yes, that was it—the change was there.*
Woolf (1929/2001, p. 13)

© The Author(s) 2019
E. Mackinlay, *Critical Writing for Embodied Approaches*,
https://doi.org/10.1007/978-3-030-04669-9_1

Fig. 1.1 And what is it to be, this book I don't write?

1.

I have a friend who loves making lists and music. He is a lover of music and making lists about the music he loves is a way to bring them closer to him; to the ways he might come to know such loved music, to how he might begin to understand the music he loves, and what he might then do with all of this understanding, knowledge and love of music all packaged up together in one neat list. One list made then becomes two, three and more; the next list is always already another list of the lists of loved music he has made. The lists he makes are made with a love of music which is naked and wanting, stripped and seeking, through a system of prompts and processes which put into motion which songs, albums and music make it onto this list or that. There is a list for the top rated 200 albums of all time; a list of songs with one, two, three, four and five stars pasted next to them; a list of music in a folder on his laptop with the tag "No, not ever". And there is a list of songs, albums and music which has not yet even been put through his paces. For Christmas I gave my eldest son the book *1001 you must list-en (sic, hear) to before you die* (Dimery, 2017), and together we are slowly making our way through the list. At last list-en we were somewhere at the end of the 1970s and each song is list-ed for later list-ing on his own set of lists.

I list-en to him talk about his music lists and I see a man in love with both. The words he writes on lists about music become lyrics in and of themselves, a song leaning ever closer to finding the feeling that sits just beneath the music he loves and that which matters most in the world. His lists of words are lilting and the very sweetest of songs. I tilt my head slightly to list-en more closely to his singing, the let(te-ring)of the words of music on his latest list fall gently into my ears like soft rain. It is not long before I am lost in my list-ening; I watch as his music lists make their way slowly and tenderly to that place which I have secret-ed away. His list-ing about music, sits softly down beside me, takes my hand, and I am in love; with the lists, with the music, with the man.

It is not long before my thinking and wondering about his list making lead to me the word itself; *list*, spelt L-I-S-T. I find the "L" words in an old dictionary I have in my hallway—my Pa's dictionary, a Merriam-Webster 1948 edition—and flip the pages over. I catch myself and stop—for a moment, a minute or maybe more—to savour the sense of homecoming that touching the leather letter tab brings; cool, smooth and aware under my finger. I close my eyes, my breath barely there and bated; tasting the scent as the fine paper turns and fills the air and my head with the very idea of going elsewhere. My lips move in a silent ritual, "Show me a-way, take me a-way, fly me a-way"; it's a whispered invocation to imagination to be, to be-come and to be-side me. I slowly open my eyes and to my surprise there are no less than twelve definitional citations of the word list. They consume one whole column of one whole page and begin with a listing of verb versions of the word. List, *v.*1, meaning to prefer, to choose or to be inclined. List, *v.*2, in nauticle parlance as to lean to one side. List, *v.*3, from hylst (hearing), to harken, to hear, to list-en to. I pause for a moment, finding myself list-ening to the ways this word is presented. List, to-lean-to-choose-to-hear. List, $v.4$, to insert in a list, as in public service, as soldiers, to en-list. List, $v.4i$, to enclose for combat.

I think and wonder of the synchrony between the man who loves lists and the verb list as listed here; a man who has chosen to willingly enter the lists, living both and loving the challenge they bring. I think and wonder whether in listing-to-lean-to-choose-to-hear he would see his love of lists and his lists of love in the same way; perhaps it is my own list-ful thinking seeking to list him. With one eye fixed on the list of verbs of the word list, the other has been secret-ly leaning, choosing and hearing the noun list. I think and wonder, not for the first time, about the wisdom of reading a-head, getting a-head of thinking and wondering in the hope(less) assumption that it brings you a-head to the elsewhere you hoped to arrive at when you first began. I think and wonder about where my desire to list him in this way is heading. I would like to think I am leaning, choosing and hearing him in my listing; my love of words and the man who loves lists touching, so close.

List, $n.1$, a row or line. List, $n.2$, a line enclosing or forming a border from the Old English *liste*. I think and wonder about the ways in which the definitions of list are now edging—leaning-choosing-hearing— towards categories; the ways that lists contain and control our thinking and wondering about the world through words. A list is a way to order, re-order the dis-order of thinking and wondering, and then to do it all again in reverse to dis-order, re-order and order the world into thinking and wondering. Lists bring our thinking and wondering so close, right up close to the edge and beyond. As I began thinking and wondering about writing this book, I had most unexpectedly and wonderfully fallen in love; in love with words once more, and in love for the first time with a man who loved words too, and especially the writing of lists. Our shared love of words and writing led us to talk at length about the books we loved to read, as well as the books he and I would love to write one day. Neither of us had yet written a word and just like that a deal was done; we made a commitment to one another to write 500 words a day. A commitment to write; a commitment to write the words we love; a commitment to word our worlds alongside each other as we fell in love. Come what may, no matter how perfect or problematic the prose, the deal was—and still is—that we would always share our 500 words with one another; no compromise, no possibility of putting words in the bank, no care for how long 500 words might take to write. You might even say that we are holding each to account, that is, to a-ccount of 500 a day.

There are days when we set ourselves a writing task; to pen a poem in the style of a songwriter that I like and he loves, to make sure we include a miscellaneous and quite random object in our daily 500, or perhaps to remember a moment where something was at once lost and found. There are days when we simply sit together in solitude and set ourselves the task of "twisting and turning our hearts around" (after Frank, 1952/2000, p. 282) as a way of sorting, sifting and settling into the words and worlds that seek to be written in that moment. One of the favourite parts of my day is when we sit together and talk about the 500 words we have shared; whether the words are working or not in the way each of us intends, the way the words are travelling and the kinds of worlds we and they are travelling through. We smile, shrug, frown, laugh and sigh as our conversation connects constructive critique with a growing sense of ourselves as becoming writers and intimately more and more entangled in each other's words and worlds. It is my love of both which brings me to writing and holds me there, intimately, so close. And it his love of lists which inspired the way the words in this book have been brought together; a number followed by 500 words or more; in and of themselves a list.

2.

Diaries and rooms, ordinary affects, dreams I tell you and the troubling secret lives of them all hold a certain kind of promise—these are the works that sit as inspiration beneath the way in which the words and worlds in this book on, with and for critical autoethnography come together as writing in pieces of 500 words or more. At this point I am caught naked and bare between adoration (yes, it's true; in love with the way you have with words to will your way) and apology (I am sorry in advance for the willful way in which I bend, twist and re-fashion your words to follow my will which may not be the way or the will you intended) for the women whose writing this piecing together of embodied emotion and experience somethings pays homage to. Virginia Woolf's stream of consciousness literary style, which I first became acquainted with when I read *A room of one's own* (1929/2001), followed by her more well-known novel *Mrs Dalloway* (1925) and perhaps lesser known collections of diary entries and essays, puts forward of a way of writing about, through and towards "moments of being". Life, as Woolf sees it, "is a long ribbon of scenes, emotions" (1980, p. 81) and finding a way to "plug into" the traces and "turn up" the sounds of strong emotion life brings through writing is a way in which we might—perhaps—become affected and attached to life once more. Writing, for Woolf, is a process of scene making and sense making and sounding syllables and sentences in semblance of the everydayness of life itself; so that we might see it as becoming beyond the "cotton wool" that holds us captive there in a state of non-being. Her insistence that writing in this way holds life close, so very close in fact that the "book itself is alive: because it has not crushed the thing I wanted to say, but allowed me to slip it in, without compression or altera-tion" (1980, pp. 297–298), draws me into thinking and wondering about Virginia Woolf as a writer of critical autoethnography—imagine, Virginia and me wording and writing and worlding critical autoethnography. This is the stuff that a girl sitting in a room of her own might give herself per-mission to dream.

3.

In *Ordinary affects* Kathleen Stewart (2007) assembles her close ethno-graphic attentiveness and attachments to life as a series of disparate scenes, each scene "a tangent that performs the sensation that something is happening—something that needs attending to. From the perspective of ordinary effects", she writes, "thought is patchy and material. It does not find magical closure or even seek it, perhaps because it's too busy just trying to imagine what's going on" (p. 5). While I can't be certain whether she would see herself in the same light, or perhaps would even like to be placed alongside the likes of Virginia Woolf—I pause here and turn quickly to see if VW is cited in her reference list; she is not—*like* Woolf, there is a flow, continuity, density and intensity to her writing as Stewart attends—slowly, without need or care to rush to conclusion—to the thinking, feelings and "stuff" in public, social and intimate worlds that have capacity to affect and be affected. They are, she contends, the things that happen that "catch people up in something that feels like *some*thing" (p. 2). The 500 words or more I write each day to piece together this book, turn towards Stewart, "wary and excited" and fully prepared to embrace the ways in which the ordinary registers intensities (p. 11). I read a page here, and a page there, in no particular order and with no particular concern for the proper order of reading. Stewart describes her text as a "tangle of trajectories, connections, and disjunctures" (p. 5) and I would like to think and wonder that she gives me permission to think and wander through her words of intimacy and sociality in much the same way. I turn to page 48 where "little fantasies pop up"; soon enough a "little world comes into view" (p. 57) and she reminds quickly me that sometimes you have to pause amidst the little experiences of the most ordinary "to catch up with where you already are" (p. 63). For the little while of wording and worlding—500 words or more upon each listing to be precise—that is this book about critical autoethnography, thank you Kathleen Stewart for pulling me into a "state of being wide open" to ordinary affects, "just to see what happens. Even if it's not much" (2007, p. 120).

4.

As the 500 words or more in this book unfold across each page and into one another, the dictionary has emerged as a faithful and critical friend. Not just any dictionary, but my Pa's dictionary. A black leather Merriam-Webster tome published in 1948. By chance, I came across another book—similar but not the same, this text a book about the secret life of dictionaries. *Word by word* is lexicographer Kory Stamper's (2017) behind the scenes account of what happens to words and how they come to be included in the Merriam-Webster dictionary. The happenstance between my Pa's dictionary and Stamper's book is one which sent shivers up and shudders down my spine; here was a woman in love with words, obsessed with what makes them tick and flick off a tongue and a typewriter in a particular kind of way, twirling and turning this way and that to present a moment of meaning in time. As I read about her love affair with words and books, I catch myself holding my breath, enraptured by the mystery, mayhem and maybe, which sits behind the ways that words come to mean something in dictionaries. Stamper describes words and language as a child we love and nurture into being, yet once it gains survival bare basics, it starts going exactly where we don't want it to go, where we don't expect it to go; it goes its own way—"we will never really be the boss of

It. And that's why it flourishes" (2017, p. 51). I am not alone in my love of dictionaries, I am sitting close beside Kory Stamper.

5.

Much of the writing that has taken place and takes its place here, comes from a moment in time of deep unhappiness; a sadness so cavernous, so consuming, *so close*, that at times I felt I would and could not possibly continue. Cessation was all that was left; I had stopped feeling, I had stopped thinking, I had stopped writing; and this more than anything, my inability to write, to write the body, to write through to life, signalled the close. I willingly conceded that I had lost my way and I watched myself in morbid curiosity crawling and crashing my way down, deeper down, ever so deeper down to the bottom to cease. With my back turned, I could no longer see the feminist writers I have come to think of friends who, with care and compassion, and without a second thought, chased after me. One voice rang out clearly above me in the chasm, a voice I recognised as Sara Ahmed's. "Quick!" she cried, "We've got to catch this willful [woman]: she has a story to tell! (Ahmed, 2011, p. 240)!" "Being willful is the best hope she has!" she screamed. Ahmed's work willingly got in the way and broke my fall; when I was ready to desist, Ahmed insistered that I persist. By becoming willful; by possessing willfulness as a claim to life; by allowing that willful part to keep standing up, to keep standing firm, and to keep standing against all that would will me away (Ahmed, 2011, p. 249). This writing that I am wording here and now, holds traces of and willfully intends to trouble that cold place of there and then in the here and now. Lillian Rubin, American sociologist, writer and sister in arms whose life's work exposed the crippling effects of gender and class on human potential, once wrote that feminist friendship evokes the "best parts of ourselves" (1985, p. 41). Ahmed and her work on willfullness is that kind of critical companion, the one who reminds me that embracing this troubling story is closely the kind of trouble I can and *will* willfully place myself in to write these words of intimate and social worlding; truth be told, I am already *the* trouble and this is indeed the best placement for and of me.

6.

"Without it—my death—I wouldn't have written" (Cixous, 1991, p. 36) and without you Hélène Cixous, I fear I would have remained forever dying and unspeakable. I read you Cixous, and with each word of yours I read I find myself "literary set free" (2016, p. viii) to write. I skim and skip my way around your words, shifting from this text to that, lingering here and jumping quickly across to there, lightly touching some and deeply kissing others, all the while allowing myself the moment of arriving in, through and of your words to dream; to *Dream, I tell you* (2006) of the words and worlds I might write be-cause and in-cause of you.

"Cixous", I think and wonder, "who are you?" I know even before it leaves my lips that my question is ignorance masked as innocence.

I ask again, "Cixous, who are you? Who are *you* in-relation to writing, to *my* writing?"

She easily sees through my thin disguise and laughs raucously at the ludicrity, "This is why I never ask myself, 'who am I' (qui suis-je?) I ask myself 'who are I?' (qui sont-je?)—an unstranslatable phrase. Who can say who I are, how many I are, which is the most of my I's?"

"'A subject is at least thousand people' (Cixous, 1994, p. xvi) I have heard you say", I cheekily cite her.

"You would have also heard me say then, 'I ask myself, but I do not answer myself' (1994, p. xvii), because the one is always the double and in each 'one' of us 'our own contrary slumbers' (1994, p. xviii)", Cixous murmurs, "Those we have been, those who we will be, those we will not be" (1994, p. xvi).

I sit with Cixous' words and give myself permission to allow the more than doubleness of the inbetween she is alluding to cross through into my I as eye-are-wareness. I think and wonder about the I who writes this text, the other I who reads this text, the a-not/her I who imagines this text, the I who watches, the I who waits for she and I to arrive. Let me then present "who are I", that is, to bring my presence/s to you as an act of pre-sentenc-ing the I's in and of the words and worlds that I am go-ing and to-ing write. The first I; Elizabeth Narelle Mackinlay. She is I. The name I was presented with at the beginning, I are becoming at the ending. Call me Elizabeth, Liz, Lizzie, or Beth or by any name you please, "it is not a matter of any importance," Virginia Woolf reminds me, for "'I' is only a convenient term for somebody who has no real being" (1929/2001, p. 5). The second I; Ruby Montrose is she. The name I present to myself at the ending, she becomes at the beginning. In much the same way as Kathleen Stewart makes use of the marker "she", Ruby as I is she "gazes, imagines, senses, takes on, performs, and asserts not a flat and finished truth but some possibilities (and threats) that have come into view" (2007, p. 5). The first name of this name I would have presented to a little girl. The last name of this name presents my past and my present in the eastern suburbs of Melbourne at the foot of the Dandenong ranges. I and she are the same but different, always in difference as she and I think and wonder as we write the words and worlds we encounter. Together, I and she go inside and outside the endings and beginnings, moving so close while at the same time standing still, far far a-way, searching for the beginnings and endings of this story she and I share.

7.

My youngest son Hamish and I go through our daily breakfast ritual. I stand on one side of the granite kitchen bench, and he is perched on a wooden stool across from me. There is no need to make small talk or ask any questions, we each know what the other needs and set to it. I place a thick slice of five seed grain bread in the toaster for him, reach for the vegemite from the cupboard and take the butter from the fridge. In the background my small Nespresso machine begins to make all of the appropriate sounds which tell me it is going through the motions of producing a much-needed cup of strong and thick coffee to kick start my day. Hamish holds the latest novel he is reading in one hand and the other moves on autopilot to take small bites of toast every now and then. For a fleeting moment I see my 12-year-old self sitting across from me; eyes and head down, legs crumpled up underneath, completely absorbed in the pages of a book, always already somewhere else and far far away from here and now.

"What's happening at school today?" I ask.

"Mmm, the usual", his voice is monotone and I can tell he is not happy about the interruption to his morning breakfast read.

"Library? Sport?" I persist regardless.

"Nope, just the usual", he says again.

"So I guess you want just the usual for lunch then?"

He nods, slowly and in a way which makes it clear that he has heard but not really taken in the question.

"Ok, the usual it is then. Mum's ordinary everyday very *usual* sandwich wrap!"

Hamish looks up quickly from his book and squints at me suspiciously. "Hang on, I know *your* usual is actually the opposite. What leftovers are you putting on my wrap today?"

"You're going to love it!" I begin to place tablespoons of last night's dinner onto the circular bread. It's Thai chicken mince; I add some mayo, avocado and baby Kale leaves for extra moisture, flavour and nutrition.

Hamish watches half in horror and half in fascination as the ingredients pile up on his wrap.

"You know this always has a good ending Mishka, it's going to taste bew-di-ful!"

He gives me a very hesitant thumbs up.

"That reminds me", he puts down his book for a moment. "How is your book coming along? Did you write your 500 words yesterday?"

I nod.

"And are you happy with it?" Hamish knows there is the *matter* of writing 500 words, and writing 500 words that *might* be usable. He can tell by my short response that perhaps in this instance, there is a little—or maybe even a lot—of editing work to be done. Hamish has been down this book-writing road with me before *and* he has the t-shirt to prove it.

"Geez, talk about dejavu!" I exhale noisily. "This reminds me of the conversation we had about my last book—except then you asked me each morning had I finished yet. Now the question is all about the beginning".

"Well, *have* you started? How much have you written?" He raises one eyebrow inquisitively.

I breathe out again, "Not enough. 500 words a day is good, but I need to write more".

"So what's the problem then?" He asks. "Just do it—just write *more*. What is it you always say Mum? A writer *writes*, no matter what, just write—easy".

I look across at the bench at him, and think and wonder, not for the first time, how it is that sometimes the most thoughtful and wonder-full words really *do* come out of the mouths of babes; welcome surprises of the strangest and softest kind that come so very near. For a moment I become lost in thinking and wondering about writing. Writing. A way of bringing those close to you closer; of bringing them write up close to you; so close that writing touches me, touches him and touches the space between us.

"Mum?" Hamish's voice interrupts my thinking about writing. "I need to get my skates on and get to school". He picks up his homemade lunch and places it in his backpack while gently placing his hand on my shoulder. "Promise me you'll write at least 500 words today?"

I smile and lean forward to kiss his cheek, "It's a deal".

"500 it is then", he gives me a wink. "*And* I expect to read it when I get home!"

A familiar dance begins inside my chest as I wave Hamish goodbye and watch him disappear on his bike up the road and around the corner. The heartlines in my hand begin to pulse, unevenly, in and out of time with the unsteady beat that rhythms of love and life have put into motion with this departure from the house. My right hand absent mindedly cradles my left wrist, gently touching the faint lines of forgetting that wait for me there, applying a tiny amount of pressure to test how close I might be to either life or death. Easy, Hamish said. Easy as one two, three, A-B-C and then onto four, five, six, eight, ten, twenty-one, one hundred and twenty-six, two hundred and forty-six, all the way through three hundred and seventy-one to 500. There can be no more hesitation, no more waiting and no more thinking and wondering without writing. And he is right; to write a book all a writer needs to do is write. This word plus that word until-; and yet, there is that question. Not any question, *that* question. *That* question I as you as we might think coulda-shoulda-woulda be an easy one to answer, but each time I try to find the words that might describe the writing that I want to write, there are none. Not one, not two, not even three. Not on a Monday, or a Tuesday, and for now I am pleased that I find myself seeking an answer to that question on a Wednesday. Any other day of the week might do, who can be sure, but finding an answer here and now does matter. The answer to *that* question comes to matter a great deal when it comes down to the matter of writing. To me as a writer, to you as a writer perhaps and always already a reader, and if truth be told, in as far as it might, to any writer. I search for an answer and find myself, once more, in the hands of Hélène. Right up next to her, *So close* (2009).

8.

The crisis ended at the beginning, or perhaps, it began at the ending, when I realised this text would become a Cixousian book-I-don't-write. I *thought* this book was going to be about autoethnography, feminism and decoloniality; and I hear my mother call from the kitchen, "You know what *thought* did Elizabeth!" I turn to look at her and laugh loud and long; she is waving an imaginary feather in the air, bobbing her head up and down, and flapping her arms in intimate imitation of a back-yard hen.

"Mum!" Her impromptu simulation of this completely charming backyard bird sends me into uncontrollable cackling.

"You *know* I never *once* dug a hole and buried a feather expecting it to miraculously turn into a chicken!"

I have covered many feathered friends with piles of dirt to rest peacefully and eternally in the ground under the shade of all manner of fruit trees but *that* kind of transformation would be a flight of fancy if ever I saw one. If I have heard my Mum use this expression once, I have heard her say it a thousand times. I never quite knew exactly what she meant, but I think and wonder now whether she was trying to tell me that whatever I *thought* I might know about wording the world, it is always already so far far a-way from the words and the worlds themselves. Mum was right about one thing, it is *almost* as if the book I was going to write about autoethnography, feminism and decoloniality was just waiting to be buried so that it might grow wings, take flight towards, and unashamedly present itself "all of a sudden" (Cixous, 2016, p. viii) as the book-I-don't-write about critical autoethnography, feminism and decoloniality. I didn't intend to write this book-I-don't-write; I always imagined I would write this book but I imagined it would be different, that the I and the book would write itself differently—this book-I-don't-write is not what I was expecting. I turn to Cixous who writes, "It's always when, and only when…the absolutely Unexpected happens. That's when:", and much like Cixous, "I found it [this book]. Just as you see it" (Cixous, 2016, p. viii).

References

Ahmed, S. (2011). Willful parts: Problem characters or the problem of character. *New Literary History, 42,* 231–253.

Cixous, H. (1991). *Coming to writing and other essays* (S. Suleiman, Ed., S. Cornell, Trans.). Cambridge, MA: Harvard University Press.

Cixous, H. (1994). *The Hélène Cixous reader* (S. Sellers, Ed.). London: Routledge.

Cixous, H. (2006). *Dream, I tell you* (B. B. Brahic, Trans., European perspectives). New York, NY: Columbia University Press.

Cixous, H. (2009). *So close* (P. Kamuf, Trans.). Cambridge: Polity Press.

Cixous, H. (2016). *Abstracts and brief chronicles of the time* (B. B. Brahic, Trans.). Cambridge: Polity Press.

Dimery, R. (2017). *1001 songs you must hear before you die.* London: Quintessence Editions Ltd.

Frank, A. (1952/2000). *The diary of a young girl.* Camberwell, VIC: Penguin Books.

Merriam-Webster International Dictionary (2nd ed.). (1948). Springfield, MA: G & C Merriam Company.

Rubin, L. (1985). *Just friends: The role of friendship in our lives.* New York, NY: Harper & Row.

Stamper, K. (2017). *Word by word: The secret life of dictionaries.* New York, NY: Random House.

Stewart, K. (2007). *Ordinary affects.* Durham, NC: Duke University Press.

Woolf, V. (1929/2001). *A room of one's own.* New York, NY: Harcourt, Brace, Jovanovich.

Woolf, V. (1925). *Mrs Dalloway.* New York, NY: Harcourt, Brace, Jovanovich.

Woolf, V. (1980). *The diary of Virginia Woolf, volume III: 1925–1930.* London: Hogarth Press.

2

Ending Writing, at the Beginning

Fate always contrives that I begin the new year in February. I ask, why another volume? (but here's an innovation: this is not a book but a block—so lazy I am about making writing books nowadays). What is the purpose of them? L. taking up a volume the other day said Lord save him if I died first & he to read through these. My handwriting deteriorates. And do I say anything interesting? I can always waste an idle hour reading them; & then, oh yes, I shall write memoirs out of them, one of these days.
Woolf ([Diary entry, 3 February, 1927], 1980, p. 125)

Here I had come with a notebook and a pencil proposing to spend a morning reading, supposing that at the end of the morning I should have transferred the truth to my notebook. But I should need to be a herd of elephants, I thought, and a wilderness of spiders, desperately referring to the animals that are reputed longest lived and most multitudinously eyed, to cope with all this. I should need claws of steel and beak of brass even to penetrate the husk. How shall I ever find the grains of truth embedded in all this mass of paper?
Woolf (1929/2001, p. 30)

The mind is like a dog going round & round to make itself a bed. So, give me new & detestable ideas, I will somehow trample a bed out of them.
Woolf ([Diary entry, 5 October, 1927], 1980, p. 156)

© The Author(s) 2019
E. Mackinlay, *Critical Writing for Embodied Approaches*,
https://doi.org/10.1007/978-3-030-04669-9_2

1.

She isn't quite sure when the ending began, or when the beginning ended. Perhaps it had always already been on its way to finishing even as it started; and she had somehow not seen the signs directing her willfully that way. She isn't certain, and neither is she comfortable with not being sure, nor the idea of not having seen. Not *being sure* signaled that she had lost which way she was willing to go right at the beginning; she had lost her will along and on the way towards the end. *Not having seen* meant she had forgotten to see the end in sight; she had forgotten what seeing was from the very beginning. Whichever it was, she senses that losing and forgetting willing and seeing as necessary endings of beginnings of endings is the kind of stuck place of uncertainty she needed to be. Each time she pictures herself at what she imagines *was* the beginning, she sees herself somewhere in the distance; blurred and out of focus, beyond and out of reach. A lone girl driving along a lonely road to a lonesome place holding hands with an academic life she thinks of as her friend. She peers in closer to stand alongside this remembering (or is it a forgetting?: once more, she can't be sure) and she sees herself at the end. A solitary woman sitting solo in her office holding hands in solitude with an academic life she no longer thinks of as the self-same kind of friend. (*Note*: self-same, *not* selfsame; written this way after Cixous [in Cixous & Clément, 1986, p. 70] to pepper and pause the a-salt of patriarchy and colonialism represented in this united empire of two times four letter words). She shakes her head; trying to shift the grit and dirt these imaginings have gifted her memory into some semblance of familiarity. Knowing where her ending begins seems like a significant part of the story she wants to tell. Knowing where her beginning ended seems like a significant move she needs to make to tell her story.

She looks over at the pile of books on her desk. These are her journals, diaries, field notes—she is never quite sure what to call them; such as they are, writing scraps of emotion, experience over, across, through and in between time. Her words-as-worlds began in black and red journals with ruled lines on the pages and ended with beautiful circular designs lettering her worlds-as-words. Her worlds-as-words ended in pink and purple notebooks with the self-same ruled lines on pages and began with lovely rounded shapes scripting her words-as-worlds. The date and author is duly noted at the end, but not at the beginning. Seeing herself at the beginning has become important now she remembers which way she is going at the end. Remembering which way she is going at the end has become impor-tant now she tries to see herself at the beginning. She imagines that if she can do both, the uncertain-ty and unsure-ty might take itself away from her and the unsettlement she feels. She has become increasingly unsettled as her ending-as-beginning-as-ending becomes her; as it becomes part of her fragmented self, written in scraps of writing inside and outside and everywhere in between the pile of books on her desk.

2.

If she and I are going to write about the ending, then we must begin somewhere and I decide she does not want to go this way on her own. She takes my hand and together we start this story in the early 1990s, when I began working with the Yanyuwa, Garrwa, Mara, and Gudanji Aboriginal communities at Burrulula in the Northern Territory of Australia. I went there as an ethnomusicology doctoral student, willing my way to document the musical traditions of a group of people whose melodies and moves had not yet become part of the Western corpus about them. Those of us working in ethnomusicology, ethnography and anthropology by necessity must locate ourselves geographically in the "field"; there is a sense of urgency and entitlement linked to naming a place to become, to settle our power, authority and privilege as academics to undertake the work we believe is our w/rite/right. It is a statement of our disciplinary belonging, a homecoming that happens before we have even arrived, and it is all too easy to stake our claim. I hear myself say the words over and under and above and around. The group of Aboriginal people. They call themselves Yanyuwa. They live in the township of Burrulula in the Northern Territory of Australia. Map 1 shows Burrulula situated approximately 970 km south east of Darwin and 80 km inland from the Gulf of Carpentaria. These are strongly reflected and notable facts. Recorded and thus affirmed, they may be said to serve and to cor-roborate. This type of examination elucidates. The significant role they play. The results of this combined linguistic and musical analysis. It is important to understand. They must stand in particular kinds of relation. The relationship is threefold. Women play too. Primarily vocal, paired, most necessary companions. Under the increased pressures of assimila-

tion. Worldly escapades thinly veil. A greater understanding (see Map 2).
Prior to contact with Europeans. Yanyuwa, Garrwa, Mara and Kudanji.
They are more frequently encountered.
3.
These are fragments of words I wrote to name the world I happened to
find myself in; she and I smile—fondness and sadness tugging at the
corners of our mouths—as we remember the happenstance that led me
that way. With first class Honours in ethnomusicology firmly tucked into
my belt, I went to work with Catherine Ellis—the undisputed grandmother of Australian ethnomusicology who had studied with Strehlow in
the Central Desert in the 1950s who by happenchance needed someone
like me to work on an Australian Research Council grant she had won.

Her voice echoes loudly in that space between the here and now,
"You'll be doing your fieldwork at Burrulula".

Field-work-Burrulula. I feel as though I have arrived—this is the naming of my belonging, the naming of my authority, indeed, the naming of
the place through which I will claim both; my *arrivance* perhaps. Work-
field-Burrulula. Burrulula-work-field. I begin immediately to work the
field at Burrulula. To work it in a way which enacts a willfulness I think
is my own. I search libraries, I visit archives, I work to piece the world I
imagine my field at Burrulula to be.

I tell my then partner, "I'll be doing my field work at Burrulula".

"Burrulula?" he asks.

I nod.

"That's where my family are from, my Yanyuwa family". In that one
moment of happenchance where our worlds became one and the same;
everything changed. She looks at me, I look at her as we remember to
un-forget and name this moment as my ending and my beginning.

In the beginning, I thought that my academic work would somehow
translate into "something better" for the women, men and children
whom I call family. Better homes, a fair education, an end to racism, and
the reinstatement of Indigenous Australians as a sovereign people. My
PhD and the journal papers I subsequently wrote about the social and
musical lives of Aboriginal women and men did not change anything,
despite how well I wrote them and the prestige of the publications in
which they appeared. I realised that while people might be hearing the

words I spoke at conferences and reading those that appeared in my writing, they were not listening—not with their hearts. Neither were the words I wrote those which my Aboriginal family wanted to listen to—they didn't tell a good story.

"Yu a Doctor now hey? What yu last name again? Mackinlay init? So now yu Dr Mackinlay", my beloved *marruwarra* (female cousin) Mudinji Isaac once asked me after seeing the large bound and red leather tomb that was my PhD I had placed in front of her as a gift. I nodded.

"Hmmph", she snorted. She turned her face away from me ever so slightly and with her toe returned my thesis to sender, "A-not/her Dr Bloody Bullshit more like it".

They were words that I will always un-forget because she *was* right. Blood and shit. The collection of words that sat in front of her were words I no longer wanted to write, read or listen to either—they didn't tell a good enough theory-story and they did not story-theory.

Sitting amongst the blood and shit of the words I had been writing, I became painfully aware of my positioning as a non-Indigenous woman in relation-to and in relation-with Indigenous peoples, knowledges and cultures, and the enormous white power and privilege I held as a white-settler-colonial-woman. If you sit with blood and shit long enough, you begin to embody it; it overcomes and becomes you. The stench of it crept into every possible crevice of skin and seeped its way into my bones. I tried my best to scrub myself clean, believing that sanitising my body of thoughts was all that I needed; all that I wanted. The harder I scrubbed the more I realised how close I was to the heart of it—all that I wanted was to come clean and fess up. My gift of cold hard words was not and never could be enough. I knew that there was more, and indeed that I had to do more, to engage the thinking hearts of my colleagues, students, and friends if I was serious about working towards a more *socially just* future for Indigenous Australians—for my children and my family. And there's that word again. The one that just keeps popping up and demanding to be heard. The trouble is, it too is smothered in thick and dense excretions and excrement; *colonial* blood and shit.

4.

Such knowing then became a-part of, with and from everything. There was no a-parting it once it had arrived; my Cixousian *arrivance* (Cixous,

1997, p. 276). It is out of such *arrivance* as a-parting that I now write in a movement towards un-finishing; for how can something ever become the end at the beginning? Or are they as much apart from as they a-part of one another? I think and wonder, trying to recall now how such knowing arrived and when did it become *arrivance*? I am sure I cannot un-forget an exact or even a roundabout kind of date, or a time precisely or imprecisely for that matter. I wrote a lot of words then and there, documenting what I knew and believed to be true about a-not/hers because I was there. Perhaps un-forgetting the moment it began its be/coming does not matter; perhaps one day I was without and the next I was within; I cannot say for sure. Besides I am uncertain I want to say it, aside from knowing that perhaps it is what is expected; it is my duty. Duty be damned; maybe I shall become Woolf's undutiful daughter after all, the one that critically dared to imagine writing in a room of her own, against convention. But just as I arrive at this knowing, Woolf's warning (1929/2001, p. 3) about writing for conclusion hangs ominously in the air as I contemplate closure on my *arrivance* at the kind of knowing that seems now always to be on its way. I can hear Virginia's torture as she speaks of how futile writing-as-fiction-as-truth is, and that in the end, all writers can do is lay bare the ideas; truths and lies mixing and freely flowing. It would be easy to lie down with the truth and pretend that in laying side by side, truth and lies slept soundly. In the beginning I thought I was telling the ethnographic truth—theirs as mine as appropriate/d. Arriving at the ending to begin I think and wonder how I was always already telling an ethnographic lie—theirs as mine as in/appropriated.

Virginia's words send me to my *arrivance*, again. I go searching for others who have arrived in this self-same place and find myself standing alongside Tami Spry. She too experienced the self-same "methodological anxiety" (2016, p. 29) in her ethnographic writing about a-not/hers. Writing sitting on the edge of a crisis in representation that until realising, accepting and embracing where it was and why it mattered, was filled with a-part naivety, two a-parts avoidance and refusal, three a-parts shame and guilt, and for a-part, four a-parts performance of power and privilege. I write to with around between for critical autoethnography because it is the only *honest* move—the only ethico-onto-epistemological line I know how to take—I know how to be/come with in this particular personal-pedagogical-political moment I find myself. I line up critical-and-autoethnography-and-heart and un-forget that in doing so, "I'm coming, I manage, I arrive" (Cixous, 1997, p. 276) because it is with a "transgressive scholarship of the body with a heart" (Spry, 2010, p. 277) that we end at the beginning of *arrivance.*

5.

I turn away from being so close to the journals piled high on my desk and glance over at the bookshelf. All of my favourites are there, waiting patiently for me to sit with them in the folds of friendship they offer. A loud blackberry sigh, sour and replete with frustration, bursts from a place deep down inside. They are going to have to wait a little longer for I have another task to do first. One by one I reluctantly remove the books from my shelf and place them carefully into a pile on the floor of my study. I stand back and glare at the empty bookshelf. It is a monstrosity and it towers above me forebodingly, a reminder that it must come to an end if I am to begin. I wrap my small frame around its awkward and angled structure and drag the large eyesore out onto my overgrown back lawn. The summer sun beats down relentlessly, even though it is still early. The bookshelf seems to grow exponentially in horror under its penetrating rays while I feel myself beginning to wither and wane in the heat. I concentrate to turn my glare into something more sinister, something that will match the evil that stands in front of me, hoping that the oft used phrase "if looks could kill" might actually turn out to be true. But there it stands, defiantly. There's no point in waiting any longer, because I know if I wait for the perfect moment it will never arrive. The bookshelf is dark and stained with memories of a life I have been forced to leave behind. I want—and need—to paint it differently so that at the close I can begin again. I stare at it belligerently; I have come to detest this unwelcome stranger of the present where once upon a past, maybe, just maybe, I called this bookshelf a close up and most necessary companion.

Gritting my teeth my resolve steels and steals away any lingering doubt; at least for now. I place my arms around the sides of the lumbering and large item of shelving in a gesture that could almost be mistaken for an embrace, but the bookshelf is too heavy and tall for my slight build. The two of us grumble and groan in protest as I roughly and forcibly manoeuvre it under the eaves and outside. We are both filled with an unbearable regret; this is not the moment, neither as strangers or friends, we might have imagined for ourselves.

The bookshelf begins to weep, it begs and pleads, and the noise soon becomes a high-pitched shriek.

"Fuck this ugly fucking god forsaken piece of furniture", I curse under my breath as it sways dangerously towards me.

My eyes spy the rusted hammer sitting on the garden bench and I begin to think about the damage such old tools can do to large and unwanted monstrosities. I imagine splinters of hard and plywood flying wildly through the air, each blow of the mallet shattering the fragments of the past this bookshelf holds. At this point the present is not a gift and the future belongs to someone else; what would I care in a time of such care-lessness. My hand reaches out to clasp the busted up blue rubber handle of the hammer and I hear the bookshelf sobbing, begging me to take pause. I purse my lips and glare at the dark combination of wood, nails and glue; the audacity! the arrogance! the insult! my mind is made up!

6.

A pause. Offensive words. Words that take offence. Words that engage in offense. Words that cause offence. The f-words. And other words that we must not say; cannot say; will not say. So *they* say. There are the c-words and the s-words and the b-words. Not to mention the *L*-words. Words that *a* for attack, assault and annoy. Words that *i* for irritate and itch at the corners of irksome, and thereby sit on the edges of infringement. Words that *r* for rattle and rile the rules of a ruse where resentment becomes the only possible result. That is what words will do; that is the want of words and the will of words. Words that mis-and-dis in all the wrong and right places; causing dis-ease and dis-pleasure all manner of mis-deed and mis-chief. Who's to say which doing of these words is more wrong, and which is more right; it depends on whether the way I am doing the word is offens-ing or offenc-ing; isn't that w/righ/te? Or perhaps whether the word is left simply offending; and pays offense and offence no mind.

Offence with a *c* or offense with an *s*, the re-turning of this word comes from the south to the north and back again, and yet their composition stays the self-same. Four or five letters, with usually one but rarely two syllables, offensive words are easily moved and manoeuvred before settling in and making a whole lot of noise. Noun, verb, or adjective; the performance of offensive words steps in and out of many part of speech. The opening of these words are undemanding and easy-going, holding carefully in their folds perhaps at times a tender caress even and slow; but the close is volatile and hot-tempered. Poised and ready to explode, such words are fickle and unstable; and become difficult to ignore. They have to be. To shock. To make sure they are noticed. To put a line under and a pin in the worlds they name. To bring back a certain kind of wide awakeness. To give anger and torment a place to call home in all their glory. To wreck the rhetorics and regulations and get beyond reserve. To laugh at the very idea of silence (Cixous, 1976, p. 886). To return from without and make a shattering entry and seize the occasion (Cixous, 1976, p. 880) and arrive vulnerable and vibrant over and over again (Cixous, 1976, p. 882). That is what offensive words *will* do.

7.

Just as I am about to deal my fatal blow I notice a small chip on the middle shelf. It happened during another move from here to there; in the dis/connection of two which had become one. I place my hand on the top shelf and I remember, my mind sliding to the next shelf and leaping from one memory to another memory all the way to the bottom. Tenderly I touch the side panel of the bookshelf which holds it together; no, I have not forgotten. The doorway to un-forgetting is opened as I twist and turn the heavy piece of furniture until it is positioned, albeit precariously, on an old flannette drop sheet. I drop down to the ground and kneel before the shelf. From here I can see all the way back into there, bookmarks of emotion and experience etched onto each wooden plank. The shelves are empty and bare; like the streets of ghost towns now bereft of the rattle and hum of meaning. Dense cobwebs now inhabit each the corner where once knowledge would flourish and grow. Sadness and nostalgic longing start whispering from the dark forgotten spaces, begging me to reconsider. I dust the temporal remnants away and raise the hammer in my right hand high into the air; for after all—thank you Shakespeare, although I so wish it were his sister I were citing—where the affront is, the great axe must fall.

Right on time, not a moment before, or after, the telephone rings; the bookshelf, it would seem, has another destiny. The hammer drops to the ground. I can't be quite sure whether I was closer to death or life "when the telephone pounced" (Cixous, 1994, p. 88), breaking and smashing its way through to my place of inbetweeness and becoming another living being in this encounter between me and the shelf.

"Hello?" I sighed. The telephone call had interrupted the intense heat, rivers of sweat and abiding urgency I now had to get this over and done with.

"Elizabeth! So glad you are alive in this moment of my telephone call pouncing (Cixous, 1994, p. 88)!"

I should have known it would be Hélène Cixous. She is very fond of phone calls that shove their way uninvited into moments inbetween.

"Yes?" I ask. "To what do I owe this pleasure?" I hide my irritation; I have no intention of sharing my secret desire to smash and slam this bookshelf away from here to there. Although, I fancy that Cixous, of all my friends, would empathise with my need to seize the occasion and wield my antilogos weapon with all my strength (Cixous, 1976, p. 880).

"I heard your fear, mistrust and rage (Cixous, 1994, p. 88) of unforgetting and needed to call. Have you destroyed it yet?"

I should have known she would know about it anyway. I sighed, "No, I was just about to".

"Well, I just wanted to make sure you are wide awake to what you are about to do. Have you thought about what it really means to undertake what I think is quite a 'violent, strange, artless exercise, an obligation without directions' (Cixous, 1994, p. 88)". She paused. "Do you really want to obliviate this shelf?"

The silence which follows brings with it a slow but sure recognition that my urge for destruction of the past held there in the shelf was not actually what I wanted. It might have been what I thought I needed to move towards here, but not what I wanted; and there is a difference. I should have known Hélène would know that this is what I thought.

"It takes nerve Elizabeth to un-forget inbetween there and here", she said. "It's a matter of slipping between two oblivions, or of leaping from one memory to anther memory" (Cixous, 1994, p. 89).

"What do you suggest then? How do I make the move when the edges are so hazy, when everything is still in draft?"

I wait, I listen; but there is no sound from the earpiece. Hélène does not respond, and I realise she has already gone. I throw my telephone onto the picnic blanket and look sullenly at the bookshelf.

8.

The bookshelf and I contemplate one another for awhile; we are trying to ascertain where we stand in relation to one another and whether or not there is still room for us both. The thought that today might be the moment of our a-parting is almost unbearable and yet its presence has become almost unbearable. This bookshelf has travelled the highs and lows of my academic flight across states, overseas, up mountains and down dales; and it decides to stand and fight. The stare we share becomes steely and stretches across the space between us; it lengthens as it thins and curiosity floats in the air as we wonder which one of us is going to break first. The seconds become minutes become hours which might in the end mean everything and nothing. The bookshelf sighs; over time it has carried the weight of many words and worlds and it tires quickly in the heat of the midday sun. The shelf is lonely, ever so alone, and longs for the company the pages and texts other imaginings will bring. It willingly surrenders, and I breathe out in relief; this war is won. There is no need to fight, no need for futility, no need to do anything at all except the very next thing.

9.

I pick up the tin of paint that has been sitting watching with interest the encounter between us on the back lawn. I carefully dip my brush into the silky substance and begin. I have decided. I am painting this bookshelf white; I am painting this bookshelf white so that it can hold the words of white ink I plan to write in homage to Cixous. It needs to match—the writing and the room, the room and the writing—the writing in the room downstairs I have come to call my own. The walls in this room of my own are painted white and the floor has cream floor tiles upon which sits her white office desk and magenta chair. I feel comfortable in this space. In summer it is as cool as a cucumber and in winter a cosy cocoon. This room of my own downstairs doubles as a sewing room and all manner of materials spill out of cupboards and drawers. There are neatly stacked fat flats, colour coded charm packs, and ready to roll layer cakes. There are half-finished quilts positioned in order of expected completion, love and importance; projects that I yearn to return to. Drawings from my two boys when they were little adorn the walls; bright free flowing painted pictures. In a small wooden frame, a handcrafted pin cushion is carefully displayed; it is the one I made when I was a little girl when I first started sewing. My Auntie Florence, Dad's sister, owned a berry farm in the Yarra Valley. Every Christmas I would spend a few weeks with her rising at sun-up and filling punnets with raspberries, loganberries, and blackberries. 33 cents for a punnet of blackberries, 33 cents for a punnet of loganberries, and 35 cents for a punnet of raspberries. Blacks and logans sat clear, bare and waiting on the vine to picked; raspberries kept themselves mysterious and out of sight, you needed to go hunting in the thick leaves to find them. After five hours in the berry patch, each punnet was washed, wrapped, sealed, signed and delivered without delay to the Vic Markets in the centre of the city.

Auntie Florence would sometimes venture into the berry patch with us in the wee hours of the morning, but most times, she would have a delicious berry dessert waiting for us just in time for lunch. Berry pie, berry jam, berry strudel, berry pudding, berry muffins, berry-berry pancakes— and berry porridge. Her husband my Uncle Bob was from Belfast and not a morning went by without an ample helping of oats to kick start our day. He never spoke of Ireland although his accent was lilting and strong; he had left the troubles long ago and did not want to return there but his love of potatoes and porridge remained. His heart started hurting one day in the berry patch; he didn't make it out and the berry farm was sold.

In the afternoons, having been sufficiently productive, sun-kissed and berry stained, Auntie Florence patiently sat beside me in the room she called her own in their four-bedroom single storeyed brick house, and showed me how to stitch. By hand, by machine and by a certain grace my sixteen-year-old self did not yet understand. On a cream Janome; model number DC3050 with 20 essential stiches, including a buttonholer. One of the first items I sewed with her was my pin cushion. Every good seamstress needs a good pin cushion she said and each time I walk into this room of my own I un-forget her. A square of navy blue cotton made in the 1980s with small white daisies and a white lacy border. The pin cushion is held together by crude and uneven back stitches in white thread. The filling was never quite plump enough but had more than enough lumps to do the job assigned to it. Over time it has held thin needles with thick eyes for seeing. Silks, ball points, plastic and glass heads, and t-pins for holding it all together. Strands of thread clung tight to the needles and pins, standing by come what may to bear witness to the truth held by stitches in time. My pin cushion now sits behind glass protected from yellowing, and boldly laughs aging in the face. I fancy that the material and my Auntie Florence have now taken on another more important role; as wise women they watch over me from near and far. I take the wooden frame holding my pin cushion from the wall and prop it up outside on my picnic blanket.

10.

The first brush strokes are runny, rough and rude; a stark signal that revolution of some kind is afoot but I am in no mind to be patient now that my mind is made up. The bookshelf moves and shakes, attempting to resist the transformation I am imposing upon it. It leans menacingly towards me, bearing its teeth, growling and roaring, threatening to splinter apart and upon me but I catch it just in time; I cradle this monstrous piece of furniture in a gentle embrace and carefully lay it down on the picnic blanket. The bookshelf stiffens at first and then finally succumbs to my touch. It sheds its anger and reveals a heavy sadness for all that has come to pass-t on its ledges; reluctantly—the bookshelf is not ready to let go and yet I sense that this is but a desperate plea. I apply the white paint with slow and smooth strokes, each application akin to a mother lightly caressing her child's forehead after a nightmare. I sing softly under my breath, a lullaby, and yet I am not sure whom this song is for. Either way, the sound is soothing, and I feel the bookshelf and me slip into a shared space of contentment. I apply one coat, two coats, three and several more and soon enough the bookshelf is transformed to a lighter shade of pale.

I step back in order to better close in on my morning's work. Three hours ago, the bookshelf was dark jarrah and despite my attempts to lull it into accepting its fate, it remains angry. It rages vividly in the midday sun and its fury signals an adamant refusal of the colour it has been forced to become. I try my best to cajole this stubborn item of furniture into be-leaving its resistance behind and believing instead that it now has the ability to transcend time, trend and space; but it's not easily convinced. Whisper white, I decide to call the new shade the bookshelf wears. Each coat of paint has cloaked the shelves in a certain kind of secrecy, the kind that is shared about truths held in words and murmured softly into ears behind cupped hands. The backwards and forwards motions of the brush stealed and sealed these whisperings in illusions of white so completely that it had become and would become forever harder to tell which words placed upon the shelves were fact or fiction. I laugh, knowing that in the end, "all manner of lies will flow" (after Woolf, 1929/2001, p. 2) from the words placed upon the bookshelf and that if one piece of writing contains more truth than the other; then it is up to a-not/her to make the call and I will pay no mind.

The white paint dries quickly in the heat of the day and before long it is time to move the bookshelf inside. Placing it carefully in the middle of an old sheet, I drag it back across the overgrown lawn. It is a slow dance. A slide to the left, a sashay to the right. Like two lovers finding their way back to one another after an ugly argument, the bookshelf and I regard each other suspiciously. We are not sure whether we should embrace or erase each other's presence. The two-step shuffle back into the spare room under the house seems to take forever; and yet, the bookshelf and I seem to accept—albeit grudgingly—that now we have begun, we need to continue this dance until the music ends.

The bookshelf slides easily across the cool tiles once we reach the hallway under the house and without fuss I have soon manoeuvred it through the doorway into the room. I gently slide it across the floor and position it plum against the left wall. It fits perfectly and looks as though that is where it has always been, standing tall and resolute painted white on white. The cruel words and baleful wishes the bookshelf and I fired at each other merely moments ago begin to fade and shift themselves to distant memory; a place of un-remembering. The bookshelf and I breathe out noisily and begin to similarly un-dress our words from the "cotton wool of daily life" which has draped and darkened our worlds for way too long. In this room of my own is where the bookshelf belongs; in this room of my own is where I belong; in this room of my own is where the I/she/we of our writing belongs and can wake itself from the dead to begin again. The heartlines in my hand begin to touch and tingle my desire to begin writing but a slow rumble from deep inside my stomach begs me to take pause. I un-forget that I have not eaten all day and I am reminded, not for the first time that "one cannot think well, love well, sleep well, if one has not dined well" (Woolf, 1929/2001, p. 21).

11.

The worlds and the words I might use to describe them are just beginning to wake. There is a quiet hush in the air as I gently slide open the back door and tiptoe down the stairs in my pyjamas and fluffy slippers. I am care-full not to make too much noise; it is fun-in-the-sun-school-holidays and my two sons are taking advantage of the opportunity to stay lying horizontal for as long as the summer heat will allow them. Balancing a delicious combination of fresh coffee and a plain croissant in one hand, and my laptop in the other, I fumble with a set of silver keys to open the door to my sewing-writing room. I am greeted by a strong odour of fresh white paint and I look tentatively across at my frenemy from yesterday facing opposite me. The bookshelf greets me with a barely civil, "Still not happy Elizabeth". I choose to ignore it and flaunt it by placing my hot beverage and breakfast on the middle shelf and toss the transformed piece of furniture what I think is a winning smile. The bookshelf stands stead-fast in its silent treatment and seethes. I sigh and gently place my laptop in the middle of my white desk; I don't have time to waste with old wooden structures that refuse to follow the will of *my* way. There are worlds and words and writing about them to be done after all. My newly painted white bookshelf represents a blank page, a new beginning for writing this book that is my ending, and I am anxious to begin.

I look at the bookshelf once more before sitting down to write. Taking a fresh look at yesterday's paint work, I am at first delighted with the result. The flat wooden panels are fresh. Clean. Blank. Even. But the longer I stand there looking, the more I begin to sense that there is something terribly wrong and horribly not right. I see that the shelves I thought moments ago to be crisp, unblemished and smooth, are now…well now, they are quite simply empty, sanitary and bare. No wonder my friend-as-furniture is still furious with me; my bookshelf is not being and doing what it knows best, it is not shelving any books. There are no books on the shelves. The shelves are book less and the books are shelf less. What is a shelf without books and where are books without shelves? What does that make a bookshelf if it is without on both counts? I think and wonder. That kind of bookshelf is lonely, and underneath the fresh white paint, my beloved bookshelf is feeling blue. I bend down low, so very low, to see if I can find the root source of this indigo sadness that has overtaken my wooden companion. On my way down, I spy in the corner of my eye the pile of books I carefully placed in the corner of my room yesterday, before I began the process of transformation. Fuck, of course. I don't know why I didn't think of this before. My bookshelf needs books on its shelves so that it can find, know and become itself—in and of itself. And not just any books. The bookshelf and I need books that we call friends, close up friends; the ones whose words and the worlds they name secret/e a language we understand; not just with our thinking heads, but with our thinking hearts. Hearts that think; hearts that write.

12.

The first book to find its place on the bookshelf belongs to Virginia Woolf. It's her classic feminist work, *A room of one's own* and one of my absolute favourites. It's a feminist coming of age book for me; a feminesto of sorts for the writing-academic-woman I wanted to be and promised to become. The pages in the copy I own are soft, almost tattered and absolutely worn, turned as they have been, many times over. The pale pink post-it notes I carefully positioned on each leaf when I first picked up and perused this copy are still there, minding and re-minding me of those places in the text where my thinking wandered this way and that. While I might have posted them many years ago, but they remain safely stuck in place; a marker of my steadfast "allegiance to the discourses of the 'posties'" (Lather, 1998, p. 487) and there I am content for them to stay, so far as they might, as Lather insists, help us to "think not only *with* but in our actions" (1998, p. 495). Every so often a pale green post-it note appears and interrupts the sameness, added as afterthought, but such discomforts of difference I have learnt to trust. I decide that the second from the top shelf is Virginia's, not the first shelf, but the one just under it. I place *A room of one's own* there because I know I can easily reach it, and that I will use it often, and often times again. *Three guineas* (1938), *Moments of being* (1976), *Selected essays* (1942/1992), *The waves* (2015), *Selected essays* (1942/1992), *Mrs Dalloway* (1925), *Monday or Tuesday: Eight stories* (1921), *Night and day* (2011) and *The death of the moth and other essays* (1974) I set beside it in close companionship. There is room on this shelf of her own for others, and one by one I set books written about Virginia Woolf. There are the two Cambridge works; *The Cambridge introduction to Virginia Woolf* (2006) by Jane Goldman and *The Cambridge companion to Virginia Woolf* (2010) edited by Susan Sellers. I whisper an apology. I do not think of myself a Virginia Woolf "expert", a literature critic or someone who would dare to assume to know *anything* about Virginia Woolf; the Cambridge texts are my "go to's" when I find myself second guessing my interpretation and responses to her works. There are others too that need to claim their place for the self-same reasons. Hermoine Lee's (1996) biography *Virginia Woolf*, Pippet's much older (1955) account of Virginia's life entitled *The moth and the star: A biography of Virginia Woolf* and a DVD copy of the British-American drama film *The hours* (Daldry, 2004), I put in place too. All of these texts ground me now, as they have since I began writing as a feminist, as an academic feminist, as an academic feminist writing a critical and embodied approach to critical autoethnography.

I stand back, the way that I seem to do frequently, to peruse the arrangement I have made on the second shelf and I smile as a sense of satisfaction washes over me. I recall Virginia's dismay as she looked in vain for books by women on the shelves of the British Museum and instead could only find texts about women written by men. "Have you any notion how many books are written about women in the course of one year?", she writes. "Have you any notion how many are written by men...Men who have no apparent qualification save they are not women?" (1929/2001, p. 32), she asks in part perplexed, in part enraged. I make a promise to her that *only* writing by women will sit upon *my* book shelf in *my* room of my own. This is indeed something I will and can do; and yet there is more still—there is still yet something more my writing will and can do. I swear to Virginia that not only will I only read books *by* women, I will only cite the words *of* women in my own writing. This is what my women's writing will *willfully* do. I feel the bookshelf groan, "Really Elizabeth? Are you heading this way *again*?" I know the bookshelf is anticipating the backlash from what might be perceived to be a radical feminist intervention into the world of academic knowledge production; fancy that! I hear titters and twitters of disbelief. To not cite men? Unthinkable! The nervous giggling is replaced with sniggers of disgust and ridicule. Really? You think you can get away with that? The bookshelf simultaneously sighs and shrugs, knowing I have no choice and that the choice I will inevitably make was written in the stars the moment I proclaimed myself a feminist academic. "Go on then, give it to them once and for all—it's not like you're a virgin at this or anything". I hesitate. Frustrated and impatient, the bookshelf rolls its eyes and gives me a shove. "Just get on with it Elizabeth!"

13.

Thinking and wondering about the matter of writing, I find myself, once more, in the hands of Hélène. Right up next to her, *So close* (2009). The question, she writes, the one that pursues—haunting and hunting her at the same time—is the one that prays and preys to ask, "What is X going to say?" (2009, p. 25). It is an interrogative sentence, it could be curious or probing or intrusive, and yet its affect is always already the same. Interruption. Falter. Prevention. Even though, as Cixous notes, the subject of the writing itself is beautiful and unique—wonder-full even—the question "What is X going to say?" is enough to position her so close and so far from beginning. Cixous is explicitly referring to her compulsion to literally, naturally, "which is to say literaturally" (p. 25) return to Algiers—a constant theme she simultaneously enters and exits, from the inside and outside, throughout much of her writing. Here she is contemplating the idea of wanting to see Algeria one last time, to take herself there, so close again yet from a distance again. She fancies that writing words about Algiers and Algeria, writing these exact words once, twice and hundreds time and more, become the visit in and of itself, and by writing of this process of visiting in return she in turn will be visited by her Algeriance.

I raise my head from her writing. Her words about writing so close, so close to Algeria that it can be touched and touches, in turn return to touch me. I can feel writing sitting beside me, fingers fluttering lightly across my skin, taunting and teasing me to begin. The sensation is intoxicating, invisible and inaccessible all at once (Cixous, 1991, p. 9); I shiver in dread-full delight. In the same but different way to Cixous, I find myself poised at the entry on the inside of a book I am writing about my work on the outside upon my exit from Burrulula as a here and there, now and then, ethnographer, educator, ethnomusicologist. I hear the voices of colleagues, companions and close up friends push and pull me towards this writing. Screaming and softly saying, this is the book, they say, you *must* write. People want to hear a story about what you now know about working with Aboriginal people there and here. People, they say, want to listen to your story about what you now and then know about writing about working with Aboriginal people. People want to take the story about how to come to know and write about and with Aboriginal people then and now here and there. This story, they say, is one that people want to hear so that your story can become our story. A story that leaves no place for un-remembering and makes room for un-forgetting.

14.

The harsh ring of the telephone makes it way into the writing room I have begun to call my own—once more. As much as I might wish it to be Virginia, I know immediately it *has* to be Cixous—again; her obsession with the telephone has not abated and no-one calls on the landline anymore, no-one that matters. This time, I pause before rushing to answer her call, because here's the thing. This, more than anything else I have written, *this* is the "book-that-I-do-not-write" (after Cixous, 2007, p. 24); because there are one, two and more lives inside and outside this writing and I do not have an answer to the question, "What is X going to say?" The facts. The fiction. The fascination. The fear. The flight forwards. The fight backwards. The first. The final. The find. The failure. The freedom. The fatal. This torment of turning and returning such around the inbetween of such "retropresentiments" (Cixous, 2007, p. 8) is k/new not and not k/new. I have known it before but not quite. You are right Cixous, I find myself on another page nine with you and know the un-easy truth that even "these passions, these pains do not…go away. They return under the cardboard cover, become silent, are silenced, have never been" (2007, p. 9). I have at once been in life and death with them and they always already finds me in trouble, troubled and troubling. And so here I am. So close to writing. So close to writing the book-that-I-do-not-write. My Yanyuw-*ance*.

15.

"Do you solemnly declare", asks Cixous, "that this is the book [you] don't write?"

"It is", I reply.

"Do you admit that you don't write them, in general, the book is not something [you] do?" She persists.

I nod my head in silence.

"Do you admit that instead of writing the book, you write 'something besides books'?"

"Yes", I agree.

"Do you circumfess to signing your name in capital letters on each of the books you do not write, of thus speaking up with an authority that darts out with dangerous assurance (Cixous, 2007, pp. 10–11)?"

I shrug my shoulders, there is no point in denying it. "I have done so in the past".

"Do you agree to be wary of this in future and not take yourself 'continuously or deeply or simply and comfortably' (Cixous, 2007, p. 11) by and for this name?"

"I can promise you I will", I say in response.

"So what is it that you think you are doing now?" Her voice cracks with incredulity. "Are you not once again being 'compliant 'and surrendering to 'this guilt by docility' (Cixous, 2007, p. 11) by writing about the worlds of others using your words?"

I turn my face away from her; of course, she is right. The book I fancy I am writing is a text full of words about other people's worlds; words and worlds which somehow when I was not watching or paying attention became my own. I *fancy* I am writing a book which brings together my work as a white-settler-colonialwoman who *fancies* she is doing social justice by reading, researching and reproducing knowledge about Indigenous Australian peoples through what I *fancy* is interdisplinary work in ethnomusicology, education and autoethnography in what I *fancy* is a relationship which is response-able and ethical because of relationship. I watch myself writing these words—full of *fancy* as they are—and catch a glimpse of a voice that speaks with authority which I had forgotten to keep a sharp ear on. The sound this academic and authoritative accent makes is one I wish I did not recognise. Of course, Cixous is right, a flight of *fancy* this book that is not yet a book it is; nothing more or less but this.

"I can see by the look on your face—'half horror half passionate compassion' (Cixous, 2007, p. 13)—that now you are divided. This book that you do not yet write, you are part of it and it is part of you", she speaks a little more softly now, the suspicion lacing her earlier questions has taken its leave.

"Our conversation is not yet finished and the next question I am going to ask requires a yes or no response", Cixous explains. "Do you call that thing you are now writing a book?"

I pause. "Well I have a book…"

Cixous interrupts, "Yes or no?"

"Yes, I have a book contract", I say confidently before hesitating once more. "So…I guess it's a book in that sense".

Cixous raises one eyebrow. "Really? A book contract? Is that the best you have?" She looks at me now long and hard, her eyes piercing their way through to the front, the back and back to the front again.

"A book!" She exclaims. "In mimicry of me and my dead woman! You have presumed to step into the shoes of me; and now, what and all that you have is that 'haggard violent thing crazy for death? That ooze of fears you don't want to run away from? That rustle of fraudulent voices from behind the pasts, through the cracks in the night?' Do you 'call that a book, that thing' (Cixous, 2007, p. 11)?"

I do not have an answer for Cixous; I am not quite sure I would call this "thing" I am writing a book for it is the book I do not want to write. I am terrified of this book that it is not yet a book; "horribly afraid of this pile of things seeping through my cracks from the other side" (Cixous, 2007, p. 14), forcing me to a place of un-forgetting where once begun, I sense it will be impossible to "stop the supervening. The returnings" (Cixous, 2007, p. 14). I know I have to make a decision. Do I write this book "into life or out"? (Cixous, 2007, p. 10).

"You are asking me questions I cannot answer", I throw my hands in desp/air.

Cixous shakes her head—in disappointment, pity or kindness I cannot be certain.

"But if you allow me, I will come to see you so that I can re/turn these questions around towards an answer", I whisper, bordering on the edge of fear and daring.

Cixous's eyes widen in surprise. She recognises this approach because it is one she herself made; not to herself, but to Jacques Derrida—"the

Book that talks", she affectionately describes him, a "nobody but anyone" (Cixous, 2007, p. 14) who she would trust.

"Let me write then in mimicry of your own writing and quote you, it's safer (Cixous, 2007, p. 14)", I say to her. I can see that Cixous is now fully wide-awake to what it is I am doing, and she decides to play along.

She asks, "Why is that you want to see me?" (Cixous, 2007, p. 14).

"I want to be able to show you 'my monsters in secret, my wounds, the limbs and pieces of my disaster'", I explain. "[My] scraps of cut tongue, baskets of sliced phenomes, traces of fauns, lots of loose sheets of paper to which I [have] consigned in vain the mad and urgent question of the real' (p. 14)".

Cixous continues with a paraphrase of herself, "I think [you] remember my memories of [me] better than I do, which is to say more or maybe less, I mean with this perhapsness which renders assurance prudent and folly wise!" She laughs then, extending the long and hard look from earlier into loud. "In writing this book you don't write, 'retelling the tale goes deeper' (p. 14)".

"And you say this I know with a 'salt of uncertainty' (p. 15)", I remind her. "'For nothing is more soothing than that which at first seems disquieting, the refinement of hesitation. It leaves everything open. Everything is…'".

Cixous holds her hand up, silently asking me to stop speaking and writing so that she may speak and write herself, her own memory and her own language, once more, "Everything is perhaps…Perhaps everything *is* perhaps. But then everything else can also be" (p. 15).

"A little, a little this or a little that", my voice takes on a sing-song tone. The repartee between goes on, note for note, and we take our self-same-other-citational turns in turn.

"My passion, my pains, my storms, my cries of anger or despair…They often give me a hand when I write" (p. 17), Cixous' voice is deeper than mine, calling up and out of writing that is how old? I cannot tell. The heartlines in my hand begin to beat in time with her words and writing. 16.

There is but one more thing to do in this room of my own so that I might begin; she would never forgive me if I didn't and besides, I wouldn't have it any other way. She has become my French *kundiyarra:* my most necessary writings words and worlds companion and with love to you Hélène Cixous I place your work on the bookshelf next to Virginia, so close. My favourites are all there: *Coming to writing and other essays* (1991), *Dream, I tell you* (2006), *First days of the year* (1998b), *Rootprints* (Cixous & Gruber, 1997), *So close* (2009), *Stigmata* (1998a), *Three steps on the ladder of writing* (1993), and *White ink* (2008). *The Helene Cixous reader* (1994) and the commentary by Abigail Bray (2004) on Cixous' work find their reserved place. A bright pink binder is the final item to be placed on the bookshelf. Inside are printed copies of articles written by Cixous of which there are many. There are three in particular I re/turn to time and time again: "The laugh of the Medusa" (1976), "My Algeriance" (1997) and "The book I don't write" (2007). All manner of pencil, ink and high-lighted colour mark these writings now cased in a plastic pocket to ensure their longevity. I look at Cixous' books and texts all lined up in a row and lovingly run my hand over the spines; from the pages of *Three steps on the ladder of writing* I hear her whisper, "The texts that call me all have different voices. But they all have one voice in common, they all have a certain music I am attuned to, and that's the secret. You may already know the ones whose music I hear. I have brought them with me, I will make them resound" (1993, p. 5). The bookshelf and I sigh in concord, content and complete in the sweet lullaby of her words; my writing at the ending can begin.

References

Bray, A. (2004). *Hélène Cixous: Writing and sexual difference*. New York, NY: Palgrave Macmillan.

Cixous, H. (1976). The laugh of the Medusa (K. Cohen & P. Cohen, Trans.). *Signs, 1*(4), 875–893.

Cixous, H. (1991). *Coming to writing and other essays* (S. Suleiman, Ed., S. Cornell, Trans.). Cambridge, MA: Harvard University Press.

Cixous, H. (1993). *Three steps on the ladder of writing*. New York, NY: Columbia University Press.

Cixous, H. (1994). *The Hélène Cixous reader* (S. Sellers, Ed.). London: Routledge.

Cixous, H. (1997). My Algeriance: In other words, to depart not to arrive from Algeria. *Triquarterly, 100*, 259–279.

Cixous, H. (1998a). *First days of the year* (C. MacGillivray, Trans., Emergent literatures). Minneapolis, MN: University of Minnesota Press.

Cixous, H. (1998b). *Stigmata: Escaping texts*. London: Routledge.

Cixous, H. (2006). *Dream, I tell you* (B. B. Brahic, Trans., European perspectives (Columbia University Press)). New York: Columbia University Press.

Cixous, H. (2007). The book I don't write. *Parallax, 13*(3), 9–30.

Cixous, H. (2008). *White ink: Interviews on sex, text and politics* (S. Sellers, Trans.). Stocksfeld: Acumen.

Cixous, H. (2009). *So close* (P. Kamuf, Trans.). Cambridge: Polity Press.

Cixous, H., & Clément, C. (1986). *The newly born woman* (B. Wing, Trans.). New York, NY: Schoken Books.

Cixous, H., & Calle-Gruber, M. (1997). *Rootprints: Memory and life writing*. London: Routledge.

Daldry, S. (2004). *The hours* (Widescreen, ed.). South Yarra, VIC: Buena Vista Home Entertainment distributor.

Goldman, J. (2006). *The Cambridge introduction to Virginia Woolf* (Cambridge introductions to literature). Cambridge: Cambridge University Press.

Lather, P. (1998). A praxis of stuck places: Critical pedagogy and its complicities. *Education Theory, 48*(4), 487–497.

Pippett, A. (1955). *The moth and the star: A biography of Virginia Woolf*. Toronto, ON: Little Brown and Company.

Sellers, S. (2010). *The Cambridge companion to Virginia Woolf* (2nd ed.). Cambridge companions to literature). Cambridge: Cambridge University Press.

Spry, T. (2010). Call it swing: A Jazz Blues autoethnography. *Cultural Studies – Critical Methodologies, 10*(4), 271–282.

Spry, T. (2016). *Autoethnography and the other: Unsettling power through utopian performatives*. London: Routledge.

Woolf, V. (1921). *Monday or Tuesday*. New York, NY: Harcourt, Brace, Jovanovich.

Woolf, V. (1925). *Mrs Dalloway*. New York, NY: Harcourt, Brace, Jovanovich.

Woolf, V. (1929/2001). *A room of one's own*. London: Vintage Press.

Woolf, V. (1938). *Three guineas*. London: Hogarth Press.

Woolf, V. (1942/1992). *Virginia Woolf: Selected essays* (D. Bradshaw, Ed.). Oxford: Oxford University Press.

Woolf, V. (1974). *The death of the moth: And other essays*. New York, NY: Harcourt Brace Jovanovich.

Woolf, V. (1976). *Moments of being: Unpublished autobiographical writings* (J. Schulkind, Ed.). Orlando, FLA: Harcourt.

Woolf, V. (1980). *The diary of Virginia Woolf, volume III: 1925–1930* (A. E. Bell, Ed.). London: Hogarth Press.

Woolf, V. (2015). *The waves* (New ed., Oxford world's classics). Oxford: Oxford University Press.

3

Writing with Cixous, in Love

When do we reach the hour when we say we have deceived everyone in our lives in order to keep what we call life going? I don't know. We go to the School of the Dead to hear a little of what we are unable to say. This is why we need to the books that hurt us.
Cixous (1993, p. 53)

© The Author(s) 2019
E. Mackinlay, *Critical Writing for Embodied Approaches*,
https://doi.org/10.1007/978-3-030-04669-9_3

Fig. 3.1 I to you Héléne Cixous

1.
Hélène Cixous how I love you. How often have I written in mimicry of you? How long have I been reading, revelling and ravishing the words you have written and sought to reproduce them in faithful, frenzied and femme fatally flawed homage? When did my yearning for your words and worlds begin with such intensity and when did the worlds you shared in words become imprinted so deeply in the heartlines on my hand? Did it begin on one of the first days of the year or was it so close to the ladder? And why, oh why, you Cixous? You are alive but talk about needing a dead woman to begin. In the space between us, something wicked this way comes and writing with you, Cixous, begins—"in one another we will never be lacking" (Cixous, 1976, p. 893).
2.
This memory, a moment this one, "the lost one" as Cixous (1998, p. 7) would say, is one I sense now I needed to find in order to begin at the end

of this story. The little girl I once knew has been weeping for years waiting for my *arrivance* back to her; one tear, two tears, many tears weeping for the world (Cixous, 1998, p. 7), a world to which I/you/we are forever are on the way (Greene, 1995) for I/she/we—and perhaps even you—are not there yet. But this is not the only lost memory and moment of one; there are other moments of one yet to write and these overwhelm me with the drive and desire to weep, these memories and moments wrap me up in the necessity of weeping. I read Cixous' thinking around weeping and there is joy, for are they not one and the same when they meet at the inbetween then and now? Could there ever be anything else when for the "hundredth time as for the first, the son [sun] would rise, rise…and break upon her hearts rock" (Cixous, 1991, p. 8)?

3.

The cool rays of autumn sun place their hands lazily upon my shoulders as I make my way across the carpark. The rusty irongate protests noisily as I enter the school grounds. I pause for a moment, stuck and squirming in the quiet discomfort of metal grating against the dirt of now and then, wondering why and yet not at all why I am there. My feet choose to ignore the scratching and snarling of uncertainty and instead carry me across the present into the past despite the complaints of the irongate. I am looking for someone, someone I have lost along the way and I need to find her. The bell has just rung for morning playtime and I walk quickly towards the place where I hope she might be. Around the corner, past the library, down the ramp, alongside the art room, under the covers of the assembly area, and into the quadrangle. Laughter punctuates soft and loud bursts of talking. The air smells thick with the dregs of reading, writing and 'rithmetic that drive thinking and thoughts about whatfore and whyfore in places of learning like this.

I scan the crowd of bubbling children and soon espy her sitting cross-legged on the concrete with a group of girls deep in conversation. I recognize her at once. Her dimples framed by simple bangs and a bob haircut belie the seriousness on her face as she contemplates the morning tea in her lunchbox. One hand plays with a homemade Anzac biscuit while the other attempts to pull her school dress further down to cover her knees.

"Hey you!" A voice rings out across the squared play area.

She looks up immediately and returns the freshly baked goods to its container.

"Hey moonface!" the boy yells and that is enough.

I watch her turn to look at the ground. I watch her body curl in abhorrence as she begins to shrivel from the inside out. I watch slow tears shed her shame and fix her in a place, not of her own making, but one she has resolved to find friendship with. Fear, loathing and familiarity catch my breath and lodge themselves roughly in my throat. I can not stand witness to this—again. This time I choose differently and run as fast as I can through now and then from here to there towards her. Crouching down, I gently place one hand under her chin and tilt her head upwards. The space between us collapses as we look at one another *as* one.

"We got this", I whisper to her as my lips gently place a kiss on her cheek. "Clear eyes, open heart, can't lose", I say as I hold her head close to mine, so close.

It might have been a moment, it might have been the many moments of here and there which lay between us, I cannot say for sure; but after some time, she pulls away. Smiling softly, she reaches forward and brushes the fringe away from my face.

"We sure do", she says. "I can't wait to be you, if this is me".

4.

The little girl as me and I stand holding one another, holding heads in our hands, holding time, holding it so tight in the hope it might stand still for we are not yet ready for what is to come next. But it does, whether we like it or not. Cixous finds her way towards us; and her writing-as-thinking-as-being-as-women envelopes us tightly within its folds. I am comfortable there and I find myself leaning into the comfort and warmth her words provide. I feel at home; I am completely homespun and in a home spin—no more and no less—than when I am with Cixous. I feel myself at ease with myself now Cixous has arrived. How could I forget? How could it be that I had turned my face against the wall as if nothing else matters, as if nothing else could ever matter? This is at once my ending and my beginning.

Her arrival at playtime in the quadrangle is quiet and unannounced. Although, if truth be told, I had been expecting her and I would like to think her appearance is for me and she only. But I know otherwise; her presence and attendance to this moment of thinking through and with I/she/we is an always already necessity. Around, through and across the heartlines that sit poised on my tongue ready to weep and burst into song; she is the bass line. Cixous looks at she, holding me, and sits down beside us.

"What is it", she asks, "that has you so terrified of writing yourself as women?"

I don't know what to say; my thinking and writing is so consumed, as perhaps it should be, with her words and worlds. I ask, "Come and join us?"

Cixous hesitates.

"I would want to but," she replies—there is a thinly veiled wariness, or perhaps a warning which now stands in the space between us.

"What happens if you don't write the ending as the beginning so that you might finally bring your story to its ending? Surely that in and of itself is dangerous?"

She pauses and grabs my hand. "You must become the dangerous woman writing, a woman writing into danger".

5.

Another woman has entered the quadrangle and is making her way towards Cixous, the little girl and me. She is young, maybe late teens, early twenties. She swings her hips and sashays confidently; her chunky black Doc Martin boots leading the way under her tartan mini skirt and red jumper. Her deeply dyed spiky hairstyle screams rebellion and revolution, her white painted face, dark shadowed eyes and burgundy lips hold a haunting that teases as it does terrify. She is not particularly tall, not particularly fat or thin, not particularly pretty and yet being particular in appearance seems to absorb her. As she comes closer, she waves her hand in recognition; I am not sure whether she is a friend of the little girl or Cixous but I am certain I do not know her. The young woman does not look like someone I would call friend. She looks like the kind of woman I have tried desperately hard not to be. A loose woman, a woman who slams shots of alcohol down her throat and shoots drugs into her veins so that she might find herself blindly on the way to false dreams as the world around her wakes up to a new day. A woman who loosely tosses her body around between men and beds she does not know in the deceptive hope that one day she will wake up held, held every so tightly and ever so securely loved. A woman who flings foul words from her mouth to fuck with her herself, to fuck the world and she does her best to fuck them all. Now this hard-hitting young woman is standing in front of me, I am certain I do not know her, I am certain I do not *want* to know her.

"Hey", she says softly as she sits down on the concrete beside the little girl.

Her voice is faint and gentle. I was expecting gravel on glass.

The little girl looks up at her in wonder. "Hello", she smiles shyly.

"Sorry I'm late", says the young woman. She sounds like a secret. "I hope you haven't been waiting long".

A sharp laugh escapes roughly from my mouth and shoots its unease directly at her. "Waiting for you? Why would we be waiting for the likes of you?"

The young woman reels backwards in an attempt to avoid my dart of dismissal and a look of bewilderment settles on her face. "I came because you called for me", she explains.

"I called you? No way, I don't even know you", I shake my head.

She moves her head in negation of me. "No, that's not right, I heard you calling me. You said, 'We got this', and I knew I had to come and find you".

In that moment, something happens, something awful happens. Time seems to stand still and yet race away from underneath my feet and I have lost control of the now and then, the ending and the beginning once more fold into one another. A memory of she and me comes into focus and I push back against her. She is the hush-hush history I have tried to destroy, and she is standing right in front of me ready to explode my world a-part.

6.

As I look at the young woman's hand in mine, I begin to un-forget the loose woman I had lost. It is summer time. The sun made its way below the horizon of this concrete jungle long ago and the blanket of darkness has laid itself upon the world. The sheets are cool on my skin as I lie in bed in my bra and undies, listening to the remnants of the dry heat hissing and spitting on the pavement outside my window. I hear a distant breeze, trying to break through the unbearable stalemate the warmth of this season brings, but it soon gives up and goes home. It's too hot for anything more and the fan above gently blows the downy hair on my face and arms. My head is spinning, slowly but surely, turning me around and around. I watch in fascination as the day, the first day of the year, unfolds before me. A day of many firsts. My first orchestra rehearsal. My first lecture in music. My first visit to the library. My first taste of university. My first toga party. One taste on the first day of the year is all I needed, I was drawn in and towards; my head is spiraling now full of it all, craving more.

"Fuck!" I am woken sharply by a knock on my door. It's late, too late. I pause, not moving, waiting, lying in wait.

"Miss Lizzie?!" A deep male voice calls from the outside.

"Miss Lizzie, Lizzie, Lizzie, *Lizzie*! Let me come in Miss Lizzie!!!"

This person knows my name.

"MISS LIZZIE!!!" He is shouting now.

"Miss Lizzie, Miss Lizzie, PLEASE let me come in". A pause.

"Pretty please?" Another moment.

"Miss Lizzie, you're so pretty, let me come in Miss Lizzie!"

Words now are flung at my door in fever pitch. Fuck. My instincts scream at me, don't, don't you dare, don't be daring and dangerous, this is not the time. I see myself looking back at me sending a silent apology as I climb out of bed and move towards the door. Don't do it Lizzie, I whisper, go back and lie down. Please don't do this. I reach out to stop her but my hand falls through hers like sand. I'm sorry I say, he's going to wake the whole fucking floor if I don't. It's Duncan. Duncan who I'd danced with at the toga party. Two years above me at college Duncan who twirled and twisted his body and hips close to mine as we gyrated the night away. Completely naked under his toga Duncan whose long legs had me wanting more, touching more, wanting, touching. Have another bourbon shot Duncan who lined them up in front of me with a wildness in his eyes I fancied a lot. It's time to call it a night Duncan who insisted that we had already had our full of one another and passionately kissed me goodbye outside my building. It's Duncan; Duncan, I say in relief.

7.

I throw myself into his arms and he catches me before I fall.

"Hey Miss Lizzie, I got you", he says with a soft laugh and stumbles us both across the threshold into my room, flicking the door closed with his heel.

I move my head slightly to look up into his green eyes, eyes that shine only for me. My legs are wrapped tightly around his waist and his hands cradle my ass. He returns my gaze and there is a shift. Ever so slight, it arrives without warning. A coolness descends upon my skin and I am keenly aware now that I am undressed, bare, and exposed; my secret is out.

"You want me Miss Lizzie, don't you?" Duncan whispers, his lips nipping my ear.

I shiver. I want his mouth elsewhere and everywhere. "Yes", I murmur.

"Say it again, Miss Lizzie, I want to hear you say it again", his teeth graze the back of my neck.

"I want you Duncan", I say, my whole-body crooning.

"I said, Miss Lizzie, say it, again!" His fingers find my breast wanting and he obliges.

"Hey!" I yelp. "What was that?" His nails dig into my nipple as he twists it, drawing blood.

"I *said*, Miss Lizzie, you have to say you want me but I didn't *hear* you properly", his spare hand grabs the soft flesh of my inner thigh and I can feel a bruise start to form.

Fuck. My instincts roar at me. Told you, told you stupid fuck, told you not to.

"Will you say it now Miss Lizzie?" Like a rag doll he flings me roughly onto the bed, my head thuds against the wall. He shoves his large body between my legs and reaches forward to cradle my face in his hands. The sweet longing of moments ago has left; the room reeks sour and dark.

"I'm sorry Miss Lizzie, I'm sorry, but I need you to say it for me". One slap, a flush of shame paints my cheek.

"Say it!" Another, pink disgrace lines match it.

"I'm only going to ask you one more". One punch, red humiliation drips from my nose.

"One more". Another, black degradation circle my eyes.

"Time!"

He fucks me then. Front and back. With his fingers, with his fists, with his hard cock that rams and raids and ruins me. Once, twice, more; I lose myself in the counting. Fight or flight, it doesn't matter for there never was any choice. I have already fluttered away.

When I wake up I am alone. There is music playing somewhere. "Why can't I get just one fuck", it's a Violent Femmes ("Add it up", 1983) song, one of my favorites. "Why can't I get just one fuck, I guess it got something to do with luck, But I waited my whole life for just one". Without warning I am trembling; uncontrollably, my body, my mind, my heart shattering into pieces on the floor. I feel a wetness trickle down my face. Blood mixed with tears; and I am laughing.

Fig. 3.2   And she laughs, a-way too easy

8.

I can't seem to stop now that I have started. Each burst of wild hilarity thinly masks a fast-rising hysteria, and it hurts. I cradle my stomach, trying to grasp all of the pain, holding it ever so tightly to keep it wrapped up inside. This is my secret; my secret to keep locked away. Bent over double I shuffle across the room and open the door to my wardrobe to peer into the mirror. I see a body broken; a wounded shell encasing a woman. I gaze and stare again more intently at my reflection, my fingers gingerly touching those parts which are no longer recognizable to me. I can't stand to look at her and yet the longer I stare and gaze the harder it becomes to tear my eyes away. I don't want to see the damage, but it is done anyway.

Watching her, watching me, I step outside myself. I take my palette of tri-coloured foundation. Green to cover the red marks, yellow concealer to hide the black and grey patches, and purple tint for those turning brown. I see the woman in the mirror raise an eyebrow, questioning as she is curious. How do I know that this is what I must do? I turn my eyes downwards, too ashamed to share with her. Each brush stroke is slow and meticulous. I become mesmerized and obsessed in this process of concealment; it is a move to protection, mine and hers. I sit back and wait for my face paint to dry before applying a final coat. A warrior woman gazes and stares back at me.

Fuck Duncan.

She is defiant. Fucked if he is going to fuck me up.

She is dangerous. Fuck him.

She is daring. Fuck them all. Using gentle downward motions, I sponge a layer of skin toned foundation on my face. I am covered. Long sleeved jumper and collared shirt. I am concealed. Jeans and boots. I am closed up and in companionship; she and me in secret. I take her hand and together we march out of my room, down the hallway, and step outside.

Fucking became ever so easy after Duncan. Sam was easy. Easy on the eye, easy to laugh with, and easy to hang around. He was all too easy to lay; easy to walk away from the next day. And then easily enough we would do it all over again the next time the weekend rolled around. Neither of us seemed to want anything less easy than that, it was easy simply being friends who fucked. Roger was not easy, even though he should have been. We only fucked once or twice although it would have been easy enough to go back for more. Being together made us uneasy because there was in fact more to it than just fucking. It was not easy being with him which made it easy in the end to say no more.

Roger prepared me for Campbell. Campbell was not easy. Campbell and I had been friends since Year 8 in high school. The word friend itself does not sit easily as I write it because he was, not quite and yet always on the edge of easy, teasing me into a place I yearned for as much as I ran from. He played tenor saxophone and I played French Horn in the combined high schools band. We played tennis, night clubs and country races became our playground, and we played whenever we could because we were desperate to move beyond this foreplay we seemed to have stuck on replay. A hum of electricity flowed between us and it was intoxicating. It would be too easy to say we played beautiful music together but in fact we never did, we never did fuck. Instead we kissed, long and hard, lots and lots, across the span of time and the last thing at night before we said goodbye under the expanse of the starry universe. With our bodies ever so close we moved ourselves near to a happily ever after because that was our destiny, we both knew it and fucking right there and then didn't matter, we had a forever waiting for us to fuck each other.

With two words Campbell stopped being easy.

"Marry me", he said. His green eyes held me tightly to him. With two times more words, his question turned into well-worn phrase, and Campbell became not easy.

"Will you marry me?" I tried to say yes, it was my destiny to say yes, yes it was, yes was easy, easy as. Yes and easy were after all almost the same word—just one letter shy, standing around the corner from each other. My answer ran fast from my heart to my head and rushed straight into my mouth before I could stop it.

"No", I said. Fuck. I just said no. I wasn't meant to say no. Saying no was too easy and it shouldn't have been. Campbell knew it, I knew it, but there it was, a two-letter word that took away our easy. Fuck. I needed to fix this. I had to make the easy between us come back.

"Campbell, I can't marry you—yet". I watched him walk away. I wanted him to come back. I waited for him. He never came. Without fucking him, I had fucked up everything. The easy was gone and so was Campbell. I wish I could replay our play and put it in reverse. I long for our easy to return, but I know there is a lot of not easy that sits between us. I should have fucked him instead of putting faith in forever, and then it would have been easy. Fuck, at this point, any kind of easy will do.

9.

The young woman gently squeezes my hand and cruelly wrenches me back to the now and then.

"I'm sorry", she mumbles. "I know this is an un-forgetting you never wanted".

"Excuse me", I stammer. "I think I'm going to be sick".

I begin to dry retch, stuck in between. Wanted, who the fuck wanted; it was the wanting that was the problem and now all I wanted was to experience fatal recall at this remembering. With each wave of vomit I imagine I was secreting my secret away; purging myself of Duncan, spewing up the pain and hurt, heaving aside the terrifying possibility that it was me. That I asked for it. That I was paying my dues. That I only had myself to blame. That I had fucked up. That I had to just forget. That this was the only way. I vomited until there was nothing more—nothing more of *me* left—and I knew in that moment that I had lost the battle. The warrior woman I had glimpsed earlier had simply given up. In the end it was that easy.

10.

Let me share a secret. Or perhaps, better yet a *secret*-ion, as Cixous would insist. "The world is full of secrets", she writes, and there are secrets "so secret and secreted away...buried in night and silence: we will never know the face of it would have if it could appear" (2008, pp. 176–177). A secret is illusive, deliberately so, constantly escaping just like writing itself, says Cixous, "a letter on the run" (p. 176) sidestepping between truth and the impossible. Writing, she suggests, "owes its life to the secret...as soon as one writes to exhume one secretes secrets" and in this way, "constantly augments itself" (2008, p. 178). This *secret*-ion is one that shares and separates the here and there of breathing, living, writing and thinking through the word fuck. This four-letter word was no longer a secret hidden, it was the secret of my existence (Derrida in Cixous, 2008, p. 178); it became an addiction, a panacea to that which I could find no other name for. Fuck was raw. It matched the million ways in which the remnants of my night with Duncan continued to tear me apart, brutally banging and bashing my brain and body around, so much so that I didn't recognise the woman I saw in the mirror any longer. I looked for her each day, hoping that she might reappear. I moved closer, and closer and closer in to the glass. But the woman in the mirror kept on stepping back, recoiling and sneering at me in disgust. With each movement she became stranger and much further and far away, until eventually she was but a smudge on the horizon. After that, I stopped looking. She was gone, and the mirror shattered.

Fuck, in the end, undressed my easy. The opening of the word is undemanding and easy-going, holding carefully in its folds a tender caress; but the close is volatile and hot-tempered. I found myself poised at the finish, dwelling deliberately in that fickle moment; I could ignore how unstable it was because each time the word exploded from my mouth, the final letters fell like a sharp and blunt blade on my skin and were guaranteed to bring me back to a certain wide awakeness. I lived fuck in the fullness of it, as noun and as verb and as adjective; it gave torment and anger a place to call home in the full glory of its orthography. I could count on fuck to do all of that and more; indeed, I *did* count them, and it did do more. A fool's fuck; I interrupt my love affair with this word at the centre of my world for just a second. Fuck had me marked as a fool at the end just as it did at the beginning; because it messes with you, fucks you over, and leaves you with fuck all.

11.

It is uneasy to un-forget how many days it was before I stopped painting my face in green, yellow, and purple to cover up my night with Duncan. Was it one, two or three? It might have been less, and it may have been more; accounting for it did not matter then and, while I would like to pretend it does not matter now, it does matter—it matters. The days folded into one another as I watched the mask of the warrior woman slip soundlessly down the sink. Splashes of colour mingled with the stench of memory, holding tight to traces of sweat, semen, tears and blood; and became dirty brown streaks. I willingly swam down the drain with them. Sitting in the depths of the sewer, I am aware that I have brought myself into close companionship with the dead woman, so close I can feel her breathing, her warm breath teasing and tickling the fine hairs on the back of my neck. The dead woman looks ups and sees the live one peering down. I watch myself for a certain while; soon enough it is difficult to tell the one from the two. I am a spectator at this scene of something lost and become transfixed by the ways in which my eyes, mouth, brow, cheeks and mouth shift and change shape in search of something found. I see myself notice me, dark, bare, and broken at the bottom; the wounds on my face, my hands, my body bearing witness to unbearable filth. The truth this sight holds refuses to be remade invisible and I watch myself recoil from me in terror.

Fig. 3.3   The monstrous woman beholds a-not/her

I beckon to me. Now that this trespass between the dead woman and the live one has begun, there is no turning back. Besides, there is something I want, something I need to present to myself. I have been holding onto this gift for some time; forever it might seem. It is the heartline in my hand; the worlds held in heart which come to matter as words written by hand. The heartline that makes me "tremble, redden, bleed" (Cixous, 1993, p. 32) in fear and combat against myself in coming to writing. I choose my pen for this battle quite deliberately. I purchase it with sand dollars, too many in number to penny pinch over; for it bears the mark of a mermaid and it is impossible to name a price for the power it holds. I hand the mermaid marker to myself and watch as the heartlines in my hand enfold it tightly. In that moment I am made to understand, "it's a double bind: either you don't render life or you take it" (Cixous, 1993, p. 32) and having the strength and courage to write through heartlines makes the rise and fall in between possible. It would be uneasy to forget the darkness; it would be easy to uneasy to forget the deadness; but the blood pulsing through heartlines renders it is easy to un-forget that "what comes back to us, no matter what our place, is a duty to truth, to know what is at stake and not deny it" (Cixous, 1993, p. 32).

12.

A-not/her confession. It is not easy. It is not easy at all. There is no *all* in easy there and then in the here and now. I am not sure I can un-forget the moment when I was able to look in the mirror and see myself as something other than the monstrous woman I believed I became after Duncan. I cannot be sure that *that* moment of recognition, acceptance, or denial—call it what you will—and arrival to this and *that* woman has ever presented itself. Like so many other moments, I sense I am still in *arrivance* because the woman of there and here that was and is, remains lost. Perhaps she is lost with the little girl I found in the school quadrangle who lay awake each and every night stone still and terrified, of the dark, of the monsters, sensing the dark monster she might become. I think and wonder now whether she is but a remnant of the material girl who became lost like the threads of cotton that fell upon the floor to lie forever beneath her sewing machine, detached and no longer fit for the weave of fabric that held the dreams of what she might become. Maybe she is lost with the young woman who despite the heavy boots and kohl eyeliner that threatened to kick ass and a-way from all of the dark places that silenced and secret-ed the little girl, did not *know* any other way and wandered a-away anyway into the abyss to keep company with all of the black and blue shades of embodied experience lost. Perhaps, becoming lost was what it was all about in the first place, to make it possible to be-come in writing. Cixous reminds me that becoming lost is "the condition on which beginning to write become necessary-(and)-possible: *losing* everything" (1991, p. 38). She pushes me further to think and wonder that "when you have lost everything…when you are lost, beside yourself [yes, I think and wonder more, it is possible to be-side your own lost, for where else are you if not there?], and you continue getting lost, then, that's when, you are unwoven weft" (1991, p. 38). Waiting to be woven; this lost body, my body is ragged—"ravaged" and "ruined" Cixous (1991, p. 39) might describe it—and yet is here in this space, undefined, detached and without borders, that "you lack nothing. You are beyond lack…Only when you are lost can love find itself in you without losing its way" (Cixous, 1991, p. 39).

13.

If I try my hardest to un-forget, I can come quite close to the moment when I fell in love and became lost with Cixous, and the connection is quite appropriately monstrous. It happened on the day when I looked in the mirror and saw myself exactly that; hideous; a woman damaged beyond repair, bruised up and blacked out. Physically, emotionally, mentally—and intellectually; there is no use pretending or pretens-ing, I was fucked over. Whoever had done this to me was indeed a monster and in return had turned me into one. The hysterics as hilarity which had erupted from within my mind out into my mouth after my night with Duncan was the laugh of a monster; a monstrous woman laughing. I became your Medusa Cixous, not deadly at all but beautiful and laughing. I think and wonder now about the Medusa myth; alive and well in the imaginary of so many women, young and old, far and wide, here and there; not so much a myth anymore. You published "The laugh of the Medusa" in 1976 when I was just five years old. At the beginning of this work you in-sister-ed that "woman must write her self: must write about women and bring women to writing, from which they have been driven away as violently as from their bodies" (1976, p. 875). The head upon my body, the body I had come to abhor, remained bent down, deeply down, to the ground in shame for I was no-one. I had already accused myself of being a monster (Cixous, 1976, p. 876) and I was *no*-one. And besides, who was I, to think that even if I was some-*one*, this no-d*one* could *read* Cixous?

"I am not a good person to ask", you reply, "how to read Cixous" (2002, p. 185). "But I can tell you…use all of yourself: not only the head, but the whole of the body simultaneously; you have to look at the text with your ears…you have to listen with your eyes…you have to see where it breathes" (Cixous & McQuillan, 2002, pp. 185–186). The heartlines in my hand began to awaken and I re/turned to "The laugh of the Medusa" to read again; indeed, to think and wonder again. "I write this as a woman, toward women" (Cixous, 1976, p. 875) you explained, and I imagined you there and then you speaking to and for me, to and for you, to and for all of as others here and now. "You are for you; your body is yours, take it", you insist (Cixous, 1976, p. 876) and I needed nothing further. I remember clearly how turning to the "The laugh of the Medusa" again, I was taken into your embrace; exquisitely ferocious and feminine, without fear. This is what women's writing *will do,* you promised, "by writing her self, woman will return to the body which has been more than confiscated from her" (p. 880).

I roared with both pain and pleasure as letter by word by phrase by paragraph your *écriture feminine* shamelessly denied, decried, defied and sought to destroy the status quo of masculinist writing. "I'm speaking of woman in her inevitable struggle against conventional man", (Cixous, 1976, p. 875) you wrote, and I nodded my head in agreement; I was that woman and I was tired of the struggle. You spoke of smug-faced men in service to an imbecilic capitalist machinery, afraid, becoming very afraid of female sexed-texts like yours (p. 877) and I laughed. "Touch me, caress me, you the living no-name, give me my self as myself" (pp. 881–882), you urged *woman for women*, I smiled and so I did. "Now women return from afar, from always: from 'without'…from below, from beyond" and we are "seething underneath" (p. 877). Take to the single battlefield, become militant, mutate power relations (p. 884) and "let the priests tremble, we're going to show them our sexts!" (p. 885). I laughed loud and hard then. I wasn't just simmering with rage, I was snorting; completely out-of-raged and poised to make "an explosive, *utterly* destructive, staggering return, with a force never yet unleashed" (p. 886). Suppressed, subjugated and silenced I would be no more; it was time "to blow up the Law" (p. 887) and "liberate the New Woman from the Old by coming to know her—by loving her" (p. 878). "The new history is coming", you insister-ed, "[And] it's not a dream" (p. 883). I was ready to arrive—to fly, steal, jumble the order, disorient it, change, dislocate, break up, empty and turn upside down (p. 887)— in and through language and writing, vibrant, and over and over again, at the beginning of the ending you promised (Cixous, 1976, p. 882). This body of women's words—your words—gave birth to a newly born woman just as you hoped they might. I picked up the shattered pieces of the mirror and looked once more.

14.

At first glance, this is what I saw. Lack, here; let me spell it for you. In capitals if you please. L-A-C-K. Again. L-A-C-K. Lack, *n*. 1. want (I confess, I had wanted and been found wanting); destitution (I was lost and as close to death as I had ever been; I didn't *need* to be pushed, I climbed willingly into the abyss); need (all I needed was a good dose of Cartesian containment and constraint, that would be sure to do the trick, trickery never fails); failure (I had lost; the predestination was always failure and therefore mission dutifully accomplished: the head of a monstrous and disembodied woman looks obediently back). The list of lack goes on. Lack, *n*. 2. A fault (after all, it was my fault wasn't it? Back to the default position; write, right, rite the same because that it is what is already known); an offense (damned if you do, damned if you don't; either way in lack you are always already an outrage of *monstrous* proportions); a blemish, especially a moral blemish; a defect in character (use all of the green, yellow and purple make-up you like it still won't hide this undeniable fact of lack). This is the list of lack that had become me—a Cixousian precocious, repressed, labyrinth, in trouble and trampled space kind of woman, mouth gagged with the sweet pollen of unheard-of songs and secrets (1976, p. 878). I was lack; I was afraid *not* to lack because that would set into motion a different relationship with my body, this and that woman over there and here. Anything other than lacking was a/nother, a woman I did not know and a different woman to be feared. Fear, difference, other; back to the default position of female lacking where I remained writing myself into petrification before the abyss it created. It is easy to become lost in lack standing there on the edge of here and there. I think and wonder now that "the miracle is that out of all this sense of lack, writing came" (Suleiman, in Cixous, 1991, p. xx).

15.

At second glance in the mirror, I saw a woman who, rather than continue to write "as a paper penis" (p. 883) in imitation of and be "threatened by the big dick" (1976, p. 892)—literally and figuratively—now pledged a commitment to breaking up the truth with creativity, love and laughter; with "an irrepressible burst of laughter" (1991, p. 41) in embodied writing and thinking, such change and surprise became an imaginary without end. I began to read Cixous then as an embodied reader—as an embodied autoethnographer reading, but not yet writing—and I sensed that the Cixousian imaginary, "a dangerous feminine position" (1994, p. 42), was one I needed and wanted to move towards in, out, above, below, up and down and around and through. I read Cixous, I read everything I could of Cixous and with each reading I felt myself coming close, so close, to the kind of autoethnography which does not "seek to master. To demonstrate, explain, grasp. And then to lock away in a strongbox. To pocket part of the riches of the world" (Cixous, 1991, p. 57). More and more I began to think and wonder that this kind of autoethnography was not *kind* at all, it was an un-kind of autoethnography which willingly or not (I cannot be sure which is worse) perpetuated an ethico-onto-epsitemological un-kind of violence which proclaimed a self which in turn dared to speak for the social. The kind of autoethnographic praxis I read in Cixous' writing was one which sought to "transmit: to make things loved by making them known" (1991, p. 57). Yes, a loving kind of *critical* auto-ethnography which insists that writing-as-thinking-as-writing is a place of love—that heart, body, hand, and blood touching in writing breathes text to life and life to text—and "under the blows of [such] love I catch fire, I take to the air, I burst into letters" (1991, p. 44). It is this kind of critical autoethnography which wants to "affect…to wake the dead…to remind people that they once wept for love, and trembled with desires, and that they were then very close to the life that they claim they've been seeking while constantly moving further away ever since" (Cixous, 1991, p. 57). This is the *kind* and loving critical autoethnography which reading and writing with Cixous makes possible.

When Cixous asks, "Who makes me write, moan, sing dare?" Cixous asks. "Who gives me the body that is never afraid of fear? Who writes me?" (1991, p. 44). I dared to position myself as the I and the me in her question, and the together as a-not/her we responded: in part it is you, Cixous: it is you who strikes, touches, agitates, celebrates and transforms. Writing against and a-way from there and then was—is—the only way to begin at the end. And now, having made up my mind, I follow Cixous willingly; "I was [now] following a woman in danger, freely, a dangerous woman. In danger of writing, in the fullness of writing, in the process of writing it, unto the dangers" (p. 90). Turning back to the mirror for another time, I gazed at the monstrous version of myself more intently that day after than ever before and since; I saw a dangerous woman, a woman I at once feared and yet had been searching for my whole life it would seem. In that moment of being, to life I vowed to refuse nothing; in one another saw I/she/we will never be lacking (1976, p. 893).

References

Cixous, H. (1976). The laugh of the Medusa (K. Cohen & P. Cohen, Trans.). *Signs, 1*(4), 875–893.

Cixous, H. (1991). *Coming to writing and other essays* (S. Suleiman, Ed., S. Cornell, Trans.). Cambridge, MA: Harvard University Press.

Cixous, H. (1993). *Three steps on the ladder of writing* (S. Cornell & S. Sellers, Trans.). New York, NY: Columbia University Press.

Cixous, H. (1994). *The Hélène Cixous reader* (S. Sellers, Ed.). London: Routledge.

Cixous, H. (1998). *First days of the year*. Minneapolis, MN: University of Minnesota Press.

Cixous, H., & McQuillan, H. (2002). 'You race towards that secret, which escapes': An interview with Hélène Cixous. *Oxford Literary Review, 24*(1), 185–201.

Cixous, H. (2008). *White ink: Interviews on sex, text and politics* (S. Sellers, Trans.). Stocksfeld: Acumen.

Greene, M. (1995). *Releasing the imagination: Essays on education, the arts, and social change*. San Francisco, CA: Jossey-Bass.

Violent Femmes. (1983). Add it up [recorded by Violent Femmes]. On *Violent Femmes* [CD]. Los Angeles, CA: Slash Records.

4

Writing with Virginia Woolf, not Afraid

Yet it is clear that she could have freed her mind from hate and fear and not heaped it with bitterness and resentment, the fire was hot within her.
Woolf (1929/2001, p. 69)

A woman must have money and a room of her own if she it to write fiction.
Woolf (1929/2001, pp. 3–4)

For the truth is I feel the need of an escapade after these serious experimental books whose form is always so closely considered. I want to kick up my heels & be off. I want to embody all those innumerable little ideas & tiny stories which flash into my mind at all seasons. I think this will be great fun to write; & it will rest my head before starting the very serious, mystical poetical work which I want to come to next.
Woolf ([Diary entry, 14 March, 1927], 1980, p. 131)

© The Author(s) 2019
E. Mackinlay, *Critical Writing for Embodied Approaches*,
https://doi.org/10.1007/978-3-030-04669-9_4

Fig. 4.1 Who's the monster now?

1.

the Woolf stands at the (in)door
to the shut library
to the closed garden
she pushes
unwisely, the door was left open
she is waved back
by a kindly gentleman
barring the way
how unpleasant it is to be locked out
worse perhaps to be locked in
the Woolf at the (out)door
going indoors
it was distressing

it was bewildering
it was humiliating
wild scribble and contradictory
jottings in riotous notebooks
truth had run through her fingers
every drop had escaped
reaching her own doorstep
draw the curtains
shut out distractions
light the lamp
narrow the inquiry
death would be better!
and the door was slammed
faster than ever
and sealed with a lock
so that she might contemplate
and gain the power
to think for herself
luncheon rooms, sitting rooms
quiet rooms, dark rooms
drawing rooms, panelled rooms
big dining rooms, common rooms
cramped rooms, scented rooms
rooms for hire
with painted windows
and gramophones blaring
everything was different
inside and outside the rooms
she has to herself
they are calm or thunderous
give onto a prison yard
hung with washing
alive with opals and silks
hard as horsehair or
soft as feathers
women's femininity everywhere
shut herself up in a room
locked up, beaten and flung about
how many rooms are needed

for her to have
the habit of freedom
and the courage
to write, to think in
a room of her own?

2.

I stand on the corner of 10th Street and State Road and contemplate crossing. It's a Saturday morning and the traffic is busy; there is busy-ness to be done now that the weekend has arrived. Cars race by and whoosh the cold air with a hot gust of movement and purpose. I wrap my thick anorak tightly around my body and pull my woollen beanie down over my ears to shield myself from the volume and vapours; I am not quite ready yet to journey to the other side. Everyone is on their way; motoring a-way to this place and that, trafficking themselves and others to here and there. I see the Volvo driving soccer Mum careen past. With one hand on the wheel, her brow is furrowed as she looks anxiously at her watch and in the rear-view mirror, trying to find the fastest weave while shouting at her children to sit down and shut up so she can concentrate on the road. The obligatory hat driver ambles by in a rusted pick-up truck, taking his sweet old time, hogging the left-hand lane while remaining deliciously oblivious to the mandatory swearing and tooting as other drivers swerve around him. I watch the cool kids cruise past in their CDs on wheels, heads bobbing in time to the beat, windows down and arms out. I turn my eyes quickly to the ground, hoping that if I can't see them it means that they can't see me.

"Heeeyyyy, wouldn't mind tapping you babe!" one of them shouts while his mates wolf-whistle a chorus in the back.

"Please don't slow down, please don't slow, please don't", I whisper silently to myself. The moment passes, they move on; I am safe and sound on solid ground again—right here and I am not, and I refuse to be, *their* traffic.

There is a lull in the hustle and bustle, just for a moment, while the lights ahead turn red. Motors idle quietly, forced to stop and take pause. I sense that perhaps now is a good time for me to cross the road but as I begin to make my move, a small hand in brown silk gloves reaches out and grasps hold of my elbow.

"It's quite intoxicating isn't it?" Her voice is English, refined and clipped. "Either suspended or swept along, there is a strange rhythmical order (Woolf, 1929/2001, p. 112) to traffic don't you think?"

As she speaks, I can feel the drum and hum of progress rising from the street; Bloomington is winding itself up once more to begin and roar again (after Woolf, 1929/2001, p. 110).

"Motor cars are like little windows", she continues, "flowing across time and space they open up moments of being, doing and knowing". A soft chuckle escapes. "Dare I say, of writing too".

The current of traffic streams past us on its way to elsewhere.

"Did you know our first motor car was a second-hand Singer? Leonard and I bought it in 1927 for 275 pounds. Things come and go now with great regularity by motor car".

I think and wonder now about the change to the ordinary and every-day that this revolution in transport must have brought to her world.

"Whether I like it or not", she explains, "'All images now are tinged with driving a motor. Here I think of letting my engine work, with my clutch out'" (Woolf, 1980, p. 149).

I think and wonder about the similarity between driving and writing, once you turn the car on, you are in motion, and on the a-way. It might become that way too with a pen in hand, in motion and on the a-way.

"What I like, or one of the things I like, about motoring is the sense it gives one of lighting accidentally, like a voyager who touches another planet with the tip of his toe, upon scenes which would have gone on, have always gone on, will go on, unrecorded, save for this chance glimpse", she waves her hand in front of her, gesturing towards the shifting land-scape of comings and goings we are standing witness to. "Then it seems to me that I am allowed to see the heart of the world uncovered for a moment" (Woolf, 1980, p. 153).

3.

Another same but different kind of yearning for freedom lead me without warning and yet not unsurprisingly to the writings of Virginia Woolf; almost as though I had finally found something lost I didn't know I was searching for in the first place. The lost girl, the lost woman of other words and worlds desperately seeks herself and my moment of being found with Virginia returns to sit with me each and every day. I turn to this moment in my world many times; I re/turn to it, and then again at the turn in and of words; perhaps, perhaps it is my re-turn at turning to the busy-ness of un-forgetting that will re/turn the lost little girl and the lost woman to me. I fear if I don't take a turn, the un-forgetting will be there and then still, just out of reach of here and now.

4.

Here is one version of this re/turning to un-forgetting. It was a cold-winters Wednesday at the end of October on the other side of the world; downtown Bloomington in mid-West America where the oak leaves had turned brilliant shades of yellow, orange and red and lay scattered on the ground. I walked along the sidewalks of this University town and allowed myself to breathe in the knowledge-making breeze, carrying as it did the thoughts of a thousand and more people thinking, and saw the colourful array of foliage doubling as a Hollywood carpet. With a skip in my step, I pretended that I had been given permission to make a grand entrance and strut my way onto the academic stage, flirting and frolicking with the leaves beneath my feet. I waved merrily at my adoring audience as I passed them by, a sea of full, half and not even near professors masquerading as smiling pumpkins sitting in doorways and windowsills in anticipation of All Hallows Eve celebrations later that week. Gorgeously grotesque, they sat quietly staring, in no need or mind to respond.

I turned this way and that and eventually found myself standing in front of a bookstore with a cosy café nestled inside. The smell of fresh coffee and baked goods gnawed viciously at my awareness and brought my attention sharply to the chill that had settled on my flesh and in my bones as the afternoon sun began to fade. A rush of warm air, the lilt of small and large talk, and an academic remainders sale table greeted me as I stepped inside. It was piled high with literary leftovers; all manner of fact and fiction that had passed their used by date. The pages reeked of being a has-been and it would not be long before they too joined their out of sight and out of mind comrades in a burial tomb made for dying and soon to be deceased books.

I sifted and sorted through the table of books slowly; care-full to be full of care for the words and worlds each text held. Maybe this one, not that one, this one I have read, and that one has read me. The rhythm of picking up and putting down soon became mesmerising and I do not know for sure how Virginia's (1929/2001) book came to be in my hand. But there it was; a paperback copy of *A room of one's own*. Fancy that, what kind of flight of fancy was it that had enabled a copy of Virginia Woolf's *A room of one's own* to find its way into my possession? I looked more closely at the text I now fancied and held tightly onto.

The cover featured a sepia image of Virginia Woolf dressed in a plain Victorian nightgown, sitting on a plain wooden chair with her back to the viewer, staring out of the window in a dark plain room towards the light. A wave of tranquillity washed over me as I peered more keenly at this image; Virginia ap-peers unmoving and resolute in her occupation of this plain space—indeed, quite obviously a room of her own. This book is one which I have had niggling at me for some time; it is a book which I have always felt I *should* read and yet it is a book which I have never felt I *would* want to read; indeed, it is a book which I felt I *could* not read because I was not a literary scholar and nor was I particularly fond of Victorian women's writing—until this moment of being with Virginia that is. The round yellow sale sticker on the front read $5 and I decided that it was time to put all of my-should haves, -would haves and -could haves—of which there seemed to be multitudes—aside to read this book. With no time left for hesitation I made my purchase. I also bought a pad of pale pink sticky notes, just in case I decided there were any nuggets of truth wrapped up and worth keeping. With a mug of steaming coffee in hand, I sank into one of the large brown leather couches at the back of the store and opened the book.

"But, you may say", Virginia begins. "We asked you to speak about women and fiction—what has that got to do with a room of one's own? I will try to explain" (1929/2001, p. 2). In the short space of 30 words I immediately found what it is I did not know I was searching for. Here was a woman writing; a woman writing and speaking to me; she was writing and speaking *directly* to me—not beyond, over or around me, but *to* me. Her words embraced me in an intimacy I was not expecting. There were so many things *they*—the others waiting just outside her room, had said which had made me pause to read her. Virginia Woolf is *difficult* to read they said. Virginia Woolf's non-fiction *cannot be trusted* they said. Virginia Woolf's vision of women and writing is fatally *flawed* they said. Virginia Woolf *fails* as a feminist they said. Virginia Woolf is to be *feared* they said. Virginia Woolf *falls* short they said. I raised my eyebrows quiz-zically. Because don't you know, they said, she is a monster? I raised my right hand and in one swoop quickly swiped they said away. I returned Virginia's affectionate hold and took her hand; she and I had some read-ing to do.

I read then from front to back without taking a breath. I was entranced by Woolf's fluid prose. My arms wrapped themselves tightly around my waist as I responded to Woolf's (1929/2001, p. 29) woman in the looking glass, watching herself shrink under the male gaze as she begins to tell the truth. I felt bile rise in my throat as the taste and tex-ture of "beef and prunes" reminded me of all that women have been denied, knowing with my "heart, body, and brain all mixed together" that "one can think well, love well, sleep well if one has not dined well" (Woolf, 1929/2001, p. 14). Tears threatened to fall as I recall the epis-temological and ontological shock of at once being "locked in and locked out" (1929/2001, p. 19) of rooms to which only men hold the key, not really knowing which is worse or more unpleasant. Revolutionary laughter bubbled up from deep inside me as Woolf responds to women's exclusion—"Lock up your libraries if you like", she taunted, "but there is no gate, no lock, no bolt that you can set upon the freedom of my mind" (1929/2001, p. 64). The threat Woolf poses as intellectual femme fatale was indeed dangerous and monstrous, I murmured in admiration—she continually escaped those who would contain her and was teaching women to fly.

When I reached the last page, there and then I felt a deep sadness creep its way towards me upon arriving at the closure; the kind of sadness that accompanies having to say goodbye to a long-lost friend when you are not yet ready to become a-part. Here and now, I departed again at the opening; this time breathing in and out the depth and breadth of her words. Before long, the pages were decorated with scribbling on square pale pink tabs of paper. Each note a mark of musing as I read and a memo to myself, of the murmurings of more that had begun to hum inside my head. I turned to the first set of notes. "No need to hurry", I reminded myself on page ix. "What is the relationship between telling stories and validity?" I queried on page 4. Page 14, "She is challenging my feelings of comfort". I turned to the final set of notes. "Lack of emotion in writing = failure", I commented on page 102. "What is it you desire in writing?" I asked myself on the very last page. Gently closing the book, I re/turned back to the cover of the book once more. This time when I saw Virginia sitting there in a room of her own, a different feeling came to sit beside me. I moved in a little closer, trying to see what it is in this image that had brought this uninvited feeling to sit next to me. I think and wonder now, just as Virginia herself did, whether this was really a room of her own making. There is such longing on the cover and this time the sensation was one of loss, of not being found and not wanting to be found.

5.

THE MOVEMENT: PERMISSIONS FOR WRITING WOM*N IN STUCK PLACES

After Woolf, V. Professions for wom*n.

But to tell you my story—it is a modest and naïve one. You have only got to imagine yourselves a wom*n in the ivory tower with mind, body and heartlines bursting with the fullness of theory, experience and emotion that is writing. I see her standing there and wonder whether she is locked in that lofty turret or locked out of a post beyond her but for now we have to only concern ourselves with what it is that she must do. She had only to craft those heartlines into an academic paper; a publication in a high-ranking journal would suffice—from beginning to end, introduction to conclusion, and life to death. Then it occurred to her to do what is simple and economical enough after all—to write from those heartlines, to write her body, herself as wom*n and slip a few of those pages into her article, quickly tap out a letter to editor, and email it away into the deep dark ether with hope as its companion.

It was thus that once my heartlines began to flow that I came to call myself a feminist academic; and my effort was rewarded on the first day of the following academic year—a very glorious day it was for me—as I watched my publication citation index grow and bibliographic data collection expand exponentially. But to show you how little I knew about what it meant to be called a feminist academic, how little I know of the struggles and difficulties of such lives, I have to admit that instead of taking heed of those around me who insisted I was too bold in daring to bite the hand that fed me, I continued to write my body, write myself, write the heartlines on my hand. Words became whimsical images became rhyme became public performances, which very soon involved me in bitter disputes with those whom I would not wish to call friends.

What could be easier than to write your body, write yourself, and write the heartlines? But wait a moment. Books and journal articles have to be something—something quite particular if you write as an academic, and even more so if you are a wom*n. My writing, had become insistent, refusing to be anything other than the heartlines but I soon discovered that if I were going to write as a feminist academic, I should need to do battle with a certain spectre.

And the spectre was a wom*n masquerading as not-wom*n, not writing her body, not writing herself or her heartlines. I observed her day in and day out, falling into step with the procession of academic men in front of her, not daring to walk to a beat of her own making because they were behind her too. The monotonous pacing saw her shift shape in mind, body and spirit and I watched in horror as she became that which she had always professed she would not. The heartlines stopped flowing, her skin began to pale and flake, the light in her eyes was replaced by a dull ache, and her voice had become but a fleeting shadow. When I came to know her better I likened her after the heroine of a famous poem, The Angel in the House, except this wom*n was a Cherub in praise of the Masters in the Academy.

It was this Cherub, Angel, spectre—call her what you will but know that she is always a refusal—who used to come between me and my writing. I can hardly believe that I once felt sorry for her but it was she who bothered me and wasted my time and so tormented me that at last I killed her. I will describe her as briefly as I can. She was immensely smart but was always proudly careful not to conceal it. She was intensely supportive, particularly of those men she saw herself in servitude to. She put herself across as utterly unselfish. She excelled in the difficult arts of office politics and baking cakes for staff birthdays. She sacrificed herself daily. If there was a committee she put her hand up to be on it and she always made sure she tidied up the action items with her trusty tea towel; if there was a course that needed teaching or work to do on weekends, she made sure to be made she did both and 100% more without complaint—in short she was so constituted that she never had a mind or a wish of her own, but preferred to acquiesce always with the minds and wishes of the Masters in the Academy. Above all—I need not say it—she was uncontaminated by the heartlines in her hand, her mind, her body, her writing was clean and the Masters applauded her. Her concentration, clarity and commitment to the Masters were her chief beauty—her blushes, her great grace, and the measure of her worth.

Then and now every department, every School, every Faculty has its Angels. And when I came to write myself as a feminist academic, I encountered her with the very first words. I felt her vice-like presence squeezing and closing my throat; the shadow of her crumbling wings fell on my page; I heard the creak and groan of shoulder pads, starched skirts and stilettos as she silently stalked me. I jumped as she slipped behind my chair and placed her clammy hand on my shoulder. I felt her sour and rotting breath on my neck as she began to whisper: 'My dear you are a young wom*n. You are writing a book for the academy. You would do well to remember that patriarchy—dominator culture of the white, imperial, capitalist kind is your Master in this tower. He pays your wage, opens the door for your publications and allows you to be promoted. Be sympathetic; be tender; flatter; deceive; use all the arts and wiles of our sex. Never let anybody guess that you have a mind of your own. Above all, be clean'. And without warning, she made as if to wash my mouth out with soap, her fingers scraping, scratching, feverishly trying to cleanse the f-word from my tongue. I bit down hard and felt the crush of bones; blood, sweat and tears burning like acid and buying enough time for something more.

I admit now it was with relish that I turned around and smashed her hard on the side of her head with an open hand. How much easier it would have been if I had had a hammer in my possession. I did my best to kill her. My excuse, if I were to be charged with a crime, would be that I acted in self-defence. Had I not killed her she would have killed me. She would have plucked the heart out of my writing. I call her 'she' but in that moment I saw her for who and what she was, an ideology, a discourse and a praxis which detested the likes of me. Don't be fooled, she did not die easily, and I cannot be sure even now that she is gone for good.

Whenever I sense her presence, the stale stench of patriarchy she exudes, the sinister sounds of domination she ushers in or the whisper of her wings that would wash me and my sisters away, I once more pick up whatever heavy implement I have at my disposal and fling it at her. She has a nasty habit of always creeping back; the blood and bruises she bears from the last assault a beacon of hope for those like me. It is far harder to kill a spectre than a reality, and the Academy is full of hallowed halls with goal posts that keep shifting. The struggle is severe, and it is bound to befall all feminist academics at some time. I raise my fist in the air and see the heartlines in my hand pounding; we are at war and killing this Cherub has become my obsession. What will remain after the Angel is dead? I cannot know; indeed you cannot know either, but such a crime is worth the freedom to begin searching for the room we may call our own in writing.

6.

When I think about the performativities associated with drawing, I am reminded of Virginia Woolf in *A room of one's own* describing herself drawing cartwheels on slips of paper (1929/2001, p. 27), sketching faces (1929/2001, p. 78) to women and fiction. According to Woolf (1929/2001, p. 105), drawing pictures, dining, looking out the window and reading books on the shelf are all part of the process of laying bare those thoughts and impressions that lead to thinking and writing. Indeed, for Woolf (1929/2001), "the whole of the mind must lie wide open…there must be freedom and there must be peace". Here she is referring explicitly to dismantling the split between the mind and the body, the masculine and the feminine, the creative and the analytic. Reflecting more on the writing processes that enable her to become as "one" she shares that, "Every morning I write a little sketch to amuse myself. I am not saying, I might say, that these sketches have any relevance. I am not trying to tell a story. Yet perhaps it might done in that way. A mind thinking" (Woolf, 1980, p. 229). I follow in her footsteps and hope that these drawings too might be "done in that way", a heart and mind thinking.

7.

Fig. 4.2 Finding

Fig. 4.3 Fighting

Fig. 4.4   Freedom

8.

The sky was clear and blue, the air fresh and sharp and everywhere I turned this Wednesday held the promise of something not yet seen. It was this sense of anticipation of going somewhere else that accompanied me—much like a giggling childhood friend, riding our bicycles with wicker baskets, our legs pedalling wildly and our minds racing towards freedom in the distance. As is my usual habit in a strange town, I lost my way and carefully steered my way through a maze of winding back to front and front to back streets before arriving at the Fitzwilliam Museum. The building was heavily guarded with wrought iron chains, standing steadfast and grave in their undertaking. So too the human shield protecting the pathway beyond the gates, a young man in a security uniform who cheerfully declared upon espying me, "Only nine seconds exactly to go until we open!" waving his watched wrist in the air. With a flourish he ceremoniously reached down and unlocked the heavy chains, the gates squeaking their own welcome. The building was grey on the outside, flushed with red and gold on the inside. The woman on the information desk looked at me in expectation.

"I'm here to look at a manuscript", I announced.

The woman looked at me in expectation once more.

"The Virginia Woolf manuscript", I explained. I said it with pride, a sisterly smile which beared my teeth warning that I would say the "f" word if needed.

"Who are you here to see?" She asked. "Virginia? We don't have anyone called Virginia here. Only Amy and she's in room nine at the top of the stairs. Turn left, go past a corridor on your right, walk through the Spanish room, past the Italian lot, go through some glass doors and turn to your left again. Just knock and Amy will let you in".

I sighed; I was destined to get lost even though I was desperately trying to find and be found. I thanked her and began to make my way to Room 9. Past Grecian vases of all sizes, painting after painting of Mother Mary with and without baby Jesus in dark aged hues, more subdued images of buxom naked women draped over safely and saintly men, quiet halls, large leather lounges placed strategically for looking. And then there it was, room nine. A room at the end of the hall with see through locked doors. What is being kept out and what is trapped within I wondered? I knocked quietly, not wanting to disturb the old books, paintings and artefacts of life once lived from their great slumber; their secrets in great hibernation from those that would invade and open them once more. As I waited, I could see the manuscripts staring back at me through the glass doors, some glaring a challenge to my authority and authenticity, others with hope written all over them desperate to be selected for perusal.

Amy unlocked the door with a large key.

"Hello", I whispered, it didn't seem appropriate to speak loudly.

Amy raised her eyebrows.

"I'm here to see the Virginia Woolf manuscript?" I paused as Amy stood and looked at me.

"I have a booking?" I added.

Amy gestured to one of the large burgundy leather lined tables, which occupied the middle of the reading room. The manuscript had already been laid out carefully on an archival reading block, book snakes coiled by its side.

"Try not to handle the pages too much; please try not to touch them", Amy pleaded.

The manuscript and I regarded each other coolly, and a momentary sense of panic washed over me. Where should I begin? How should I begin? And what if I begin in the wrong place? There was nothing else I could do except that; begin.

Time had a mind of its own that morning, cheekily stealing from the very pages of the manuscript. It raced past, blowing raspberries, teasing and taunting, reminding me that all too soon I would need to take my leave. There was simply not enough time to do what I had wanted to do, which was what exactly? I had wanted to sit with the manuscript and imagine that I was sitting next to Virginia Woolf. I wanted to find that moment of being by being with her words; the page a physical remnant of her thoughts that would grant me a moment to enter into being with her. I wanted to tell Virginia Woolf-the manuscript of Virginia Woolf how inspirational the words it held were. In October 1928 Virginia Woolf gave her infamous lectures at Newnham and Girten Colleges Cambridge; in October 2003 I first discovered and read the published version of these lectures in A room of one's own in Bloomington, Indiana; and now it is October once more, 2013, and I find myself in Cambridge retracing Virginia Woolf's steps to read the original manuscript. A circle is made complete, but I cannot be sure if I have arrived at that moment of being I was searching for. Perhaps, that was not the point; perhaps my relationship with this manuscript, this book and Virginia Woolf is "forever on the way". The manuscript and I came to know each other for the rest of the day. I noted the jottings and the notes on the side; reading and re-reading passages, translating and decoding the purple inked handwriting that adorned its pages; hoping that my noting would, in the end, be notable.

With great sadness I looked at the clock and closed the manuscript. My moment of being there was over. I walked quietly to the desk.

"Amy? Unfortunately, I have to go now", I whispered.

"Really, you are leaving so soon?" Her voice was loud and pierced the quiet sanctuary of the reading room. I fancied I heard the books behind the glass doors grumble and moan in protest at the noisy interruption. I made arrangements to return to the archives next Thursday, but I could already sense that time did not wish to be my friend. I was already late for my meeting and as I pushed my bicycle away from the kerb, I wondered whether or not I should have followed Virginia Woolf's lead and made my rendezvous with the manuscript Monday or Tuesday?

9.

the Woolf writes a letter
and offers the gift of a guinea
not one, nor two but three
because, on behalf and bravely for
we who have been shut out
from the universities so repeatedly
we who are only admitted
to the universities so restrictedly
how we feel to be shut out
to be shut up
because we are women
an outsider, moreover, who has no right to speak
what is this "civilisation" in which we find ourselves?
what are these ceremonies and
why should we take part in them?
the Woolf declares
we believe that we can be most effective
by refusing to join your society
by working for our common ends
outside your society, not within
the daughters of educated men
will make their own
the outsiders society
the Woolf vows
we will be indifferent to yours
we will not participate in yours
we will omit everything of yours
women of the outsiders society
will not repeat your words like a stuck record
we will not repeat your methods

References

Woolf, V. (1929/2001). *A room of one's own.* London: Vintage Press.
Woolf, V. (1980). *The diary of Virginia Woolf, volume III: 1925–1930* (A. E. Bell, Ed.). London: Hogarth Press.

5

But First, a Love Affair with Words

It is words which are to blame. They are the wildest, freest, most irresponsible, most unteachable of all things. Of course, you can catch them and sort them and place them in alphabetical order in dictionaries. But words do not live in dictionaries; they live in the mind…And how do they live in the mind? Variously and strangely, much as human beings live by ranging hither and thither, by falling in love and mating together.

Woolf (1937, n. p.)

It is the rapture I get when in writing that I seem to be discovering what belongs to what; making a scene come right; making a character come together. From this I reach what I might call a philosophy; at any rate it is a constant idea of mine; that behind the cotton wool is hidden a pattern; that—I mean all human beings—are connected with this; that the whole world is a work of art; that we are part of the works of art…We are the words; we are the music; we are the thing itself.

Woolf (1976, p. 46)

© The Author(s) 2019
E. Mackinlay, *Critical Writing for Embodied Approaches*,
https://doi.org/10.1007/978-3-030-04669-9_5

Fig. 5.1 Word by word, in love

1.

My love affair with words and writing began with a large black leather book (Merriam-Wesbter, 1948). I reach my hand forward, close my eyes and run my fingers over the embossed lettering on the front. I know it by heart, "New 20th Century Dictionary Unabridged" it reads. I move down a little and trace over an outline of the map of the world that is featured there and I un-forget the moment words and I became sweethearts. The dictionary belonged to my Pa, my mother's father, and it sat on his brown laminated drinks cabinet right next to the equally as sizable Teacher's Whisky bottle. This hard covered 1948 Merriam-Websters with 2006 pages, measuring 21 cm wide × 28 cm long × 14 cm deep, complete with carved indentations to mark the beginning of each letter was the most wonderful book I had ever seen.

Visiting my Pa was always an opportunity to explore its contents. I never bothered to stop and look for very long at the introductory pages. The preliminary pages contained a portrait of Noah Webster; pages and pages of photographs of American passenger planes, fighter jets and various kinds of army and navy vehicles; and maps from an atlas of the world with particular attention to the United States of America. These were not enough to hold my interest for very long and neither did I worry about going over again the introductory outline of the history of the English language or the listing of new words and meanings right at the beginning. The real logophilic adventure began after the preliminary pages.

I always began my flight into word fantasy in the same place—the letter "E". E. The second vowel and fifth letter of the alphabet seemed the perfect place to start—my name was Elizabeth, I was the second child born in the fifth month of the year. I glance quickly at the entire page. There is an illustration of an eagle, an ear and a coronet of an earl on the first page of E. Page 539. The dictionary tells me that E can sound open or long, and when placed at the end of a word is generally silent, yet after letters such as s or j, changes the sound completely. A clever and necessary letter I thought, and another quickly followed—that because my name started with the letter E that maybe one day I might become something other than normally quiet and instead find a crafty and needed place in the world. Perhaps if I read enough words I thought, just maybe it would be that easy. I turned to the definition of easy. (1) At ease: (a) quiet, being at rest, free from pain, (b) free from anxiety, care or peevishness. P-e-e-vishness. Double ee. I step then across the carved indentations to the letter P, curious to learn more about this word with two letters I have claimed as my own next to one another. Page 1236. P-e-e-vish, to whimper, probably of onomatopoeic origin the dictionary says. O for onomatopoeic; a difficult word to say, a tricky word to spell and it grabs my attention. Page 1168. It takes me a little while to find it but once I do, I am captivated. A "name to make" the dictionary tells me; literally "name making" or "word making". My heart and head somersault around together, I am in love with this dictionary and I lose myself completely to the worlds that words and their meanings open wide.

2.

The dictionary was not the only thing I loved about visiting my Pa and it was not the only thing he did to fan the flames of my love affair with words. Crosswords; not words that he said which were cross, or at cross purposes, but crosswords. The grid of black and white squares with up and down clues to words and their meanings attached which appears in every newspaper worth reading—at least that's what my Pa said. Crosswords were part of his morning ritual. A thick slab of white toast with real butter and home-made plum jam, a cup of strong white tea, then the crossword and a second cup of his favourite brew. I loved this time of the morning in the kitchen with my Pa. Just me and him and the crossword. NO interruptions allowed.

The Herald Sun was his favourite daily and the daily crossword his favourite puzzle. It arrived with clockwork precision in the driveway with a thud courtesy of the local paperboy called Dave at exactly 6:30 am every weekday morning rain, hail or shine. Pa wandered out to collect it in his stubbies work shorts and bonds white singlet, regardless of the weather. After a cursory glance at the news of the day, he sat down in the kitchen at the round red speckled laminated table with a satisfied sigh; paper in hand, ready to begin.

"Get me a pen would you love", he'd say to my Nana, each and every morning, in exactly the same way.

I loved hearing him speak to her like that. So much of the talk between them was filled with something else—niggling over rapidly depleting money on the one hand and beer consumption on the other, over what we were having and then being late for dinner, over the Playboy picture in his backyard shed and the time spent there outside instead of here inside, over everything and nothing at all.

Pa had a method for doing the crossword. There was only one way to begin a crossword according to my Pa—at one down and/or one across, whichever answer came to you first.

"Always start at number one", he would say to me. "Don't just pick a clue any clue, you've got to have some rhyme and reason to the *way* you do a crossword, else it will never get done!"

If starting at number one was rule number one, then rule number two was always build from the clues you have completed. Words standing on their own without being attached to other words, even if you knew the meaning, were simply not acceptable. Each word on the crossword grid was in relationship to every other word; being a word alone on the grid was not a possibility and completing the crossword in this way without connection made the all the more task harder. My Pa never let me help him with the crossword, my job was to sit beside him, watch and learn. One of my last memories of my Pa was watching him do the daily crossword. He did the same crossword over and over again, the cruelty of dementia kicked in and provided him with a never-ending source of word entertainment. We just had to make sure we had a never-ending supply of daily newspapers.

3.

I loved loving words alongside my Pa. Sitting with a crossword in my hand over my second cup of coffee first thing in the morning brings him back in, so close to me. I can feel his logophilic heart beating right up next to mine. My own children know the rules now too. Do not, under any circumstance, interrupt Mum while she is doing her crossword, failure to comply is bound to result in cross words. Crossing words, wording that crosses there and then to here and now, my Pa and me. Our love of words and crosses and words crosses a mark on my Mum too. She's a lover of crosswords as well and each morning she follows exactly the same ritual as Pa and me; she remembers and reminds me that once upon a time she and her Dad did exactly the same thing. Perched on the stool at the kitchen bench, ABC am radio playing a mixture of static and talkback in the background. A second cup of weak black tea in front of her, a pen in hand, and a blank black and white grid ready and waiting for another person to cross over into the world of words and meanings. We take it in turns to do the crossword. Five clues each and then we swap over. Back and forth until all of the words are crossed. We do exactly as my Pa taught us, always start at number one up or down, always build from words, and always make sure words are in company on the grid.

We talk quietly to one another about this clue and that. How the crossword in the local paper is so much easier than the one in the New Idea. How the New Idea clues are sometimes so obscure and disconnected from the answer that it beggars belief, and how we prefer the Woman's Day crossword over all of them. We nod our heads in agreement, yes, we only buy the women's magazines so that we can do the crosswords. And we always have a crossword book on hand, because you never know when you might have a spare five minutes here or there to sneak in a quick crossword and never under any circumstances do you want to be found lost, wanting and confused without a crossword.

"What's a three-letter word for mature acorn?" She asks. She doesn't really want me to respond, she knows the answer. This is how it goes between us, playing with words, being playful around words, we know how to wordplay well.

"Aside from Mum?" I reply, not afraid to give her a little bit of cheek this early in the morning, especially over a crossword and a cup of tea.

"Mmm, no. It has 'a' as the middle letter", she murmurs without blinking but smiling softly.

I look over at her as she concentrates on the crossword.

"Hey, only five clues remember Mum!"

She shakes her head, "I know, but someone (she raises her eyebrows and looks at me pointedly) put in a wrong word—that gives me an extra one back. A five-letter word for 'stupid' is not 'silly', it's apish. The 'a' connects to 'oak'". Her arm gently reaches around my waist and she leans forward to kiss my cheek. "I love loving words with you Elizabeth", she whispers.

4.

"I don't want them", she says and throws the two small white pills back in my face. It's first thing in the morning and she is in pain, her back has seized up after a long night of lying down but she is stubborn and refuses to take her medicine. It's taken her a lot longer this time to bounce back from her latest fall and she is frustrated with and by herself. I pick the Panadol up off the floor and put my arm around her.

"It's ok Mum", I kiss her cheek, trying not to take notice of the salty tears which have begun to appear there. "I don't like taking medication either, but this will help. If you take it now, you'll get on top of your aches and pains early".

She hastily wipes her eyes with her soft well-worn cotton hanky and looks at me with distrust; she is not pleased and places me in the naughty corner as her undutiful daughter. We are standing next to one another but in this moment, we are on opposing sides and regard one another in an uncomfortable stand-off, not least because here and now our roles are reversed. No, she is not happy at all and neither am I; I am not ready for this. I hear one of the songs she used to sing to me when I did not want to take my medicine when I was a little girl start to play on repeat in my head; "Just a spoonful of sugar" from Mary Poppins. I break the stale mate with my best and sweetest smile.

"Here you go Mum", I place the medicine gently in her hand and pass her a glass of juice. This time she doesn't resist. I give her shoulder a slight squeeze; she has lost weight since I saw her last, her muscles have wasted away to make room for her bones to protrude. She feels like a fragile little bird.

"Besides, we've got to have you in good shape for Christmas shopping today!"

"Shopping?" Confusion shadows her face. "Do I have a list?"

"Yes, you're almost done Mum", I reach across the bench and pass her a white piece of scrap paper with my neatest writing on it. There are names of all close family on the left-hand side, and on the right, the gifts she has bought.

"Why is it stuck together with sticky tape?" She asks, her face crumpling into a frown.

"Oh, that's me", I shake my head and my voice is soft. "I thought you'd finished with it and I accidentally put it in the recycling". I quickly think of a cover story; I don't want to remind her of why it was ripped up—that would tear us both apart all over again.

"Do I need to make a new one then?"

"No, I don't think so. Let's take it with us and we can go over it while we have a cup of coffee to kick start our shopping".

Mum smiles at me, the tension which passed between us moments earlier now no longer even a distant memory, "Café first, then the shops, the best plan".

5.

"What are you going to have Mum?" I ask.

"I'll have what you're having".

"Two lattes thank you—one large and one regular", I place our order with the waitress at Fika. It's a new coffee shop in the centre of Ballarat, and all the hipsters are there. Today Mum and I are joining them to begin our festive spree.

"Here's the list Mum", I pull the scrap of white paper taped together from the depths of my handbag.

"Are sure that's my list?" Mum raises her eyebrows, At the piece of paper which by now is looking pretty shabby and worse for wear.

"Why is it stuck together like that?" She asks.

I hesitate, unsure of how to reply.

"Oh, that was me", I explain. "I thought it was recycling".

Mum starts reading the list.

"Do I have everyone?" She pauses. "What about Sally's kids?"

"George, Harry and Lyza are there", I point to the bottom.

"Yes, that's right," her voice is quiet. "George, Harry and Lyza". Mum's hand reaches into her bag for her hanky. It's the same one from this morning, white with faded pastel flowers and so very soft from overuse.

"Oh Mum, what's wrong?" I gently take her hand in mine.

"I think I might be going the same way as Pa, losing my memory. He had dementia you know", she blows her nose. "There is so much I can't remember. Sometimes I just don't know anything anymore. I don't even know who I am". Her thin shoulders shake thickly as she begins to cry. I hold her hand ever so tightly.

"I'm so scared", she whispers. I lean my head onto her shoulder so that we are touching.

"I know Mum", I say, knowing even before I speak these words that I can never know and that these three words are empty, so shallow and hollow that they clang and crash noisily about in the despair I hear in her voice.

We sit like this together, so close, so much passing between us as our heads and hearts touch that we do not need to say anything.

"Your coffee?" The waitress places a large and a small cup on the table and the moment gently fades.

"Thank you", my Mum smiles. The waitress turns to walk away. "Excuse me?" She calls the waitress back.

"Yes?" The waitress looks as bewildered as me.

"You don't happen to have today's newspaper do you? It's just that it's Saturday and there's a large crossword in the weekend paper—we can make a start on it Beth", she winks at me. The waitress returns with the daily broadsheet and hands it to Mum.

6.

I look down at the solution I have quickly handwritten into the grid. My love of crosswords, once decried as a passing fad fit only for those only with the mentality of child by the church, means that often times my writing is hasty. Once I know the answer, I feel an urgency to write the solution down; almost as if the only way to ensure I have captured and can hold onto the meaning and wonder of the word is to write it in letters from the pen of my own hand. The word and me are inextricably connected to one another forever more and ever after, and there is no time to wait. Number six down. An eight-letter word and the clue is "remiss". I watch the letters form hurriedly on the thin paper, taking no notice of the heartlines in my hand beating steadily, asking me good-naturedly in their quiet way to reconsider. It should be CARELESS but I have written C-a-R-e-L-e-S-S. Too late I see I have broken one of my Pa's crossword rules and shake my head in irony at my care-lessness. I can hear his instructions as clearly as if he were sitting beside me.

"You have to write your answers in capital letters, Elizabeth", he explains as he completes the next clue. "There is no excuse for no CAPS".

I look up at him in wonder. His knowledge of words and why they are crossed the way they are in a crossword seems endless. "Why Pa?"

"Well, it means that proper nouns can have their initial capital letter checked with an intersecting non-proper noun which does not usually have a capital letter", he squints his eyes and looks at me to make sure I have understood. "It makes it easier to cross-check meanings, clues and whether you are on the right track".

"I guess it also means that words that are not in English can also be cross-checked too and there is no confusion", I add, half questioning, half elaborating, half giving him back everything he has taught me. Pa reaches his arm around me and gives me a squeeze.

"That's my girl, my little word warrior", he kisses me lightly on the cheek. "The usual rules about capital letters are ignored in crosswords—we break some, we make some. That's why I love crosswords Elizabeth—we can take words and the world becomes ours all over again, never mind the bloody English". He chuckles, his British colours in stark contrast to his dislike of the Crown shining ever so brightly. Pa was an infantryman and never hesitated to curse and cuss against the rules and regulations of the army.

"It also means it's much easier to read. Capital letters means block writing and no running writing".

I return my gaze to my writing on the grid that has run care-lessly away between CAPS and no caps.

"Sorry Pa", I whisper. I notice then that the crossword is numbered 1917, the year of his birth and the date on the top of the newspaper is 27

July, the day and month he was born. I pick up my pen and try my best to fix it, but it's messy. "C-A-R-E-L-E-S-S", it now reads in block letters. "I tried", I murmur. "Next time I won't forget Pa".

7.

Wednesday, not Monday or Tuesday, has become one of my favourite days of the week. It's the day when I am able to leave work early and meet Hamish after school. Every other day he walks or rides home but today is Wednesday. It has become *our* day of the week. I happily close the door to my office at precisely 2:50 pm and arrive at school by 3:20 pm. The timing is critical; I need to be there before 3:30 pm when I will receive a "Where are you?" phone call from the Principal, but arriving well after the 3:00 pm mayhem of parents in a panic to park and pick up is equally as important. As I turn the corner to the school I catch myself smiling; an expression of deep regret, intense hope or inexplicable joy I cannot be sure for Wednesday is the one day of the week when I feel like maybe— just maybe—I am a *good enough* mother.

Unlike Wednesday, the rest of the week passes by in a blur. On Monday, the first day of the week, those all too familiar working nine-to-five blues wash over me, and I let my children down by staying back late. On Tuesday, I am firmly focussed on the week ahead, and leaving them to fend for themselves before and after school is simply how it has to be to satisfy my fixation with doing *and* being better in my life as an academic. On Thursday, I see myself tumbling dangerously close to the weekend and the pressure to finish something, anything lest it becomes nothing, consumes me and my children are deserted once more. On Friday, the end of the week arrives with appropriate amounts of gratitude and I put on my favourite "pants off" clothing in an attempt to begin the weekend wind down; denim, converse and always red fit this purpose perfectly. In the process of uncurling myself from work, I am finally in a position where I am able to raise my head to see if everyone is clear and present. There is nothing quite like the sheer relief to find that all three of us are— in a fashion which is as ordinary as it is remarkable—still breathing.

8.

I think and wonder that it's been awhile since I spoke to my Mum. When I first left home to go to university 600 km away we would talk routinely every Sunday night. I would sit and wait by the bright orange landline in the corridor of my college dormitory at precisely 6:00 pm for the tele-phone to ring. Mum always rang me; she was never quite sure whether I would have enough or the right change to make the long distance call and neither of us wanted to risk the telephone not ringing. The telephone was always free at 6:00 pm on a Sunday night; most of the other residents would be lined up at the bay Marie in the dining hall for the standard end of the weekend-hangover cure meal of hot chips, pies and peas. By 5:58 pm I was seated on a comfy chair next to the telephone waiting, snuggled in a quilt if it was winter and waving a fan if it was summer. Without fail Mum would always call; and without her call I am sure I would have. One day, long after I had left university, the telephone stopped ringing on a Sunday night at 6:00 pm. The silence was a call that signalled that something had changed, and it was now my turn to telephone.

"Hi Mum! It's Beth!"

"Oh Bethy, it's you—I was only just thinking about you and that I must give you a call. How are you love?"

I breathe out; it's Mum, the voice on the other end of the telephone is still my Mum.

"We're all OK Mum, busy as always but good. The boys have started back at school and the footy season has just kicked in", I explain.

"Oh, that's great they are playing footy. What kind of footy are they playing? AFL I hope!"

My breath catches in my throat. The boys have been playing AFL for the past five years and love this particular football code as much as me and our Victorian family do. Mum has seen them play for the Kenmore Bears each time she has travelled to Queensland in winter and has shed tears of pride and joy upon watching them kick goals. I swallow back equal amounts of uncertainty, panic, and something which tastes a lot like grief.

"Of course, Mum! I wouldn't have it any other way! Maxie has had a great start—he's definitely living up to his nickname of 5 goals and Hammer…"

"Hammer?" she asks, "Who's Hammer?"

"That's Hamish Mum—that's what his team call him, he's coming along really well in the backline but it's funny, he's such a gentle little soul off the field".

"Well, I haven't ever seen them play and I wish we didn't live so far away so that I could come and watch".

I can hear tears begin to choke her voice and I do the same, trying not to focus on everything I can feel slipping away.

"I know Mum, I wish we lived closer too".

We say our goodbyes and make plans to telephone again next Sunday. I place the telephone back in its cradle with a promise not to fail her.

9.

I glance over at the clock and can't believe how quickly the weekend has flown by. It is now 6:00 pm on Sunday night and time for me to telephone my Mum. I pick up my mobile and call my Dad, not on the landline and not my Mum. Mum has a smart phone, but she rarely uses it. She carries it with her in her handbag for emergencies which mostly means she can call my Dad. She can't and doesn't want to understand the way it works; it's too small and fiddly, and besides, it's almost always out of battery.

"Hi Dad, it's Beth!"

"Oh Bethy—hi! Is it 6:00 pm already?"

We make small talk.

How are you?

Have you had any rain?

How is your car project going?

Are you busy at work?

How are the boys?

And then I get to the most important question.

"How's Mum going Dad?" I hold my breath as I wait for him to answer.

"Oh, she's still the same Beth, not any better, not any worse and the blessing is she doesn't remember in either case", he replies with a laugh.

It's a sound not intended to ridicule or demean my Mum, it's a soft and joyful recognition of the 60-year-old love he holds for and shares with her.

"You know what I'm going to ask next Dad don't you?"

He chuckles, "Yes, I know exactly, and the answer is still yes—she is doing the crossword every morning".

10.

I see Hamish standing waiting for me outside the school gates and his grin mirrors mine. He hastily climbs into the front seat and reaches over to give me a kiss. "Hey!" We both say in unison, and with nothing further to add, we are on our way to experience our Wednesday after school nirvana at Café Bliss in down town Kenmore. We choose our regular booth in the corner by the window and place our regular order; a vanilla thick shake and dotty biscuit for Hamish and the largest latte on the planet for me.

Hamish looks at me expectantly. "You brought a pen didn't you Mum?"

I nod. "Yes, I think I have two—right there in the front pocket".

He eagerly dives into the leather bucket I have which doubles as a handbag and retrieves one; he's chosen my favourite, the pen which has a mermaid on it.

"Shall I go and get it?" he asks, sliding out of his seat.

"For sure, I think it's somewhere over on that bench", I point to the front counter.

He races over, nods briefly at the man behind the coffee machine, and slides in next to me upon return.

"Got it!" Hamish smiles broadly, the daily newspaper in hand. "Now", he says under his breath as he carefully turns the pages. "Where are the puzzles?"

I look over his shoulder as we both eagerly scan the newsprint, hoping that one, the puzzle page isn't missing, and two, that no one else has beaten us to it.

"There they are!" His grin mirrors mine; lady luck is our café companion today—*all* of the puzzle grids are empty, including both crosswords.

"Shall we read the comics first? What's Garfield up to?"

We lean in to take a closer look. It's a classic. Garfield is trying to find a word for the first day of the week—Monday—and the way it makes him feel. After having a bowl of porridge flung in his face, "dreary" is the word he decides upon.

"Yep, that's so true!" Hamish gives a thumbs-up as a sign of solidarity with this particular cantankerous feline. "What would be our word for Wednesday Mum?"

"Mmm, I'm not sure. What is the best word for a Wednesday feeling? How does Wednesday make *you* feel?"

He giggles softly. "Well, I know we come to the café on Wednesday to have a milk drink, eat something sweet and do the *cross*word, but it definitely doesn't make me feel cross". Hamish pauses for a moment, thinking and wondering, wondering and thinking.

"Do you know what the word Wednesday means Mum?" He asks.

I shake my head; I have no idea.

"It comes from Wodens-day", he explains. "Woden is the English equivalent of the Roman god Mercury, god of the sky and wisdom. Mercury is also the god of poetry, commerce, travel, thievery, eloquence and science".

I smile at him and his love of Greek and Roman mythology.

"Doing a crossword together on Wednesday fits the meaning of this word Mum—every part of it—it's perfect! Plus, you know that Wednesday's crosswords are medium difficulty, not like a Monday or a Tuesday which are a cinch."

"So, after channelling the god of the sky and wisdom, which one are you Hamish on a Wednesday? Poet, thief or scientist?"

"None of them—I'm a word warrior, just like you Mum", his small hand squeezes mine. "Let's get this crossword started!"

He picks up the pen from the table.

"Shall we go the quick crossword or the one with the double clue list?"

"You choose".

"Well, number one across in the quick crossword is…huh! Would you look at that!"

"What?"

"Eight letter-word for Melbourne suburb and an AFL (Australian Rules Football) team—surely, it's got to be Richmond" He gives me a prod.

I nudge him back. "Well, you know the way we work, see what the other connecting clues are".

"Six down is, a five-letter word for journal", he gives me a wink. "This is totally your crossword today Mum, do you know that one?"

"You know it", I reply. "Put them both in".

11.

I watch him carefully as he begins to fill in the solutions.

"Make sure you can read what you write and make sure …", I begin, noticing that like me he is rushing to get the letters down on paper.

"You use CAPS. I know, I know Mum", he sighs. "But remember, this is meant to be a *quick* crossword".

"Oh, trying to get a PB today are we?"

Hamish tries not to smile but his dimpling cheeks give him away. He ignores me and keeps working away at the crossword. While he fills out the small grid, I cast my eye over the double-clue puzzle. I focus on the regular clues, not the cryptic, mentally completing each one so that when it's my turn to have the pen, I am already halfway there to completion. Occasionally I take a peek at the cryptic clues, but my gaze does not stay there for long. Cryptic crosswords are not part of my word play; my family has always stayed firmly aligned with the straight puzzle word playing tribe, finding enough satisfaction in the other than literal, sometimes metaphorical and often times lateral wondering and thinking required. I often wonder and think about the two crossword types, cryptic and straight, and whether my inability to complete cryptic clues must necessarily mean I am intellectually lacking. Already missing in so many ways, I console myself with the common train of thought that straight crosswords are harder than cryptics because there is only one answer and only one way to get there, whereas cryptics have two. Singular and double, solvers and non-solvers, and never the twain shall meet; another chain of thinking around word play. My breath catches ever so slightly, training and chaining thinking, is this what crossword puzzles do?

"Mum, I'm stuck on this last one", Hamish taps me lightly on the arm, an interruption most welcome.

"Look at that, you're almost done! What's the clue?"

"Right here, 22 down", he points to the crossword. A five-letter word for soul ending in T".

"Any other letters?"

"Well, there's an A in the middle", he explains. "But I don't know what the other letters are".

I reach over and take his hand in mine.

"Can you feel that?" I ask, placing his palm against my chest. Our eyes lock together and a whole world of wondering and thinking passes between us.

"H-E-A-R-T", he sounds the letters out as he pens them in. "I'm thinking that its heart—that's my heart thinking".

"Yes", I whisper, tears choke my voice. "That's right Hamish, heart thinking".

I look in wonder at my 12-year old son; he is right. This is what cross-words will do; crosswords when played alongside those you love unchain the trains of thought that would have us think otherwise; crossword play-ing that brings right up close together the families of words with families of word lovers; crossing words in ways that un-forget the meaning of both; this is the kind of heart thinking that crosswords will do.

12.

The chickens are chuckling and cackling noisily below, busily scrapping and turning and scratching the garden over. Their clucking signals a charm and contentment for a sunny Sunday morning, deliciously warm, plain and idle with no expectations. I stand on the deck and breathe in the day, so close, so very close to something a little or maybe a lot like perfect. Holding hands with an almost seam/seem-less Sunday morning like today, there are two more companions I need beside me to inch even closer to perfection; a strong coffee and the daily crossword. I carefully balance the puzzle on my lap and my cup rests on the arm of my chair. A deep sigh escapes my mouth, an audible announcement to the world that here and now is exactly where I want to be—and I will not be moved until both are complete; so mote it be. The first few clues of the crossword fly by. One across. A four-letter word for close. N-E-A-R. Two down intersects with the third letter of one across. The clue is, a four-letter word for prayer end. I pencil in A-M-E-N. Six across intersects neatly with the third letter of two down; a five-letter word for a type of duck feather used in bedding. I write in the solution without even thinking. I stop my cross-wording for a moment and smile. Here's the thing. If you sit with crosswords long enough, there are certain clues and solutions that return and make their way into puzzles both near and far away. The ways in which the clues are written might differ, but the solution is always the same and across time they become part of your crossword vocabulary; they become words placed neatly inside your head for easy retrieval. It is only when you search for them that you realise that they have also been embedded tightly in your heart, a fine thread of memory, ready as it is for thinking and wondering its way through your very own crossword story to trace your way back to now and then. I carefully sort my way through these lines of remembrance and find one I did not know I had been searching for.

13.

The traces of breakfast have been cleared; the slab of yellow butter is back in the fridge, the jar of dark brown vegemite is back in the pantry, and the loaf of white bread has been placed back into its box. The only thing that remains is a small tin teapot snuggled up in a warm and once brightly quilted cosy. The material is now faded and stains of English breakfast are a testament to the hundreds and thousands of cups it has poured. "The cup that revives", I hear my Nana say, and if I close my eyes tightly I can see her sitting there. She is wearing her fleecy dark pink button up winter dressing gown, her soft and short red curls gently frame her face and she yawns sleepily, not yet ready for the day to begin. Her hands are gnarled and twisted—rheumatoid arthritis has been a cruel companion since she was a 16-year-old girl, one kick of a football was all it took so they said—and cradle the steaming brew carefully. The smell of the strong white tea fills my senses and I find myself there once more; sitting at the red and white speckled round laminate kitchen table in their suburban home in the Dandenongs.

The daily crossword is spread out before us and today it is my turn to begin. Pa sits patiently beside me, black ink biro in hand and poised ready to help if I find myself stuck. It is no small thing for him to have given the crossword over to me; the morning crossword is his territory, his turf, his time to be at one in the word of worlds. My grandfather's urgency for me to start pulsates from his body, tensed and straight in his chair and it makes me nervous—I don't want to ruin the joy of another crossword solved without cross-outs and most of all I don't want to him to feel cross with *me* and the word ruin I have wrought. It's a wondering that doesn't bear thinking about, my Pa being cross with me over words.

My eyes turn towards the black and white puzzle. First clue. One across. A five-letter word for a northern duck. I look across at Pa.

"Yes, you know this one", he smiles encouragingly. "We've seen it before".

Reassured I boldly ink in the solution.

"E-I-D-R-E, Eidre duck", I say.

"Correct!" He exclaims then adds, "Mostly".

"Mostly?" I ask.

"The solution is indeed an Eidre duck—you know the feathers are as soft as snow and I bet you'd find them stuffed tightly in your pillow if you opened it up—but there's something not quite right with the way you've written it", he shakes his head.

I look again at the letters I've written. He's right; it doesn't look *quite* right but I can't be sure what is wrong with it, only that it can't be left.

"Ah ha, dictionary time Elizabeth", he gestures to the lounge room.

I retrieve the much-loved tome of words and plonk it heavily on the table. My fingers easily find the "E" tab and I start searching for "Eidre". I see my mistake immediately on page 552 alongside the small sketch of a bird.

"It's the spelling, I've spelt it wrong", I know he knows but I need to say it out loud; my face flushes red, embarrassed by my mistake and sorry to have ruined his crossword. "The correct spelling is 'Eider', E-I-D-E-R".

"What else does it say about an 'Eider' duck?" He asks and always already accepts my apology.

"It says, 'A large species of duck of the genus'", I pause. "Genus, that means a family of living things right?"

"Do I look like a walking dictionary to you? It's sitting right in front of you—take a look". My Pa had no patience for word laziness and today was no exception.

I carefully place my finger on the "G" tab and turn to find "genus". There is it on page 733.

"One. In biology", I groan. I have always hated science; my least favourite subject at school and the subject most likely to send me thinking and wondering to worlds far far a-way.

"Keep reading", Pa says, his patience now restored.

"A group of species agreeing with one another in the broad features of their organization but differing in detail", I stifle a giggle and I think again about the word eider. I imagine a plump of waterfowl—ducks, geese, coots—perched down noisily quacking and quabbling about their sameness-es and differences, trying to reach agreement about feathers and family.

"And back to the northern duck?" Pa gently puts my thinking and wondering back on track.

"Oh right, the definition of Eider", I say. "'A large species of the genus *somateria*, especially *somateria mollissima*, which is found on both sides of the North Atlantic'".

"There's the clue, right there!" Pa says.

"And here's where you were right again", I nod. "The dictionary says the Eider duck's down is 'much valued from its superior warmth, lightness and elasticity'—which is why it's in my pillow!"

"Yes, and that's another clue you'll often see for Eider", he adds.

We have come full circle in our search for the spelling of Eider.

"How do we fix this?" I ask Pa, looking at the mis-spelling I have pencilled in.

He peers across and lowers his glasses on his nose to take a closer look.

"Mmm, it should be easy enough", he pulls the paper across to his side of the table. "The 'R' can become 'E' if we add three horizontal lines to mask the capital, and the 'E' becomes 'R' if we add a bubble and a crooked leg".

I watch him intently as he makes the corrections.

"There, all better now!"

"Better Pa?" I raise one eyebrow.

"Well, we can work with it", he says and pats my hand reassuringly. "Now, onto the next clue".

"Okay, one down. A four-letter word, starting with E for an Italian volcano", I read aloud.

"Oh, this is another one of *those* clues", Pa says.

I look at him blankly. "Those?"

"Yes those", he says again. "It's a repeat offender, one of those words which keeps coming back. Each time it returns you write it again and before long the clue and the solution become intimately connected— they become crossword partners in crime and impossible to forget. Eider is one of those words".

I am not sure I like the association of words with illegal activity but then I think and wonder about words and danger and the necessity of writing them both; and feel a certain kind comfortable to sit with this discomfort.

"Is this a word I might know?" I ask. "Have I heard it before?"

Pa shakes his head. "No, I don't think so. I don't even think *we've* come across it in our crossword adventures together and we've been to a lot of places—but it seems that Italy has been outside of our realm so far". He puts his black ink biro to the puzzle and pens in the solution.

"E-T-N-A, Etna", he says as he writes.

I reach for the dictionary before he says another word. I am not sure whether I can expect to find a proper noun like this one inside—for some reason I think that they are not *usually* found in dictionaries but this dictionary is no *ordinary* dictionary.

"Here it is Pa!" I find it the second column on the top of page 600. "Etna, a volcano in Sicily".

There are no pictures and my fingers traces a path to neighbouring words. "E-toile" is below it and oddly I know this word; it's a star shaped embroidery stitch my Mum taught me as I was just beginning to learn the joys of being a material girl. I keep wandering and move across to the first column on the page. My eye is caught by the uppermost word, "eth-ˈnä-grə-fər". It's a word I am sure I haven't seen before but it rolls familiar and sweet from my tongue. The definition reads, "ethnographer, *n*. A student of or authority on ethnography" and I begin to roll so close, so very close away from here and now to there and then. But I am not ready yet to leave this place of un-forgetting; I am not ready to move away from the memory of my Pa and me and crosswords and comfort and carefree companionship in the world of words. I push back and resist the time turning for a little while longer. Just like my Pa has taught me, I continue to follow the trail and my finger shifts down to land on "ethnography"; "that branch of anthropology which has to do with the classification and description of the various races and nations".

14.

The threads that loosely tie this memory together are subtle and strong, like the spider web in Virginia Woolf's room of her own (1929/2001, p. 48), attached ever so lightly but still attached to life at all four corners. Knowing how fragile yet determined they are in this moment of un-forgetting, I hold onto them tightly and watch a little girl sitting next to her grandfather, our bellies full of breakfast, marvelling upon the strangeness of this word beginning with the letter "E" that she has stumbled upon. I can see by the curious but uncertain creases which begin to creep their way across her forehead that in this moment of then, she does not yet know this word in the way that I know it now. She does not know then that ethnography and being an ethnographer is what I do now and that both will become our end and our beginning. I watch myself reaching out to touch her, to stop this ethnographic train of thought from embedding itself in her head before her heart is caught, censored and finds itself as herself cowering in the corner by this ethnographic way of thinking in a room that is most certainly not her own.

I make one last try for it but she slips away; the strings of remembrance that held us together, so close, have been cut. An ugly cry pierces the quiet comfort of moments before as I helplessly watch them fall away. I see a short movement in the shadows around the corner of my memory and hope keeps me hovering on the edge of possibility. Is it her? No; not her; not her at all and without warning slim tendrils of fear find an easy escape into my arms. I shiver as they begin to wrap their cold arms around my waste and tentacles of ice freeze the warm nets of blood that lie criss-crossed on the inside; the very inside of me, the part that is secret, that I have easy-come-easy-go secret-ed away. No; not her at all, but him. The sour smell of the night before that follows him everywhere hangs in the air like the heavy dew that will become frost just before dawn breaks; just before the thread is rendered broken. I stand still; not moving, secret-ing myself back into that place where I can withstand the cold; where all of the easy-s in this world cannot find me. I am too late. It was that easy; the moment where the possibility of then and now becoming now and then is gone. She has vanished. There is no way of stopping her now; she is on her way to ethnography. I am in fear for her. I am in fear of her.
15.
I turn back to look up at my grandfather who has been waiting patiently for me to finish reading the dictionary.

"Ethnographer", I say slowly. "Do you know any ethnographers Pa?"

He looks at me and time between there and now collapses in a heap to the very last time I saw him.

"You know Elizabeth", he says, "I think I just might have met one".

References

Merriam-Webster International Dictionary (2nd ed.). (1948). Springfield, MA: G & C Merriam Company.

Woolf, V. (1929/2001). *A room of one's own.* London: Vintage Press.

Woolf, V. (1937, April 20). *On craftsmanship* [Radio broadcast]. London: British Broadcasting Corporation. Retrieved from https://ebooks.adelaide.edu.au/w/woolf/virginia/w91d/chapter24.html

Woolf, V. (1976). Moments of being: Unpublished autobiographical writings (J. Schulkind, Ed.). Orlando, FL: Harcourt.

6

Writing, in and to *Arrivance*

Fig. 6.1 "Under the sea", by Lily Terzo (2018). *Dream, I tell you* (Cixous, 2006)

© The Author(s) 2019
E. Mackinlay, *Critical Writing for Embodied Approaches*,
https://doi.org/10.1007/978-3-030-04669-9_6

1.

I am poised, ready to begin at the end.

"Cixous", I write my first six-letters, "A woman who arrived at my ethnographic door at a time when I didn't know I needed her".

Yes, that's exactly how it felt. I knew it in a way that goes beyond knowing; it was an *un*knowing, I could *not* know because I had become a dead woman; I felt it deep deep down inside. My words were brittle and on the verge of breaking, my sentences no longer flowed with life, and each book a tomb which held out its arms to cradle the skeleton of me. Such a death was inevitable; you see, my writing as an academic in ethnomusicology and education had become stuck, stalked and "partially submerged" (Greene, 1994, p. 109) by what the "One-Eyed Father" (Haraway, 1997, p. 45) had said and continued to say about acceptable writing-as-research practices. I struggled to reconcile the mixed up personal-professional-political-pedagogical locations I found myself in and how I might come to write these worlds of shared, material, embodied and affective experience in a way which responded to an ethical call for something more than a reproduction of colonial "monovocals" and "master narratives" (Solórzano & Yosso, 2002, p. 25). The black words I wrote on white paper claimed to be "working towards social justice" for Indigenous Australian people, but I felt trapped and frustrated by their inability to engage in the kind of decolonial work in ethnomusiciological, educational and ethnographic contexts that I espoused. I turned my back on everything I knew and placed myself in the "school of writing" with Hélène Cixous in an "attempt to unerase, unearth and to find the primitive picture again, ours, the one that frightens us" (1991, p. 9). I poise myself again, ready to begin at the end.

"Cixous", I write the same six-letters again, "A woman who arrived at my ethnographic door at a time when I didn't know I needed her".

2.

"I thought this was going to be easy", I mutter. "Fuck, it *should* be easy", I mutter again. "But then, I should have known, that would be *too* easy wouldn't it?" I laugh roughly at myself. Easy is a word I am all too familiar with, albeit in not familiar to this context, and the task I have given myself today is surely is all that and more. I am searching for the first; the first letters and words and notes and memories that write my *arrivance*. I bend down and pull out a bright purple archive box appropriately labelled "field notes" sitting on the bottom of my office cupboard and dump it on the floor. They are the remnants of thinking and wondering in 1993 and 1994 before and after what I once thought of as "arriving" at Burrulula. One by one I pull out the contents and before long, the carpet is littered with sheets and reams of variously yellowing and browning loose A4 paper. There is nothing un-forgettable about these documents; the paper is old and plain, the handwriting is plain and neat, the ink is blue and plainly clear on thin, faint and straight blue lines, the staples which hold some together are plain and the paper clips on others are plainly rusted, and they smell quite plainly like papers which have been secreted away at the bottom of a cupboard for quite some time. Perhaps the only un-forgettable thing is the un-forgetting they document, and, that despite the discolouring of the paper itself, the writing is legible.

"Hmmmph", I grunt in surprise. "I wasn't expecting that. *This* should be easy".

Crossing my legs underneath me, I start sifting through the sheets of paper—and I know immediately that *this*, whatever I think *this* is, is *not* going to be easy. *This* is writing-thinking that is twenty-five years old, *this* is me writing-thinking twenty-five years ago and none of *this* then was easy. "Fuck, how stupid was I?" I chide myself, caught in a painful un-forgetting that plainly I never was nor will be any good at systematising my ethnographic record keeping. It was one of those things in my academic training I always shied away from and shoved to the bottom of my to-do list. I couldn't quite bring myself to give file numbers and indexes to the field notes I took because it felt—and perhaps there is the problem, too much feeling again—like I was stifling and stealing a-way the very heart of my work. Numbers, indexes; the dead heart of ethnographic work; and all too easy.

The little girl taps me on the shoulder and passes-by into this moment of here and now from the past.

"Lizzie, look what I found!" Grinning broadly, she hands me a hard-cover book. It's a copy of Enid Blyton's "The Magic Faraway Tree" (1943/2016) and my heart leaps to join her back then.

"Do you recognise this? Look!"

The little girl turns the book over and on the rear side in the top left-hand corner there is a sticker. I recognise the three capital letters printed in blue ink as my handwriting. It's my version of a call number in letters; "BLY" it reads. One summer I decided to turn the contents of my book-shelf into a library, so in love was I with the ways words would fly me a-way to worlds way far a-way. Cataloguing my books was a-way for me to always be certain I could find my way back to those worlds through those words. I didn't need to worry, I would always be able to find my way through.

The little girl gently turns my cheek so my gaze comes to rest upon a small archive box. It is so faded I can no longer tell whether it is purple. Stacked inside are hundreds of catalogue cards. Each one has the author, date, title and publisher printed in very tidy handwriting on it; along with the call number. Underneath the bibliographic material the date I borrowed the book is dutifully printed along with the date I returned it. Writing neatly was important to me; I knew that good librarians needed to have good handwriting so that the way back to the words and world in books would be good and easy. I sigh deeply. The evidence that my record keeping of words and world decades later stopped being good and easy is plain to see. I sigh again. Certain colleagues of mine like Amanda and Mark would be finger wagging and shaking their heads in a gleeful kind of "I told you so" gesture; they had never been fond of the likes of me who fell all too easily into heartline work.

"Fuck you", I whisper softly to them. "These are my words and worlds and I will fucking sort them whatever way I like, systematic ethnography be damned".

But this kind of dismissal too is all *too* easy as I continue my search for the writing that begins my *arrivance*. The order the papers are placed in the box is not easily recognisable; they seem to have been thrown in with-out remembering rhyme or reason and they probably were. Most sheets have a date entered on the top right-hand corner, but some don't. Some papers have the names of people and places scribbled in the centre not far away, but most don't. A quick glance down one of these pages tells me that this detail is hidden, living in secret somewhere under the academic story that wants to hide these memories. The type of writing I decided might belong in this purple archive box labelled "field notes" is similarly forgetful. There are letters to family and friends, faxes to colleagues, notes from advisory meetings, writing labelled "journal entries", fragments of musical transcriptions, quotes from academic papers, and drafts of research questions.

3.
Diary entry, 23rd August 1993.

> *My meeting with my advisor on Friday went very well. We only had enough time to discuss two items or sing verses – B1.12 and B1.11/9 (or B1.6a and B16b, B1.18). B1.6a and b were fairly straight forward and my advisor had nothing new to add really to my analysis.*
>
> *One thing she did mention though was that if you are having problems finding rhythmic section or segment division, to turn to the transcribed version of the song text, in this case John Bradley. There may be some clue in the way the transcriber divided the text into lines as to how rhythmic division should take place. With rhythmic section division, it is also a good idea when having difficulty to listen for the rise in the melodic contour (not as dramatic as at the beginning of a cycle) which may also indicate a level of interaction with the rhythmic structure. These are all handy hints for future analysis!*

4.
A letter to John Bradley, one of many notes to a here and now dear friend and there and then linguistic and anthropological colleague which fly out of the bright purple archive box in my search for; even then and there a search for *arrivance*.

13th September, 1993.

Dear John,

Thank you for your letter dated 6.9.93. Firstly, to answer your question in regards to the syllabic division of the song verse in question (and in fact all song verses), the linguist here did check over these and she is confident that the divisions are O.K. Aside from anything else, these divisions are based upon the way in which I hear the performers dividing the words, whether this is linguistically accurate or not. Even so, the division you suggested does not alter my analysis considerably to be a problem. Thank you for your comments in relation to this.

In terms of my question on the text and rhythm, and how the two fit together, I am not sure whether or not I made myself clear, but your answer does at least tell me one thing – the performers are very consistent in the way in which they perform the songs! I still wonder whether or not just because they start the song in the same place all of the time, whether that starting place is actually the beginning of the song.

Thank you once again for all of your help – I know you must be a very busy man and appreciate your time spent on this. Looking forward to hearing from you soon,

Regards,

Liz

5.

Diary entry, 14th October 1993.

I had a meeting with my PhD advisor today, a good discussion about where I am at with my thesis work and where I need to go next. And that place is a research question. I need to find one. I could start with "Have Yanyuwa women taken over custodianship of men's song?" Very quickly this becomes "Have they also taken on the musical structures of men's song?" A number of sub research questions arise from this, concerning matters that I have been dealing with in my research so far and these may form chapters. My advisor and I thought this was a good beginning list:

What are the performance rules for Yanyuwa women's song?
Is there any rhythmic encoding?
Which came first—text, rhythm or melody?
What is the relationship of Yanyuwa music with Central Australiam or Arnhem Land?
What is the history of Yanyuwa culture, Yanyuwa women's culture and their position in relation to men?

I am ever so keen to gather some more Yanyuwa musical material for transcription. My advisor mentioned that I should be doing an hour of transcription a day—the ethnomusicologists rule—I'll start tomorrow, I promise! And that includes analysis. Tomorrow I will follow up with a search for material—tomorrow.

6.

Another scrap of writing finds its way into my hands. I am staggered by how many snippets of this and that there are, and not only *how many*, but *how much* I wrote before I had even arrived. There is *so much* writing about Borroloola (sic Burrulula) sitting in the bright purple archive box. "The following is an account of issues", I read at the top of one sheet. "Questions to be answered in fieldwork, headlines another. Here's the catch; I know that there and then when I wrote these words on paper, I held them to be so much more than snatches of thinking and wondering. They were pieces of writing which declared a certain knowing about a place I had never been to, people I had never met and songs I had never heard. I take a closer look at the particular notes I am currently holding onto, they are from a research meeting dated 20th December 1993 with my linguistic and anthropological colleagues. They begin like this,

> It was decided that fieldwork will not be carried out until the middle of May, when the wet season will be well and truly finished, making access to Borroloola and associated areas much easier.

See? Just look at the grammar, spelling and expression; it's *all* wrong. *All* of it, and it continues,

> Also at this time of year people are more relaxed and at ease, more willing to sing and perform as the weather becomes more tolerable.

It is an interesting word isn't it, this word "more"? *More* relaxed, *more* willing, *more* tolerable; it seeks to go further and farther than what is to become another, added to and greater and: wait. All of the more-s here— I see the word "more" now as more than one and turned towards the multiple it speaks a different kind of meaning, one that whispers ever so gently and yet with warning, words about encounters and elsewheres and ethics; most loudly and insistently words about ethics.

> It is hoped we will be able to stay on outstation called Wandangula…not a good idea to stay in town due to alcohol and associated problems. There are some knowledgeable people staying at Wandangula including Dinny McDinny, Eileen, Nancy and Rachel McDinny…quite willing to help us in our work. I am going to write to them, asking permission to come and stay with them, to study their music further.

And there they are, the words I wrote. In black and white. So much less than the more-s I had been looking for. There and then the words that followed all kinds of academic rules in relation to researching and writing that were not, in fact, *kind* at all. *These* words assumed and assured me of my authority to arrive and any being in-relation association they might have held was absent and a-way. Here and now the words blanket shame on me, and shame it is. Un-forgetting these moments of white-settler-colonial-privilege is excruciating, even more so because how can I be sure I am any different here and now writing *these* words than I was there and then writing *those* words?

7.

There is an interruption and it arrives as a knock on my office door.

"You've got to be fucking kidding me!" I hiss, refusing to answer.

"Doesn't anybody no how to read the signs anymore?"

I shake my head, what had happened to the "DANGER: WOMAN WRITING" warning I had carefully and deliberately hung from the handle a few moments earlier?

I turn my back and turn back to my task. But here and now, another knock, more persistent this time. I throw my hands in the air and scraps of writing fly high into the air, fluttering down and around and down. Some catch themselves before it's too late on books and folders of more writing that protrude from shelves, others land awkwardly on the archive boxes which now I sense have never behaved in the way intended.

"Oh, that's just fucking brilliant, *more* mess", I throw my now empty hands in the air again. "As if things aren't messed up enough!" And another rap at the door arrives. It propels me like the blast from a cannon to the door and I wrench it open violently, ready to start the revolution.

"What the fuck do you wa…" I begin, but then I see her. It is *her*.

"Entering has never been my forte" (Cixous, 1997, p. 277) she explains, and bows her head ever so slightly in a gesture of apology. She gently pushes past me and steps inside my room. I watch her pause and take in the mess of papers on my floor. She turns back to me and raises one eyebrow.

"I know I once suggested a writer needed 'to crawl on the text' (Cixous, in Cixous & McQuillan, 2002, p. 186) but I was not ever sure anyone would surely *ever* take it so literally", she smiles. "Is that *what* is going on here?"

I don't know what to say; so, I say nothing. She stares at me; so, I stare back and think and wonder whether I should ask her to leave and then I think and wonder whether I should ask her to stay. Leaving as one, staying as two; perhaps the best option is in-between; so, I say nothing.

"Or perhaps, it is better, I ask, *who* is going on here?" I know she is curious. I am too, because this is a question that has been lurking, "waiting, alert, pulling itself together" (Cixous & McQuillan, 2002, p. 412) ever since this moment of un-forgetting began. It is not just *a* question, it is *the* question.

8.

Questions to be answered in fieldwork. A list of Yanyuwa knowledge to collect and document. Who knew then what I know now about loving lists, lists that are lovingly made and yet this one shows no love at all.

Number one. Yanyuwa musical terms. What is the Yanyuwa word for music? For song, for dance, for melody? How do Yanyuwa people describe the correct beating accompaniment associated with the singing of a song verse? Is there a Yanyuwa term for isorhythmic pattern? Rhythmic segment and/or text line?

Number two. Yanyuwa knowledge of the song creative process. What are the origins of song in Yanyuwa culture? How is each song genre created? Do men and women compose song in the same way? Is song composition in the form of visitation by a spirit during a dream an expected experience in Yanyuwa culture? How many dream state songs are there? Is there a strong distinction in importance between Dreaming songs as opposed to dream state or newly composed songs?

Number three. Yanyuwa perceptions of knowledge, power and song. What is the Yanyuwa definition of knowledge? How does it function in their society? How do people obtain knowledge? How does song impact knowledge? How does knowledge as song as power work in Yanyuwa culture?

Number four. Yanyuwa women and song. Is there a difference between women's singing and men's singing? Are the differences musical, social, cultural and how are they interconnected? What kinds of songs do women compose today? Do men still compose? What kinds of knowledges does women's singing hold? How is it used and for what purposes? Where does the power of women's singing rest? What is empowering *for* women *about* women's singing?

9.

Before I had even *arrived* at Burrulula, there was *this* moment. I watch the little girl from a distance; she is in that place of further away I am trying to get to. The family car pulls into the driveway of the shack that would become their home for the next two weeks. It's a blue/grey Ford GXL—Betsy, her Dad's pride and joy. They had left the big freeze of a Victorian winter and driven long into the night get here. Every now and then the little girl would be woken up by the comforting sound of eight cylinders growling and rumbling them north along the bitumen. In that moment of quiet she would glance sleepily at her Dad, hands resting lightly on the wheel at 10 and 2 o'clock, eyes peering straight ahead into the blackness; just him and Betsy, the sweetest relationship there ever was, rolling through the night while his wife and two girls slumbered beside him.

Grabbing her towel, she has the door open and is running across the road towards the beach before the engine even stops. Her family has been coming to this place by the ocean for as long as she can remember. She kicks off her shoes, peels away her socks and steps bare foot onto the fine golden sand. Her feet squeak as she runs wildly down to the edge of the ocean, the fine grains lodging themselves deliciously between her toes and tickling the back of her legs with each step. She squeals with delight as the first wave of the holiday season teases and touches her with a carefree splash. The little girl stands on the edge of the shore, closes her eyes and stretches her arms out wide. The sea breeze blows gently on her face and begins to fill her up; she has been away from the saltwater for far too long and with each breath she is becoming alive again. Standing in the shallow water she sheds layer upon layer of heavy clothing to bear her bikini-bather-clad body to the sun and signals her arrival.

She turns away from the water; there is something she must do before she dives into its depths. The little girl is looking for sand dollars; the skeletal remains of sea urchins and starfish, which the ebbing tide deposits on the beach as intricate patterned white shells. Her Mum had told her that these beautiful coins belonged to mermaids and she scooped up as many as she could in both hands before diving into the clear ocean.

Tucking the precious pennies into her bikini bottoms, she clasps her feet tightly together like a fish tail as she swam out to the sandbar. The cool salty water flows in and around every fold of her body, wishing and washing and wishing her towards something beautiful, a certain place of daring and freedom. Each time her head rises up out of the waves, the little girl opens her mouth and sings her siren's call. She is singing to the mermaids, waiting for them to come to her.

10.

I find what I am looking for. It is a copy of a letter dated the 2nd of January 1994 addressed to Dinny, Eileen, Nancy and Rachel McDinny at Wandangala (sic) care of the Borroloola Post Office, BORROLOOLA, Northern Territory, post code 0854. The letter is from me to them. Miss Elizabeth Mackinlay, care of the Music Department, The University of New England, ARMIDALE, New South Wales, post code 2351. It is typed in large times new roman font.

> Dear Dinny, Eileen, Nancy and Rachel,
>
> I am a friend of John Bradley's, studying Aboriginal song at the University of New England, Armidale NSW. John has kindly let me listen to some of his recordings of Yanyuwa *walaba* and *akuriya* (sic) performances. I found the singing and performances to be most interesting and exciting, and would like to have the opportunity to hear more Yanyuwa song.
>
> I am wanting to know if it would be possible for myself and a linguist at the University to come and visit you at Wandangala, to learn more about Yanyuwa song and Yanyuwa song performance.
>
> I am looking forward to hearing from you soon.
>
> Yours sincerely,
>
> Elizabeth Mackinlay

I turn back to my bright purple archive box looking for a reply from Dinny, Eileen, Nancy and Rachel McDinny. There is nothing there.

11.

"Here she is!" An elderly man ambles over to the camp chairs where my mother-in-law Jeannie and her mother Hilda are resting. It has been a long hot day sitting in the back of a troupe carrier to get to Burrulula, and with a cup of white sweet bush tea in hand, the two women are beginning to feel their bodies shed and mend the dust and dents of the long hot drive.

"Oh, my boy, Dinny!" Hilda stands up slowly, but her smile is fast. She embraces Dinny McDinny, a senior Garrwa man, and the moment they touch there is a subtle shift in the air. Time stretches out of shape; the heat of the sun grows soft, the crows quieten and croon, and the essence of family in kinship on country is all of a sudden everywhere.

Jeannie waits to be welcomed, she knows the Law.

"And who is this?" Mr McDinny asks, pointing his lips at me.

Hilda waves me over to them.

"This is my grandson's wife", she places her thin arm around my shoulder.

"Yu! I've got to call you granny then", he chuckles. "You're my *kukurdi*".

I see the Yanyuwa kinship diagram I've memorised in my head; if I close my eyes and I can see the chart clearly, the names and the relationships. Yakamarri marries Nungarrima, our daughters are called Naminyanma and our sons are called Kangala. Jeannie is Nulanyma and Hilda is Nimarrama. The chart tells me that Dinny McDinny is my maternal grandson; I call him *wukuku*.

"This is Liz", Hilda continues, "She's the...what did you say you were?"

"I'm the ethno-", I stammer. "I'm the ethnomusicologist from the Univer..."

Hilda interrupts and translates. "Yes, that's right, she's the, the...the music researcher that wrote to you".

Dinny reaches forward and shakes my hand.

"Welcome to my country *kukurdi*," he says, placing his hand on his heart. "To her country", he holds Hilda's hand in his other.

He steps to one side and takes a look at the luggage and supplies piled high inside the back of the troupe carrier. He is looking for something.

"Well, did you bring your tape recorder my girl?"

I nod.

"Good, that's good", Dinny seems pleased. "Because I have some songs that I want to sing for you, we can start tomorrow, *bawuji barra*". Dinny turns then and walks away, humming loudly not quite under his breath. 12.

This is the moment I arrived. I was introduced as some-*one*, I was named some-*body*; I was called some-*one*, I was given a some-*body* in Yanyuwa. I was no longer a stranger. Not being a stranger was a necessity. I was given the Yanyuwa "skin" name Nungarrima which linked me to the Rrumburriya clan. It was the proper "right way" name for me as wife to a Yakamarri man and it meant that others would know how to relate to me *as* an-other. Being Nungarrima meant I was now in-relation to people and country, a stranger no more. The *feeling* of being introduced, named and called in Yanyuwa has imprinted itself heavily and permanently on my un-forgetting, a living and breathing in-memoriam tattoo. At first, a rush of warmth from head to heart becoming a smile dissipating fault and fear. And then, not long after, an itching and scratching which became a burning of discomfort asking,

"Really? Did you think you had *arrived* because you were introduced, named and called? Did you *really* think that this moment you think of as arrival meant acceptance? Think *really* did you about arrival?"

A Yanyuwa man I once knew and thought to be wise and loving once said that being given a skin name was like being granted a visa; a skin name was a stamp on a passport page which gave approval for movement and action in an-other place, a place where being without permission, was to be a stranger; but so much more than that, a stranger intruding. This Yanyuwa man I once knew explained that being given a skin name was an assertion of power by Yanyuwa people to give outsiders provisional entry into and onto their country, and a way to control, via a relational ethic, the scope of activities by strangers like me within this system. Like a visa, like the stamp on a passport pages, a skin name came with the expectation of operating within and according to Yanyuwa Law.

I wish I had understood then and there what this meant, what this *really* meant, when I thought I had arrived; but I didn't. I was named, no longer a stranger in name, but ways of being Law-fully Yanyuwa were strange to me; I was a stranger. I was still *outside* Yanyuwa Law; and they were outside to me and inside the research drive—my desire, there is no use pretens/ding—and demand to uncover, translate, know and fix the others in their otherness. I see myself there and then a naive researcher. Trespassing blindly, heavily. Filled with right. Replete with privilege. I see myself there and then covered in coloniality. An ethnomusicologist and ethnographer. Recordings, notepads, cameras. I hear you ask myself there and then, will you sing? For me now? Fires, dust, melodies. I want to. To know you. To know me? Who am I? You ask me? I see myself there and then take hold of your hand. Teach, watch, wait. Patient and generous. I see myself there and then travelling on country. Always on country. I see myself there and then in words that are written in collision with worlds. Strangers become friends. Friends become family. Family becomes *kundiyarra*. Most necessary companions. I see myself there and then *a-mijii* no more. Nungarrima and a-Yakibijirna. I see myself there and then a newly born woman. Dance, dare, dream. Time passes by. Laugh, love, cry. Birth, death, renewal. A sisterhood beyond. And mermaids sing. I see myself there and then with Law-full women. Forever a reminder. To be Law-full. On this country. In this country. For this country. With this country. A decolonial yearning. Can you hear? Will you un-forget? I see myself there and then here and now, and Cixous' question places a mark next to my skin name, the one I was introduced, named and called, *who* is going on here?

13.

We sit quietly together, content for now to lose ourselves in the comforting flickering of the fire. It is just the two of us; everyone else has retired for the night and the sounds that mark the days end occasionally escape from the houses that surround us. Dinny McDinny stays across the way and I can hear him singing *kujika*, low and strong. He has been singing every day since I arrived from sun up to sun down and listening to him now, I think and wonder how he *truly* lives and breathes in a sung world. His daughter Myra lives next door to him and I can hear her crooning softly to calm her niece's baby. In the distance, the latest

2Pac track thumps and pumps from the single boy's shack at the end of the road.

Jemima sighs and tsks, "Can't they sleep?"

She looks across at me. "And what about you? Are you sleepy yet baba?"

I look up from the fire, "Not yet".

"Maybe you and me are the same; too much happening here", she gently taps the side of her head with her finger, "And here", she says, pointing to her heart.

My eyes meet hers, and some-thing passes between us. I think and wonder now what it was. Recognition? A yearning for connection? An awareness of our relationship as sisters and what it might become? I cannot say for sure; just as I will never know if she felt it too; but when I try to un-forget my *arrivance* at Burrulula, it is this night around the camp-fire with my baba Jemima that I re/turn to.

"So, you and my son, you married hey?" she asks.

"Well not properly…", I start and then stop. "We live together if that's what you mean".

"Married then", she nods. "No kids hey?"

She is not asking but rather confirming what she knows.

"And what about your family, where you from?"

"Ballarat, just outside of Melbourne. I grew up in a little town called Creswick; it's goldfields country—and cold", I add.

"Any Aboriginal people live there?"

In the pause that follows I see the face of my kindergarten teacher, Mrs Clarke. I didn't know she was Aboriginal back then, it was only later as life happened to her, cruelly and publicly with pursed lips and pointed fingers in our small town, that I knew she was not the same as me. Mrs Clarke smiled from the inside out each and every day. She simultaneously sparkled and spoke softly as she read and cuddled me when Michael Savage pushed me off the swings. I didn't know many things back then. That the country I grew up on is was, is and always be the traditional lands of the Dja Dja Wurrung people of the Kulin alliance of Aboriginal nations. That an explorer called Thomas Mitchell passed through Creswick in 1836 and paved the way a year later for squatters to establish a sheep station. I didn't know then that these white mostly men brought many things with them aside from rams, ewes and lambs; they brought smallpox, guns and hatred. That led by their clan head Munangabum, the Dja Dja Wurrung people resisted European settlement and the dispossession of their lands at every turn and paid the price. That there were 11 reported massacres on Dja Dja Wurrung country from 1838 until 1846. That in 1841, less than five years after white people arrived on Dja Dja Wurrung country, they were rounded up and placed for their own "protection" on the Loddon Aboriginal Protectorate Station on the north side of Mount Franklin. That after the squatters came the government and after the government came the missionaries and after the missionaries came the miners and after the miners came; well, after that, the Dja Dja Wurrung people were moved and moved on. That at first contact the population of Dja Dja Wurrung was estimated at 2000 and by 1852, 15 years later, the population estimate was 142. I didn't know then that when my history teacher told me that there weren't any "full-blood" and real Aboriginal people left in our town, she was wrong; she was so very wrong.

"I don't know, baba, I think there was only one family...I'm not sure", I am whispering and lower my eyes to try to hide the shame that has crept in to sit beside me and my not knowing.

Jemima's voice breaks my discomfort, "Most whitefellas don't know baba, most don't know *us* at all". Her words are said with care and kindness—with a generosity I did not then and do not now deserve, of that I *can* be sure.

"Let me tell you about me and my family", she begins.

14.

The view from the city airport is literaturally miles away as I watch myself in *arrivance* there, in the southwest Gulf of Carpentaria. A place so far fly away that it has become a place I might think of as home. This time I am searching for something quite particular; I am looking for the beginning. The moment when I sensed that I had arrived there. I am sitting perched high behind the wheel of a grumbling and growling mechanical monster—a white Toyota troupe carrier I've rented from the North Australian Research Unit associated with the Australian National University for exactly this purpose. This particular troupie is no different to any other I have driven; it has energy, grunt, and a certain kind of tenacity which I have learnt to respect and trust over the years, knowing that it will deliver me, come what may—and maybe a little late and dirty—to the place of my *arrivance*. The corrugations on the red road rattle and rock the 4WD out of time with the rhythms playing on the stereo, and every so often the troupie lurches to one side or the other in an effort to return to some kind of synchronicity. I know am driving too fast; but I am anxious to get there and let the wheels glide. The wet season has not yet begun and for now I can tear up the road without care for watching the mud slide me and the troupie in slow motion into a bog. I look in my rear vision mirror and smile at the clouds of red dust kicking up behind me as I drive along the dirt track. I know my family at Wandangula will be scanning the horizon for the tell-tale billows and they will know I am now not very far a-way. I open the driver side window and feel the sea breeze blow through my hair. A song begins to circle and cycle around in my head. It's a Yanyuwa song I know well.

> *Karna-bulma ngarna-ngurru*
> *a-munji munjingu ayu ngurrbungku*
> (breath intake)
> *bulma ngarna-ngurru*
> *a-munji munjingu ayu ngurrbungku*
> *karna*
> (a little bit longer breath intake)
> *a-munji munjingu ayu ngurrbungku*
> *karna-bulma ngarna-ngurru*
> (a deep breath)

It's a Yanyuwa *women's* song I know well—an *a-nguyulnguyul* song; a tricky and clever kind of song all over. Tricky to say, and clever enough to sound old (read traditional) enough but tell a story about the here and now of women's lives. Tricky to sing, and clever enough to move you in a passionate way—laugh, cry, scream or dance, it doesn't matter. What matters most is that the song speaks to your heart, a heart that lives and breathes through these words and the world itself.

A-nguyulnguyul songs are indeed tricky and clever; they grew me up as an ethnographer and before I could say no, they had moved me from there to here. This genre of music became the topic of my PhD in ethnomusicology; not at first. Over and across time I heard, saw and felt how powerful *a-nguyulnguyul* were for women because they became a place where women's ways of being, doing and knowing in the world were documented, shared, celebrated—and mourned. I recorded many *a-nguyulnguyul* songs and seventy-one of them made it into Appendix D of my doctoral thesis with full text translations and musical transcriptions. It is not the Yanyuwa way to name songs—the English word music itself has no correlate—the names given to songs throughout are a rough summary of the topic each covers and were named by Yanyuwa family with full awareness of the women who created them. Neither is it the Yanyuwa way to write music down—the notation is mine. In Appendix D there is one unknown *a-nguyuln-guyul* song; we talked around and over possible composers but in the end, it was better not to say for certain. And the final song in Appendix D is named "Elizabeth's song". The *a-nguyulnguyul* song flying a-way with me in the troupie along the dirt road was made by Elma a-Bunubunu Brown.

Although she is now gone, Elma is very much a powerful and performative present/ce in the social, spiritual and sung worlds of Yanyuwa women. Elma is famous for many reasons—and when I think of her, the three words which come to mind are totally-kick-ass; her reputation as an independent, wise and "boss of herself" kind of woman is legendary. She had never had children and was said to have sung her womb to stop herself from becoming pregnant. Elma was one of only two people who had been given a ceremony by ancestral beings during a dream; the *Ngardirdji* mermaid song. *Ngardirdji* is a constant in my *arrivance* story at Burrulula, and over time, became the focus of my ethnographic writing about Yanyuwa women's song performance. I look over at this list of publications proclaiming to know and I can't help but shake my head now thinking of how easy it was to pro-claim and position myself as a pro(fessional) claimer. "Blurring boundaries between restricted and unrestricted performance: A case study of the mermaid song of Yanyuwa women in

Borroloola" (Mackinlay, 2000a) was one of the first academic papers I wrote proclaiming to knowledge of *Ngardirdji*. "Of mermaids and spirit men", I penned with my anthropological colleague and friend John Bradley (Mackinlay & Bradley, 2003). And then, questioning my knowing and the ways I was proclaiming that knowledge as an academic in classrooms, talking about *Ngardirdji* became central to "Moving and dancing towards decolonisation in education" (Mackinlay, 2005a). The "d" word had willowed and wisped its way into my vocabulary and it was making damned sure it wasn't going away. From then on, any kind of proclaiming was done at the in-between and it had become a Cixousian kind of "undecidable" thinking that "thinks all the possibilities, all the positions" and returns to writing as recycled and reconsidered (Cixous, 1997, p. 84). The title, "Crossing and negotiating borders of identity, knowledge and tradition: Coming to an understanding of Aboriginal women's performance in educational locales as a white woman" (Mackinlay, 2008) need say no more of the kind of reviewing and reflecting about.

Elma had died by the time of my *arrivance* in Burrulula. In the one photo my family and I have of her, she is smiling widely and holding a packet of Aspirin. Every time I look at this picture I am reminded of the writings of anthropologist Marie Reay whose work I came across early in my PhD research. Before going to Burrulula, I did what every "good enough" researcher in the field of ethnography does and went to the archives to see what materials relating to Yanyuwa performance already existed. A search of the Australian Institute for Aboriginal and Torres Strait Islander Studies (AIATSIS) catalogue revealed that some of the earliest sound recordings of Yanyuwa, Garrwa, Mara and Kudanji women's performance made at Burrulula were done Reay when she visited there from 1959–1962 for 20 months of fieldwork. Approximately 10 tapes deposited into the archives after her first trip to the Northern Territory were documented by Reay as including Anyula (sic) and Garawa song and language. The notes accompanying the tapes are vague; no names of people are noted, no names of songs are noted, and the only note-able notes are those which indicate the genre of song. Most of the songs she said she recorded were restricted, women's only *a-yawalhu*;

and I knew immediately that *these* songs should, could and would never be note-able.

Wrote and note Reay did however; two research papers— "Subsections at Borroloola" (1962) and "A decision as narrative" (1970). Her words about Yanyuwa people, place and performance horrified me then and they fill me with the same abhorrence now. In 1962 she called Burrulula "a decayed township" (p. 90), by 1970 she condemned it as "that sick segment of Gulf-Barkly Tablelands" (p. 172) and always already a "poor relation of [her] New Guinea material" (p. 166). I can't help but think as I read her writing that despite broadcasting publicly that she went to Burrulula to document women's secret ceremonies (1970, p. 165), Reay never expected to find anything of import to her field. I watch myself, head bent over her papers highlighter in hand, looking and looking and looking for words that signal her *arrivance*; words that draw a line between hers and the heartlines of mine, because after all, are we not in some senses the selfsame (*Note*: written this way and *not* self-same to evoke the violence of empire after Cixous [in Cixous & Clément, 1986, p. 70]), just thirty years a-part? The more I read I am not sure she ever wanted *arrivance* but rather desired arrival at some kind of anthropological truth she could write, right and have rites about. Her words (p. 164) about being incorporated into the kinship system at Burrulula are silent on relationship—there is no naming-as-in-relation, only naming-as-classifi-cation which in and of itself is given.

I can feel my thinking heart tensing and apprehensing. Her absolutes and assumptions about *her* anthropology, authority and acceptance by simply *arriving* at Burrulula have me wanting and needing to argue a-way through my abhorrence for the likes of her. Perhaps if I focus on her 1970 paper, the one that claims a narrative turn in the title, my thinking heart might begin to find some affinity with this woman who only moments earlier I thought the selfsame as me. In this latter piece, Reay uses a cre-ative style of writing she names a "dramaticule" to describe the process of placing her within the Yanyuwa kinship system and the naming of her with the Yanyuwa female subsection Nangalama. It's a literary genre I am not familiar with but immediately I am expecting a story which includes elements of mimicry, mockery and perhaps even derision. Being a dedicated anthropologist, Reay dutifully wants to know why, why was she given that particular subsection name? The response to her question is not one she was expecting. "The only explanation they would give me", she writes, "was that anyone could tell by looking at me that I was Nangalama. My physical imperfections, which enumerated ruthlessly, were typical of Nangalama women". I imagine Reay huffing and puffing with insult. She continues, "And they told me, looking me straight in the eye, that women of this subsection always tended to be a 'little bit silly'" (1970, p. 164). Oh, the insult! How dare *they* use "an unsuspecting anthropologist to help them carry out their evil purposes in the moral theatre of their paltry world?" And with these words, Reay begins to take revenge.

My breath catches in my throat as I read the next section of Reay's paper. During fieldwork Reay relates how she made explicit enquiries about women's ceremonies and talks about "a girl who was somewhat an expert on the myths" told her about them whenever the "resourceful" anthropologist could "persuade her to do so by satisfying her addiction to Aspros" (1970, p. 168). I look at the picture I have of Elma sitting beside me on my desk and can't help but think and wonder. She calls this girl "Clytie" and gives further detail about her data collection methods: "This girl, whom I shall Clytie, gave beautifully full accounts of the Mungamunga [Women's Dreaming] on eleven Aspros each morning. (more than that, I found her silly as a rabbit and her stories unintelligible)" (1970, p. 168). The vitriolic comments continue. An informant Reay names as one of the leading female singers of women's secret ceremony is described as a "slovenly dancer" (1970, p. 169) and another is characterised as "surly" and "sluggish" with lesbian desires for Reay (1970, p. 169). I shake my head at Reay's arrogance. She continually positions herself as the innocent anthropologist whose only wish was "to record the ceremonies in notes and on tape" (1970, p. 170) and what did she receive in return for such academic nobility? Dis-respect, dis-missal and defiance. In an era where the missionaries at Burrulula did not allow Aboriginal people to perform ceremony, Reay felt mis-used by the Yanyuwa, Garrwa, Mara and Kudanji women "who desired strongly to hold the forbidden ceremonies" and took advantage of the "unsuspecting anthropologists" (that is, Reay) own desire to record their performances and thereby "escape censure for doing so" (1970, p. 172). Although she thinks it unlikely that her informants were unlikely to have "systematically misled" her (1962, p. 92), Reay admits that the "Borroloola natives" were hard to work with and that "during 1959–1960 several of the men and at least one of the women deliberately tried to prevent me from finding out anything of significance" (1962, p. 92).

15.

I finally find the set of field notes that document my conversation with Karrakayn about Yanyuwa musical words and worlds. I smile, partly in shame, partly in sadness at my naked naiveté. I needed to have this "interview", instilled as I was there and then with the disciplinary knowledge that one of my first duties as a dutiful ethnomusicologist was to document all of the Yanyuwa words I find that related to music and to bring them "into view". Getting this list of words, I was told and trained, was an important step in becoming an ethnomusicologist; every academic I knew working in this field had a musical word list just like this one and being able to cite from this kind of list meant that you were on your way to becoming the expert in your field; it meant your status, authority and privileges as an expert had *arrived*.

I carefully read my way through the thin pieces of notepad paper I hold in my hand; they are yellow now and aging, the blue ink is fading fast to grey and the lines are barely visible. "TRANSCRIPT OF CONVERSATION with ANNIE KARRAKAYN" is written neatly at the top of the front page. It's dated the 17th July 1994 and we are sitting on the front porch of Myra's house at Wandangula outstation. Just below the date, the title, "Yanyuwa musical terminology" is loosely scrawled. A column on the left-hand side lists the English words I must have thought I was going get to translated: words like music, rhythm, scale, metre, style, song, genre.

As I leaf through my field notes, a waft of smoking ironwood rushes up from inside and takes me there, back *there* and then, to Wandangula. The open fire outside the house has been burning all day. Wisps of smoke puff slowly and steadily from the hot ash and drift their way into tresses and dresses. Billies of tea have simmered, johnny cakes have risen and fallen, and fillets of gummy shark have been charred and consumed. As the sun sets on the day, the coals continue to smolder.

"You ready for me now?" Karrakayn calls out as she wanders over to the blanket I have laid out under the shady tree.

I nod, "Yu marruwarra! Come and join me!"

She settles herself into a cross legged position, pops a piece of chewing tobacco into her mouth and looks at me expectantly.

"So, what you want to know marruwarra? Ask away", she smiles at me broadly and chuckles. "After all, that's what you mob do best innit? Ask questions?"

"Well, I guess we could start by talking about music", I say slowly, looking down at my list of questions to be asked on fieldwork.

"In my language we say *ngalki*; that's every song got *ngalki*. When you sing different song, different *ngalki*. Same tune, same *ngalki*", Karrakayn explains.

I recognise the word "ngalki". I have not heard it spoken until now, but I remember reading about it in a paper by linguist Jean Kirton (1977) who worked at Burrulula in the mid 1960s. She writes that the word *ngalki*, while literally translating as "skin" refers more centrally to the concept of "essence" (p. 321), that is, the quality of a phenomena which makes it unique. My ethnomusicological mind starts whirring around, trying to equate *ngalki* with Western musical concepts.

"Ngalki's just the melody, not the rhythm? Or is it the rhythm as well?" I ask Karrakayn.

"Yeah, with that one now", Karrakayn explains.

"And does rhythm have a special name?"

"No", she replies patiently.

Here and now I begin to squirm as I read this transcript. Aside from the glaringly obvious interviewing mistake I have made by asking for a yes or no response, my question there and then shows that I wasn't listening to Karrakayn. She told me clearly that melody and rhythm are all part of the one concept, the Yanyuwa concept of *ngalki*, but I did not hear her; I did not *want* to hear her. I think and wonder how I proceeded to duck and weave my way around to ask over, and around and over again the same kind of single response questions. "What's that called when…"

I ask. "Does that have a name?" I ask. "Is there a word for?" I ask. Not once, but over twenty-four times. I walk away from our conversation with a list of Yanyuwa words for the world of Yanyuwa music that is over twenty-four lines long.

"You can have more words", Karrakayn says. "I can tell you more things so that other people can listen to what I'm talking to you".

She pauses.

"But tomorrow I want my friend with me, my *kundiyarra* there beside me". Her lips point in the direction of Dinah. "I'm older than her but my partner, she knows what I'm talking about".

16.

Later, as I learned what it meant to live and love within the boundaries of this word and world of Yanyuwa women's being-in-relation, I would think and wonder and write many times (e.g., Mackinlay, 2000b, 2005b; Mackinlay & Bartleet, 2012) about *kundiyarra*. Karrakayn had tried to explain it to me that day on the porch but I didn't know there and then what she meant, what she *really* meant when she explained, "Yinda a-ngatha mara". This phrase translates loosely as "you are my most necessary companion" and *kundiyarra* taught me the centrality of love, care and compassion to the ways in which are born, live and die in this world as women. *Kundiyarra*, she taught me, are those women who talk, walk, sing and dance beside you when you are a young girl and hold you close as you enter into womanhood. Karrakayn was *a-wirdi*, a big boss woman, and I remember how often she reminded and growled me that I was not just a young girl but a baby on Yanyuwa country with much to learn. "You right *marruwarra*", she said, "I'll show you proper way". *Kundiyarra*, Karrakayn taught me, lift their voices up in song and kick up the dust on the ceremony ground alongside you. Sometimes when I am lying in bed at night, thinking and wondering, I close my eyes and I can hear her singing, "Ngardijarra, ngardijarra, yaka jamala, mala bila mala bila". Her voice rises higher and higher, calling up and out to the mermaid women, the a-Marabarna women who gave Yanyuwa women their own Law. In song as *kundiyarra*, she told me—most especially in song and in ceremony—we are strong women, women ourselves, bosses ourselves. *Kundiyarra*, she taught me, nurture your body, heart and soul as you give birth to children and watch others pass away; they will hold you close as experience both the tears and sorrow, and love that is life.

Before Karrakayn died, she asked but one thing of me. While my then husband was visiting Burrulula to attend the funeral of senior Garrwa Law man in 2004, Karrkayn spoke to him quietly but with a sense of urgency.

"You tell your wife", she said, "that I want her to record my story before I die".

In that moment Karrakayn's request overflowed with recognition that with the recent deaths of several senior men from her community, the old women were now carrying a lot of culture and that it was important to pass on their stories. When he came back and told me what his kukurdi Karrakayn had asked, I sat down alone to think and wonder. I had been working with the Burrulula community since 1994 when I began my PhD work in ethnomusicology documenting Yanyuwa women's song traditions. Karrakayn was my marruwarra and my kundiyarra who took me firmly and willingly by the hand and heart into strange and unfamiliar places where our relationship and our research could come to life. I knew I had to fulfill Karrakayn's wish; I felt ever so strongly that with all the power and privilege I held as a white-settler-colonial researcher and in return for all of the gifts she had given me—how do I begin to make a list? Where do I start? Knowledge? Law? Friendship? Love? These words seem grossly inadequate—that surely this was one thing I could do for my marruwarra, to help this old lady get her story down for her children's children?

17.

"So, what have you got planned for us this afternoon kujaka?" Nancy McDinny asks, stretching out across her blanket in the late afternoon sun. Jemima, Annie a-Karrakayn Isaac, Dinah a-Marrngawi Norman and Rosie a-Makurndurna Noble lay nearby, their eyes closed and ears open.

I look across at her and I think and wonder if this is the right time do it. I have been agonising over it ever since I arrived, about when would be the *right* time, knowing that perhaps there would never be a right time for it. I take a deep breath.

"Well, I wonder if we might…", I struggle to find the right words. "You see, there's an archive down in Canberra and…and there's a woman who came here and placed tapes there…and now…well I have…"

"What you talking about marruwarra? You going down to Canberra with what woman? Hmmph, you leaving so soon, you only just arrived," Karrakayn growls softly but impatiently.

I pause and take another breath, deeper this time, so much further, in a failed attempt to lower and swallow my nerves. I was told when I agreed to bring the tapes from the archives back to Burrulula; no, not just told, *warned*—to be careful. I remember the earnest look on the archivist's face when she spoke to me about what it was she wanted me to do. There was no need, I could read and decode the implicit warning for myself; the tapes were recorded by *Marie Reay*, nothing more to say. I had read her work before arriving at Burrulula and they were the only two names as words I needed to know to be warned and to take care. I know that Nancy, Karrakayn, Jemima, Dinah and Rosie are waiting for my reply and I imagine as I un-forget this moment that the world similarly places itself on hold, waiting. Waiting for me to make a decision about this narrative, the one that I am going to tell here and now about the narrative that Marie Reay left behind there and then and deposited in the form of cassette recordings in the archives in Canberra. Accession numbers 004023A–004028B; 009250–009251. 16 audio tape reels, duration 8 hours and 43 minutes. Women's yawulyu song series including topics of horse galloping, necklace song, songs about sweethearts, and shaving whiskers. Performers include Florence; Helen; Molly Bungurimera; Agnes Budgamara; Jingle; Maggie Yuendya; Gilbirr; Rosu; Elphine; Josephine; Rosemary; Spider; Jack Williams; Jemima; Willie Ngawuji. Access conditions apply, some tapes may contain restricted material. I think and wonder now about how easy it was for me to gain access; all I needed to say was that I was a researcher with an interest in sound recordings from Burrulula and they were made available to me. There were no restrictions and even though Marie Reay noted the material as "restricted", I think and wonder now who that particular notation was for. I think and wonder about *that* notation and the subsequent way that Reay noted and wrote and about her experiences at Burrulula. I realise I always already know the answer. I decide here and now that the time is right.

18.

I reach over and gently press the stop button on the cassette recorder.

"That's it", I whisper, "finished now".

The silence that descends upon us sings loudly into the starry night above and returns the songs and spirits of those we have just been listening to into the present.

Kulha Nancy wipes her eyes. "Kurda! My old grandmother. Such beautiful songs, she was a really deadly singer hey?"

"Yu! She had the sweetest throat", Jemima adds with a soft and sad smile.

"And you too nhilla!" Karrakayn sniffs and reaches for a tissue, her voice chokes more than a little. "We heard you running, dancing and crying in the background, might be when you was just a little girl".

We have been sitting huddled on a cotton blanket around a small tape recorder listening intently to the Reay tapes since late afternoon and now we are done. The quiet echo of the past in the present decides to stay with us a little longer.

"So many songs, all the women's business; the proper sacred songs", Karrakayn's voice begins to trail away. "We haven't sung them in a long time, kurda, poor things, we forget them and they dying too now…kurda".

"And this mijiji kujaka, that one that made these cassettes. What's her name again?" Nancy asks.

"Marie Reay", I say quietly. Saying her name aloud feels like I am betraying an unwritten and unspoken ethnographic code to always protect our own; but *not* saying her name is no longer an option. In that moment I watch myself cross over to a/not-her that says being-in-relation is the only ethico-onto-epistemological possibility.

"Uh huh…mmmph, I remember that old lady", Karrakayn begins. "Mijiji is right, a-murdu a-mijiji too".

"What do you mean kukurdi?"

"Well that old lady Marie she broke the Law. She was all the time breaking the Law. Going where she should never have gone, listening to songs she should never have heard. She was proper a-murdu that one", Karrakayn points her finger towards me. "Are you listening to this story marruwarra? You listen hard my girl, women's business is for women only, only for us ladies to know".

Nancy shakes her head, "Why didn't the old people stop her?"

"They argued and tried", Karrakayn explains, "But she was stubborn and the old people didn't understand what she wanted. They let her go and do those things because they didn't know and that mijiji didn't tell them".

"You mean they didn't know about these tapes and the archives?" Nancy frowns.

"No, none of us knew".

The quiet turns around uncomfortably.

"Until now, I didn't know either", Nancy pauses and frowns at me. "I didn't know kujaka, but *you* did".

19.

The tardis-like phone box at Wandangula station rings out plaintively in the early crispness of a Sunday morning in the bush. I am sitting quietly on the porch, contemplating life and the day ahead while enjoying a hot cup of tea while I watch the world around me wake up. At first, I don't want to answer it, who would be ringing so early anyway? But then, something stirs and I know instinctively that the phone call is for me. It's my Dad. His voice is strange, strangled; he tells me that my grandmother has died. I cannot speak; I drop the phone and run for the hills. I stand on top of that rocky outcrop where only the day before we had hunted for porcupine and scream, my voice cries out until it can be heard no more. My voice is gone. I leave Burrulula, my baba (sister) Jemima speaks for me—she hears the words that I cannot say and speaks for my heart. I go back to Melbourne. I see myself standing at the grave of my grandmother and still I cannot speak. I cannot say goodbye to her, I refuse to say goodbye to her. I close my eyes to shut out what I know must be done and I can hear the old men at Burrulula singing around the Yalkawarru funeral pole, feet thumping in the sand, firesticks flying in the air, and all around me the haunting sounds of grieving. Someone close by is crying in rasping gasps and for awhile I am unsure of where I am. I look up and see that it is my father. His entire body is shaking uncontrollably and my mother weeps beside him.

20.

The little girl finally reaches the sandbar and pulls herself out of the saltwater. She stands to rest awhile on the ledge and her eyes scan the ocean which stretches out before her. Her chest rises and falls in time with the ebb and flow of the waves. Patiently she waits; she is certain the mermaids are close by. One by one she throws each sand dollar as far as she can back out to its belonging place in the sea, wishing and wanting and wishing for the mermaids to come and take her away. The little girl closes her eyes and continues to sing at the top of her voice, calling the mermaids to her. "Ngardijarra, ngardijarra, yaka jamala, mala bila mala bila", the words are strangers to her and the notes taste rough as they leave her throat. The more she sings this song, the more smoothly the melody falls from her tongue and with each repetition, the little girl is taken forward in time to a place she did not yet know she was destined for.

The place is called Balamini. It is about 10 km outside of Burrulula travelling east towards the Queensland border, where a large deposit of soft white clay has always sat since Nangurrbuwala (Hill Kangaroo) placed it there and named it Rrumburriya country. Dust settles around us as our car pulls up on the side of road. It is late afternoon, dry season time in the Northern Territory, and the sun lazily makes it way down to the bottom of the horizon. Carrying our digging sticks and dilly bags, my big sister Jemima a-Wuwarlu Miller and I climb out of the troupie and carefully scan the ground upon which our bare feet stand, searching for the whitest clump of earth to take with us. We are looking for a-makirra, the white ochre that we will later grind up into a soft powder to mix with water and paint our bodies for performance of *Ngardirdji*, the Yanyuwa mermaid song.

"Wunhaka? Marnaji nganin-nyanji baba!" my sister Jemima points to a spot just to the side of her.

As we gently pull the a-makirra away from the ground, Jemima and I laugh as we remember how in the rush to board the plane last time, our bag of a-makirra had been left behind on the porch. We had to resort to using white body paint purchased from the local art supplier. But it wasn't the same. The texture was *too* smooth, the colour as it dried on our bodies *too* white, the smell *too* synthetic and there was *too* little in the bottle to paint all the dancers bodies. Jemima takes a small sample of a-makirra from the dilly bag full we have gathered and rubs it between her fingers. The chalky powder falls softly into the palm of her hand and she tips a little bit of water from her bottle to mix the a-makirra into a wet and silky texture. She reaches forward and gently takes my face in her hands.

"Marnaji a-wunhaka", she says.

With her forefinger she lightly traces a line of a-makirra across my cheek.

"A-mangaji a-makirra yinku".

She turns my face to the other side to draw another streak, "A-mangaji a-makirra yinda wardjanantha yinku awara baj-ngulaji la Brisbane".

"Yinku awara maraka a-Ngardirdji".

21.

Today I park the car just metres from the beach. Here and now collapses with there and then, so long ago and yet so close, when I first visited this small coastal town as a little girl.

Today the air tastes sour as I breathe in the sound of the ocean and the sun has a cruel bite which no longer warms my skin.

Today the sand beneath my feet is cold and coarse; it scrapes against my flesh like fingernails running down a blackboard, and I cannot bring myself to run. I think and wonder now I am here why I bothered to take my shoes off in the first place. I find myself adding layers of clothing on the outside but somehow find myself subtracting on the inside.

Today I am alone, without my family, and beneath the weight of un-forgetting I begin to shiver. The company I keep is a pile of papers and I shove the bright purple archive box roughly onto the sand to wrap myself up in the un-forgetting that once cradled it. Some of the pages catch in the wind and blow up and up away over the dunes. I pay them no mind.

Today I sit on the edge, hugging my knees close to my chest, and stare at the waves rolling in, grey becoming grey becoming grey again. The darkness of the water folding in and over itself is mesmerising, yet there is no calm to be found.

Today I am silent as I gaze out to the horizon and beyond; I have no song left to sing and the mermaids too are soundless. I remain as still as still, barely breathing, hoping that maybe if I listen hard enough, I might hear them again.

Today I whisper otherwise than here and now and wish for there and then. All of the murmuring and yearning begins to circle in on itself; it becomes too entangled and in frustration I toss the dishevelled moment into the ebb and flow of time.

Today is the ending of all of this un-forgetting and I roll up the pants of my jeans to begin. The bright purple archive box is necessarily heavier than when I carried it from the car and I walk slowly down to stand in the depths of the salty shallows. I close my eyes and arms tight around the bright purple archive box; the rough surf pushes and pulls but together we hold our ground.

Today the tide is coming in and with each ebb and flow, the waves grow louder, bigger, stronger. The sun will set in a few moments, its beams fall like shards of glass on the water and the spray cuts the dimming light like a knife. The bright purple box and the papers inside are now soggy and a streak of dark violet dye runs from the left-hand bottom corner into the sea. It mixes and swirls the words and worlds they contain in and with the flow of water like blood pooling in the rain.

Today the weight of a life without mermaids singing has become unbearable; I feel the heartlines in my hand begin to slow in tandem with the heaviness of the waves. I cradle the bright purple archive box close, so close, as a large breaker rolls over its body and mine towards the shore.

Today it took a dead woman to begin and now the live one brings it all to an end.

References

Blyton, E. (1943/2016). *The magic faraway tree*. London: Egmont Books Ltd.

Cixous, H. (1991). *Coming to writing and other essays* (S. Suleiman, Ed., S. Cornell, Trans.). Cambridge, MA: Harvard University Press.

Cixous, H. (1997). My Algeriance: In other words, to depart not to arrive from Algeria. *Triquarterly, 100*, 259–279.

Cixous, H. (2006). *Dream, I tell you* (B. B. Brahic, Trans., European perspectives). New York, NY: Columbia University Press.

Cixous, H., & Clément, C. (1986). *The newly born woman* (B. Wing, Trans.). New York, NY: Schoken Books.

Cixous, H., & McQuillan, H. (2002). 'You race towards that secret, which escapes': An interview with Hélène Cixous. *Oxford Literary Review, 24*(1), 185–201.

Greene, M. (1994). Postmodernism and the crisis of representation. *English Education, 26*(4), 206–219.

Haraway, D. (1997). *Modest_Witness@Second_Millenium.FemaleMan©_Meets_ OncoMouseT: Feminism and technoscience.* New York, NY: Routledge.

Kirton, J. (1977). Yanyuwa concepts relating to "skin". *Oceania, 47*(4), 320–323.

Mackinlay, E. (2000a). Blurring boundaries between restricted and unrestricted performance: A case study of the mermaid song of Yanyuwa women in Borroloola. *Perfect Beat, 4*(4), 73–84.

Mackinlay, E. (2000b). Maintaining grandmothers' law: Female song partners in Yanyuwa culture. *Musicology Australia, 23*, 76–98.

Mackinlay, E. (2005a). Moving and dancing towards decolonisation in education: An example from an Indigenous Australian performance classroom. *The Australian Journal of Indigenous Education, 34*, 113–122.

Mackinlay, E. (2005b). The personal is political is musical: Reflections on women's music making in the Yanyuwa Aboriginal community at Borroloola, Northern Territory. In E. Mackinlay, S. Owens, & D. Collins (Eds.), *Aesthetics and experience in music performance* (pp. 221–233). Cambridge: Cambridge Scholars Press.

Mackinlay, E. (2008). Crossing and negotiating borders of identity, knowledge and tradition: Coming to an understanding of Aboriginal women's performance in educational locales as a white woman. *Journal of Australian Studies, 32*(2), 179–196.

Mackinlay, E., & Bartleet, B. (2012). Friendship as research: Exploring the potential of sisterhood and personal relationships as the foundations of musicological and ethnographic fieldwork. *Qualitative Research Journal, 11*(2), 75–87.

Mackinlay, E., & Bradley, J. (2003). Of mermaids and spirit men: Complexities in the categorisation of two Aboriginal dance performances at Borroloola, NT. *The Australian Pacific Journal of Anthropology, 4*(1/2), 2–24.

Reay, M. (1962). Subsections at Borroloola. *Oceania, 33*(2), 90–115.

Reay, M. (1970). A decision as narrative. In R. M. Berndt (Ed.), *Australian Aboriginal anthropology: Modern studies in the social anthropology of the*

Australian Aborigines (pp. 164–174). Perth, WA: University of Western Australia Press.

Solórzano, D., & Yosso, T. (2002). Critical race methodology: counter-storytelling as an analytical framework for education research. *Qualitative Inquiry, 8*(1), 23–44.

7

Writing, A-Way to Un-Forgetting

I find that scene making is my natural way of making sense of the past. A scene always comes to the top; arranged; representative. This confirms me in my instinctive notion—it is irrational; I will not stand argument—that we are sealed vessels afloat upon what it is convenient to call reality; at some moments, without a reason, without an effort, the sealing matter cracks; in floods reality; that is a scene—for they would not survive entire so many ruinous years unless they were made of something permanent; that is a proof of their reality.
Woolf (1976, p. 145)
Instead of remembering here a scene and there a sound, I shall fit a plug into the wall; and listen into the past. I shall turn up August 1890. I feel that strong emotion must leave its trace; and it is only a question of discovering how we can get ourselves again attached to it, so that we shall be able to live our lives through from the start.
Woolf (1976, p. 81)

© The Author(s) 2019
E. Mackinlay, *Critical Writing for Embodied Approaches*,
https://doi.org/10.1007/978-3-030-04669-9_7

Fig. 7.1 "Tell un-forgetting I said high", she says and because of words she laughs and lives

1.

The woman with the lilting accent whispers to her from the past into the present across the dead of night; for she knows that it is here, in this descent into writing when the coldness of day departs that secrets find safe passage among the warmth of dreams—bad reputation be damned! (Cixous, 1993, p. 107) The woman speaks to a/not-her to remind her that the "story [she has] to tell is the story of writing's violence" (Cixous, 2002, p. 403), the one that pushes and pulls her to be written even though she knows she cannot write what she wants to write. The woman warns and words against the selfsame as she gently brushes the hair aside from her forehead, reminding her that writing this book is her un-forgetting, "the instant-scene at once already 'remembered,' already coming back (to haunt) [her] already a dweller in the memory-cabinet" (Cixous, 2002, p. 428). The woman does not hesitate for there is no room of an on her own; she places her hand on her heart and feels her chest rise and fall. With each breath the woman senses her a/not-her turning and tumbling deeper and deeper down towards her un-forgetting. The woman takes one last look and walks a-way; the hour has come for her to race and struggle against and for memory so that she can "seek to bear witness to what [she] keep[s] secret" (Cixous, 2002, p. 425); these signs and sentences of un-forgetting.

2.

> Well it's 33 Burke Street
> And the house on the hill sounds like
> An exploration
> But there is only one man here not two
> And he is working eggs over easy towards closing time
> To find that place that he set out for
> Without asking his mother for permission
> It takes him back to that house on the hill
> Over and over and over again
> He watches and marches in time full of duty but empty of dare
> And the orchard keeps on flowering and fruiting
> He sits down with a cold piece of Christmas pudding in hand
> In the shade of an abundant lemon tree
> Eyes closed and the silver bullet in his hair
> Shines and lines the night road
> Warmed as it is by the summer sun
> He picks up a rifle and rests it on his shoulder
> Waiting for the vermin in his mind to come close enough
> That he might he take a pot shot, any shot will do
> And then a small voice touches him where it is oh so tender and fine
> It's a little girl reaching out and calling and pleading
> He stops and forgets what it is he was about to do and listens
> And listens ever more closely
> Hold my hand, she says, hold me she says
> Sing to me, sing to me she says and take the dark away with your gun
> And he lays next to her, cradles her head in his hand
> The rifle beside them, folded up in the sheets of friendship
> And he strokes the hair on her forehead
> "If I could find you a diamond ring…"
> And he ceases his crooning for he knows the future is lost
> Sleep finds and falls them away

3.

When McDonald's first arrived in my home town it was sold to us locals in the country as a family restaurant; the kind of place Dick, Jane, and their two children of the same would dine regularly on a Saturday night to share quality time together over a fine meal. If you couldn't afford a weekly visit, then McDonald's became the place of choice to celebrate a birthday. The joy a table set with just the right number of party hats, whistles and happy meals could bring was beyond measure. If it was your birthday and you were celebrating it at McDonald's with ten of your friends, in my hometown you were *someone*; a girl to be remembered long after the cheeseburgers, small fries and soft drinks had been consumed— you were a girl who was going places and if you were someone she happened to call friend, she *might* just take you with her.

The last time I was at McDonald's for a birthday party, my best friend was turning ten. We had giggled all the way in on the 20 km drive into town, oohed and aahed in delight when we saw the table set in her honour, screwed up our noses at the gherkins on our cheeseburgers, and burped our way through a, b and possibly c as we washed down the last of our fries with lemonade. It was time to play hide and go seek in the kid's playground while we waited for the surprise chocolate birthday cake her Mum had made to be lit and we could sing happy birthday hopelessly out of tune at the top of our lungs. The kid's playground at McDonald's was full of large plastic twists and colourful turns juxtaposed with dark tunnels and shadowy corners. My best friend was it, that's the way it always went—if it was your birthday, you had to be the first seeker. I found myself the perfect hiding place right in the middle of one of the underpasses and sat stone still, not moving and barely breathing. "Hey!" I half-giggled as I felt cold fingers grab hold of my ankle. "You found me!" I laughed and quickly spun around expecting to see my best friend. In that moment I found out they got the marketing wrong, hopelessly wrong, because McDonald's was not a fine family restaurant after all.

I pull into the service road and make my way to the nearest fast food outlet that holds at least the promise of a decent up of coffee. I am going places and I still have a long way to go before I arrive.

"Excuse me miss?" The girl at the counter of the McCafe is calling me forward to the front of the line. "Can I take your order?"

I stare back at her.

"Is there something you'd like from our fine family friendly menu?" she asks.

I stand stone still, not moving and barely breathing.

I feel the cold fingers of yesterday wrap around my ankle and I begin to scream.

4.

He reaches forward and brushes the hair from her forehead. She closes her eyes, lost in the intimacy. It is the most tender of touches and for a moment she remembers the words and worlds of a/not-her. She holds her breath in, holding it tight, as it delicately curls its way to the secreted part of her, the part where all of the fragmented pieces lie, and gently, ever so gently, begins to put her back together again. She dares not move. The sweetest air fills her lungs and her head swirls faintly; she begins to un-forget what it is like to feel such tenderness and soon finds herself drifting and dreaming of other days. Before she realises it is too late; her temporal wandering has tamed her into foolish contentment and trapped her between the horror of there and the hope of here. She stays still, momentarily alarmed and on high alert, unsure of where to place herself. The sweet air of moments ago is now thick and saccharine, clogging her throat in fear. She thrashes and screams: fight or flight! Flee, before it's too late! And then he touches her and there becomes here. She flinches. He touches her again, this time there is tenderness but something more, something she thinks that maybe she once knew. It feels close to a memory, so close to familiar, and she tries her hardest to focus. His fingers gently stroke her cheek and she breathes out, knowing in his loving hands she is no longer a-part.

"I don't want you to do this", he says softly. His eyes search hers, looking for reassurance. He needs it as badly as she does.

"Please", he says again as he pulls her towards him. "Please, I'm begging you. You don't need to do this".

She wraps her arms around him and holds him tight, drawing his lean body so close. She can feel the strong muscles in his back and shoulders twitching as his heart beats faster with each second that passes by. His skin is smooth and cool under her touch; it calms her. She rests her head on his chest, wanting to hold onto this moment now and for ever; because, he is not her there and then but her here and now.

"You know I need to", she whispers. "I have to do this",

He holds her closer.

"But you don't need to do it alone. Let me come with you".

She shakes her head; not in denial, not in defence but as declaration. She loves him—yes, it is no longer there but here, a love, in love, with love. Her love for him has arrived, unexpected, and now announced; to herself.

"I know you want to", she replies. "It means the world to me that you would want to come with me".

A pause, she tries to find the right words, the words that will convince her and him that what it is she is about to do is not going to end the wrong way. She is prepared for tears, but she does not think she could bear a wrong ending, particularly as it is in and of itself only the beginning.

"I can look after myself; I need to be able to look after myself, to prove to myself that I can. It's time—it is a-way past time—for me to step outside of the darkness and be more than myself".

The look on his face tells her he is not persuaded. She tries again with a different set of words, words that do not belong to her but spill instead from the lovely mouth of a woman who does not brush her aside at the scene but anticipates and inspires her. I hold him tighter.

"And now—now, I have arrived; I have found my *arrivance*, here, in writing".

He gently pushes me away so that we are standing face-to-face, our foreheads touching, touching ever so close. I can feel his long eyelashes quietly brush kiss my cheek.

"Writing", I pause. I am whispering on purpose, not wanting these words I have found so hard to find to be broken up with the harsh sounds of the world crashing in uninvited. "Writing as a-way of un-forgetting through and around the past as present to un/entangle the dis/embodied moments before, between and beyond. Writing through the a-way is shocking, but it is a-way I am willfully choosing to go in my words and worlds as a critical *kind* of autoethnographer so that a return to love in writing through the body is possible".

5.

She waves him goodbye and turns back inside the house. She walks slowly to her room and lays her head down on her pillow. She cannot remember a time when she felt this tired before. She turns some words and phrases over on her tongue, searching for the right taste, Bushed, burned, buggered, shot, spent, drained, plum tuckered, wiped out, washed up, exhausted, dead on her feet. The truth is, she is quite plainly and most simply tired, from her head down to her toes and everywhere in-between inside and out. She cannot find the right taste because lately she is in no mind for tasting at all. She closes her eyes and sighs, drawing the air in as deep she can, hoping it might blow away her tiredness but leave her bones in place. That's what she worries most about. Her bones. She knows what she needs to do but her bones are way too tired to carry her there.

She shifts her body into a more comfortable position on the bed, trying to move away from the dis-ease that has decided to fill the empty space where only moments before he lay down with her. She closes her eyes and soon finds herself floating in and out sleep, drifting through the past sea to the present see and beyond. She watches herself being carried along by a boat made of bones, and she breathes a sigh of relief knowing they are hers. The sun's ray kiss her softly and warm her bones gently as they subtly shift in colour from light grey to white. She rests her head back into the curvature of pelvic bones, content to be cradled there as the boat made of her bones continues to lull and dull her along its way. Slowly but surely the tiredness and exhaustion she feels lay down beside her and are replaced with an unbearable ache. She sees she is at peace in her boat of bones on the sea; and feels a deep yearning to stay.

Without warning, a shadow falls across her face and the boat made of her bones begins to rock. She freezes and feels a trickle of water wet the back of her head. Her pelvic bones rudely reveal their porosity, and the crude boat begins to leak. She opens her eyes, wide and searching, and the outline of a man comes into view. She knows instinctively it is not him, the one she now loves and lays with, but another who only ever lied about both. He reaches out to grab her and in her sleep sea she moves too slowly. Her boat made of bones begins to crumble and the see water rushes in as he crushes her body to him. She can feel pieces of her bones breaking away, becoming nothing more or less than flotsam and jetsam in her sleep sea and she thinks and wonders that she should be worried about them. Her bones. She knows she needs to find a way out of here to there but she her bones are way too tired to carry her.

6.

"What do I care if it's shocking? I am shocking. What was done to me was shocking. I am outside the boundaries forever, no longer decent," says Judith, the main character in Julie Berry's novel *All the truth that's in me* (2013, p. 34). Judith is a young woman who was mutilated by her captor, her tongue cut out to stop her from speaking; to silence her cries. She lives in a world sometime in the distant past; I can't be sure when. Judith cannot speak; aside from various kinds of grunting and moaning, she has no voice. In her voicelessness Judith is doubly bound and freed; there but not here, then but not now. She stands outside the present and looks in; being on the inside is a gift that was snatched from her, cruelly and without invitation. Judith watches her outsideness with a certain clarity and acceptance. She can be and do whatever she chooses because no-one can hear her, no-one cares to hear her and she decides that she in turn no longer needs to be care-ful; being and becoming shocking is at once the everything and nothing that she has left. I am only halfway through reading Judith's story but it has moved me in a-way I was not expecting. The words, her voice, are clipped, sharp, and stilted; somewhat crude or simple and matter of fact some might say. But silently they edge ever so close to a truth that folds itself into familiarity.

"I told you to shut the fuck up!" He raises his fist. "Don't say another word", he slams his fist on the table.

"I'm sick of hearing your nagging-fucking-whining-fucking-voice", he clenches both fists by his side.

"It's my turn to speak you fucking slut and you *will* be fucking quiet", he stands up and towers over me.

"You think you're so fucking smart. Your ass is way too fucking smart and you've always had a smart mouth", his left hand lands a bruise on my breast.

"Not so smart now are you?" His right fist follows swiftly with a blow to the soft part beneath my ribs.

I secret myself away and silence my voice; he knows to hit the quiet places, those out of sight parts of my body that no-one will see; and I know that if I am smart I will not speak a word. I decide not to use my voice and instead say the words I need to say in silence.

Except for that one time; that one time when I decided to scream. Somehow screaming seemed better than speaking. Screaming was easier because I didn't have to use *any* words; I didn't want to use words because then they would become tainted, used up, and in the end, voiceless just like me. I find it hard to remember now why I started screaming; what it was *exactly*. Were we arguing over what was for dinner and who was going to cook? Was it something to do with parenting teenage boys and how to respond to backchat? Or perhaps it was about what we were going to watch on television? Perhaps it doesn't matter, in the end; what matters in the end was that I screamed. And that's part of the shocking; the shocking part of this story; the part that shocks me as I watch myself speaking it.

It might have been any night, an ordinary night some would say, and it was quite ordinary, ordinary for us at least. He came home early; not an unusual occurrence these days, and at 4:30 pm he opened his first brew, took one long sip and then topped the brown bottle up with dark rum. In my head I begin to sing a familiar song but with a twist, "There was one brown bottle, sitting in his hand; one brown bottle sitting in his hand; and when one brown bottle gets thrown into the can, then there'll be two brown bottles, sitting in his hand". Two brown bottles stand tall together on the bench like washed up and rusted tin soldiers, soon enough there are three side by side and by 6:00 pm he was onto his second six-pack. And who was I to question why; I had stopped asking a long time ago. The beginnings of dinner lay splayed all over the kitchen bench and that old sinking feeling had made its way to my stomach. Time seemed to stand still, content to pause and watch awhile, just like it always did on ordinary nights like this. That old sinking feeling sat there like a lead balloon, heavy as it waited, dreading what was to come because the ending to this scenario was always the same. Every now and then I would ask how long, how long until dinner; and yet the question begged another, how long until *this* ends?

"Is dinner almost ready?" Max has emerged from his room. It's late now and he is hungry.

"I don't think dinner will be far away", I say, "Dad is almost done". I hope he hasn't heard.

"What are we having?"

"Tonight, it's Dad's special, Thai chicken curry".

"Oh nice", Max says. "Let me know when it's ready". He starts to walk back to his room. But I realise a second too late. His Dad is not pleased. He is not happy that his son dared to ask a question, the question, any question which might be seen to question him.

"What did you say?" his father says.

"What Dad?" Max looks at him, unsure what is happening.

"I said, what the fuck did you say?" His Dad looks at him directly in the eyes, daring him to respond.

"I said Dad", he emphasises each word. Please don't, I whisper silently in my head, please don't say any more Max. But he persists. "I *said* Dad, when is dinner going to be ready?"

I watch closely and I see his father's eyes turn red; but Max has not seen it. He does not know he has crossed a line, a line that was drawn without him knowing.

His father pounces on him, fast and furious, across the room. He grabs hold of Max's shirt collar, and pulls him close, so close that their noses are touching.

"What the fuck did you say, you little cunt!" His father's eyes are blazing and in my head I keep saying please don't Max, please don't.

His father pulls him and raises his fist above Max's head. And that's when I scream. I scream and scream. Not my child. Not my son. Not ever.

7.

The clock outside the room ticked noisily in the dark; marking the nothing-ness of the everything-ness that this time of night always seemed to have capacity to hold. The whole world seemed to be dead, or maybe the whole was asleep; asleep she thought and wondered as she tried not to feel alive. She sighed; and the day done, dust and dirt-ed, decided to put itself on repeat; she gave in because in truth she was done, dust and dirt-ed too. Another day ruined. It was that easy, another kind of easy and yet a whole different type of easy altogether that was not at all kind. One glass became two snaps became three hits became her on all fours. Beaten and broken, no desire to move or shake, no freedom to be found there to do either, even if she had chosen to. Sometimes it was easier to let the ruin happen, to fall into and under the unbearable weight, buried with no easy way out and no energy to look for one. Finding a way through, over and out was never going to be easy; for her it was taking the easy alternative, which was never an-other option at all.

She looked over at him sleeping beside her, a long way over on the other side of the bed and not beside her at all. He had not been on her side, any kind of side with her for a long time; not with any kindness that she could remember. She hugged her thin body and tried to un-forget the last time he had touched her, touched her in a way that took her side. The day before there was the sideswipe when she asked how long dinner was away. The day before that she had tried to help with dinner, but that had ended in a kick to the side. The day before the day before that she had looked at him side-ways and had landed roughly a-way over on the other side of the room. She sat there, lone alone alongside the wall and thought and wondered how she came to be there, outside on the inside here of her world with no one on one side or the other.

She winced as her cold and bony fingers brushed ribs, sore and wasted. Fuck! Did he hear that? Fearing the worst she slowly opened her eyes to stare at him; waiting for the ruin to repeat the ruin of the day before, the day before that and the day before the day before that. She breathed out, this time in silence. He was dead to the world. Dead. To. The World. Dead. A lone alone tear escaped and fell onto her pillow; a solitary friend she had learnt to trust. She had never felt so cold, so very cold. She had never felt so alone; so very a-lone. She had never felt so cold and alone, so very cold and alone in the world and in the words she wrote. She had never felt this close to both before and thought and wondered how much longer until she was found. Her longing for the dead woman to arrive droned loudly and deeply in the darkness. She listened and waited for the dull hum to lull her to sleep so that in the dead of night she might begin to live.

8.

This moment took place before the un-forgetting began, before the dead woman found herself alive. It might have taken place, but it may not have. And for now, that is a secret she does not wish to reveal; there are some unbearable moments of being which are not possible or permissible to share, not according to the rules and rights she has always played by and exercised willfully. The dead woman rustled around in the bottom of her cupboard where all memories dwell to haunt to dwell, searching and searching, reaching forward in search of a small cardboard box. Her hand scraped and scratched the sides and bottom of the cardboard and she remembered that she had carefully hidden it away; secret-ed it away in the darkest depths of this closet lest it be found, not least of all by her. She needed to go deeper inside. Her fingers brushed lightly against a dried-up spider, a remnant of life now shrunken and alone. She felt all manner of dust beginning to coat her hand and she struggled to maintain her resolve to keep looking. Dust and dirt, dirt and dust, the most unwelcome of companions but they cling to bodies of thinking, foundering and wondering; her body thinking, foundering and wondering all the same, no matter; yet, precisely that which matters all the same.

She sneezed loudly. Particles of dust and dirt search and found an unwelcome home inside her nose; and her body lurched forward with the unexpected force produced by this loud and abrupt wave of sound. Her fingers bumped against the corner of a hard package and she thought and wondered if maybe she had found it after all. Encircled by memories and backed into the depths of the cupboard without return by the passage of time; she fancied that minutes, hours, days, years passed by the small cardboard box in this way. She paid them no mind as they began to scratch and screech at the thought of being pulled away from the comfortable cushion of un/remembrance that had embraced and secluded them for so long in the back of the cupboard. She fancied she heard them scream, no, please no; not again as she began to tug and pull at the small cardboard box. But she was ruthless in her perseverance and pursuit of the small cardboard box; she fancied she needed this small cardboard box now more than ever before. With one final grab she finally held the small cardboard box in her hand and wrenched it into the light on the other side where she might then be finally free to do with whatever she fancied.

The small cardboard box winced and tried to screw itself up tight into its hard corners; resisting, revolting, returning to the depths of itself and the cardboard; but to no avail. Outside the cupboard was too bright and too dim, too real and too imaginary, too close to being all at once dead and alive, alive and dead.

She tried to console the small cardboard box and whispered gently, "How do we advance? In darkness, says the author, and we call it broad daylight" (Cixous, 2002, p. 50).

She gently placed the small cardboard box on the wooden floorboards in front of her. And there it was; in the day of light, stark, bare and wanting in the light of day, and all she needed to do was open it. Like the bookshelf from words and worlds away with which she had spent a whole minute, hour, day, year, life of time arguing with, the small cardboard box threatened to do exactly the same. But in this time of life she knew better, she knew how easy it was to be and do harder and so she did, and she was. Without warning, she reached down and tore the lid off the small cardboard box. And this is how it was done; done, dusted and dirt-ed. The secret that the small cardboard box had held onto forever and a day was out in all of its darkness in broad daylight and there was no turning back.

She watched herself in slow motion; not wanting to continue but unable to stop, the small cardboard box a force beyond herself to which she was now intimately connected to and controlled by. She could almost taste the way it felt to be pushed and pulled by the small cardboard box to bend to its will; a cold hard steely tang clung to her tongue, teeth and tonsils and warned her of the consequences if she refused to do its bidding. Not for the first time the dead woman was overcome with remorse, regret—and revolt—for what she was about to do. She gave herself a rueful smile; they were a tripartite set that rebuked any suggestion of separation. A less than holy trinity for how could it be otherwise? Maiden for revolt, mother for remorse, crone for regret, she fancied that would suffice.

One by one she carefully reached inside and pulled the contents out of the small cardboard box. A tattered packet of tough fabric bandaids was the first to appear. One, two, three, she counted. It was almost as empty as it was done, and she made a mental note to add this basic necessity of revolt to her shopping list. Her hand went inside the small cardboard box once more and pulled out the second object. Her heart filled with dread, she knew what it was even before it appeared. Dust became the rusted taste in her mouth as she looked at the silver blade. It was thin, no longer sharp, and tarnished beyond measure and use. She held it tightly between her forefinger and thumb; poised, as it was to make its mark once more. The dust in the dead woman's mouth became grey, dry, and thick as she stared at it, transfixed by the rapid way it had begun to solidify. She watched it harden and slowly but surely block the passage from her heart to her head with remorse, she knew it would not be long before it became a wall of stone. Struggling now for breath, her hand fumbled its way back into the small cardboard box, desperately searching for the last item. She grasped it and roughly pulled out a white floral handkerchief made soft by use over time. The dead woman hastily drew the cotton square to her face and began to wretch, trying her hard-est to dislodge the regret that had hard-set in her mouth. Parts of the handkerchief crinkled and cracked as she held onto it and it was then, but only in that moment, she felt the dried brown stains interrupt its purity. This handkerchief was dirt-ed; and she was done and dusted.

9.

"Is this the kind of easy way out you were looking for?"

The young woman still has hold of my hand. She gently turns it over and exposes the under-side of my left wrist. One by one, she traces the faint lines. They are spider thin, faded and most days I almost forget they are there; almost. There are too many to count but I remember each one and not one of them was easy. I snatch my hand away; I am not ready to un-forget these lines and the young woman crossed them uninvited.

"Fuck off", I say, and it was easy to become someone else; a-not/her. "You have no fucking idea".

"Tell me then", she is ready to punch back with fighting words of her own. "Tell me about them".

"What?" She really has stepped over the line. "You want me to tell you it was as easy as pie? Some kind of fucking elementary?"

The young woman shrugs, "Yeah, why not—if that's how it was".

I want to rip her fucking head off, so she will just shut up; shut up and shut out where this talk about and through time is headed. This is not *easy* to talk about.

"So?" She dares to ask again.

I'll give her that much, she is persistent, and I admire that kind of perseverance.

"Let's just say it was dead easy. I took a walk down easy street along the lines of least resistance", I give up.

"To what?"

"The dead woman", I say. "The one that's preventing the live one from breathing."

The young woman is stationary and unmoved.

"For a woman of easy virtue such as me, it was just like taking candy from a baby. All I had to do was paint by numbers and find the sweet spot", I laugh; it's raw and tainted with metal. It is much easier to make light of it, easy is as easy does.

The young woman raises her eyebrows, "Really? Not buying it and I don't believe you".

"My scars, my story, I can tell you whatever the fuck I want. It's up to you whether you want to take notes and turn it around into some kind of truth. After all, there is a fine line isn't there?"

I hold my white streaked wrist in front of her face, so she can look again—and look harder this time. I want her now to really see, to now see how fucking many lines there are and now know that these were my lines in the sand, the ones I had to draw so that I could somehow find a way for living to become easy *now*. She and I stare at one another; I am preaching to the converted. She knows, she recognises because these are the scars that will become her life. She needs to know so that the living of them is easy; so she can become the woman who wants to wake the dead, who wants to remind people that they once wept for love and trembled with desires, and that they were then very close to the life that they claim they've been seeking while constantly moving further away.

The lines fade as does the sound of the young woman's voice in complete surrender to a listless and lifeless kind of easy. Despite how easy it may have seemed earlier, I am not ready to be woken awake. It is easy to secret-e the lines away under a large black watch, a silver charm bracelet and as many bangles as I can cram onto my arm. I willingly take the easy way out and accessories are an easier a-way. Ten classic stainless steel double-edged blades, a packet of baby wipes, one of Dad's old handkerchiefs, and a jumbo pack of extra-large and-aids become a daily necessity for living. Day in, day out, blade in, blade out; it becomes easy and this kind of easy becomes addictive. How easy it is to cut through; I am mesmerised as the life-blood trickles from my veins and across my skin. This is how easy it is for heartlines to flow.

"You fucked around didn't you?"

One more line appears.

"You fucked so many guys when we separated, I can't fucking trust anything you say".

Another arrives in companion.

"How do I even fucking know they are my children?"

It's hard to keep count.

"Come here and let me fucking finish it for you!"

There is no pain anymore; just blessed release—easy, easy, just release me; just.

For a long-time I lived through these lines of easy. Yes Cixous, like you, they were my only assets; they put me to the test and became the one and only thing that reminded me to and made me live (1993, p. 11). Secrete-d away by and under all manner of accessories, these heartlines were my "strange and monstrous treasure" which silently and dangerously kept me trapped in a place where it was easy to forget. In that easy forgetting, complacency lurked. It skulked and sulked its way around me; glaring and burning its hatred of me; that in the end, I am still alive.

10.

She takes a deep breath and opens her cupboard. She feels a soft swish of air on her face as the doors opens and the sensation flicks a switch. In that instant she changes from respectable-white-middle-class-six-figure-earning-university-professor into soon to be ex-wife going to visit her soon to be ex-husband in a maximum-security prison. She shifts into autopilot and goes through the motions. She stands in front of the mirror and gently applies unscented moisturizer to her face and body. She can't and won't be bothered with putting on any make up. She looks without wanting to see but notices anyway that her eyes refuse to let go of the dark rings that encircled and apprehended her sleep; and even though she washed it the night before, her hair is tangled and torn. She sighs; no amount of hair straightening is going to tidy her up this morning and she soon decides it is time to move onto the next part of her routine.

Her feet drag heavily cross the wooden floor boards, and she can feel all manner of dust clinging to her even though she has only just showered. She stands naked on tippy toes in front of her wardrobe and reaches for the clothes on the shelf she has mentally marked as her prison gear. Like him, they too are in protected custody. Quarantined from the real world so that nothing might contaminate them; not perfume vapours, nor petrol clouds, nor petty glares, not pretty looks. The t-shirts are chic but baggy and reveal nothing while her jeans are now three sizes too big. She is but a shadow of herself and she prefers it that way. In the dark corners where she used to be she can hide from herself; and him. She bends down, pulls out her underwear drawer and chooses the sheerest knickers she owns; a silky jungle patterned pair, not quite a G-string but near enough. She smiles wryly to herself, if they are going to extend their search that far she might as well give them something to look at. Besides, it helps her cope with the indignity of it all; her mother always said you should never the leave the house without wearing your finest your pair of panties just in case you end ass up and legs spread out somewhere you weren't expecting. She glances at the clock and struggles to swallow the ball of shame that is beginning to swell up in her throat. She hasn't got long before she needs to leave to make it in time and you never can trust the traffic on the freeway that leads to this place of no return. Her hands tremor as she carefully removes all of her jewellery, sterling silver here and there in her ears, around her neck and on her fingers. She is allowed to keep her wedding ring on, but it is dented and damaged; it carries the pain and wounds of their marriage and she prefers to leave it lying there at the bottom of her memories.

11.

> Well it's 5 Coogee Street
> And the house on the suburban street
> A chore
> There are four females here
> But she is the only woman
> And she is easily working time and a half towards closing
> To find peace in that place
> Without anyone asking her anything
> She reaches out and holds hands with un-forgetting
> It takes her back to that house on the suburban street
> Without thought she catches the click clack train
> And still they keep asking for this and that
> She is a dutiful daughter and hands this and that
> Over and over and over again
> She sits down at the red laminate table

The quiet haze blushes her pink
To match the wrapper of the caramel columbine
That floods the sweetest of memories into her mouth
She sees her daughter standing
There is an audience
Grandmother, mother and daughter smile and watch
From yesterday's image behind her
And then there is singing
Holding her there and then
Blue ribbon in her hair
A baby on the way
She learned to do the same
Roast chicken, apple pie and plain sponge cake
But they are old and out of date now
Tears carry the bitter tastes away
Lost forever to her now that
She has swallowed them whole
Who is the girl standing at the front?
She reminds her of someone
She once loved

References

Berry, J. (2013). *All the truth that's in me*. Sydney, NSW: Harper Collins Publisher.

Cixous, H. (1993). *Three steps on the ladder of writing* (S. Cornell & S. Sellers, Trans.). New York, NY: Columbia University Press.

Cixous, H. (2002). The book as one of its own characters. *New Literary History, 33*(3), 403–434.

Woolf, V. (1976). *Moments of being: Unpublished autobiographical writings* (J. Schulkind, Ed.). Orlando, FL: Harcourt.

8

Writing Decoloniality, with Cixous and Woolf

It is one of the great advantages of being a woman that one can pass even a negress without wishing to make an Englishwoman of her.
Woolf (1929/2001)
The diamonds of the Imperial crown blaze on my forehead. I hear the roar of the hostile mob as I step out on to the balcony. Now I dry my hands, vigorously, so that Miss, whose name I forget, cannot suspect that I am waving my first at an infuriated mob. "I am your Empress, people". My attitude is one of defiance. I am fearless. I conquer.
Woolf (2015, p. 32)

1.

The heartlines
In danger
Shrug off
Old lies
Your hand
Writing autoethnography
Through critical

© The Author(s) 2019
E. Mackinlay, *Critical Writing for Embodied Approaches*,
https://doi.org/10.1007/978-3-030-04669-9_8

Decoloniality in
And with
Hélène Cixous
Virginia Woolf

2.

It's quiet as she steps onto the carpet of pine needles. Above her the wind whistles a sad and forlorn melody, searching for a place to call home in the lofty branches of these natural skyscrapers. There is no movement here on the ground, where she finds herself to be found, and the stillness becomes the bass line for the breeze playing its tune above. The woman stands, motionless and in vigil, prepared and patient to wait and watch. She closes her eyes, soaking in the completeness of being here in this moment and feels her body begin to gently sway. Like a mother rocking her baby from one hip to the other, her body keeps time with the symphony that swirls and sashays in the treetops high above her. Here, in the quiet by and by, she does not have to explain. Here, the belonging she yearns for is close, so close. Here, she settles in to the comfort of now to wait just a little longer. Now, the sharp snap of a twig breaks her reverie. Now, a crow screeches a warning, piercing the quiet and beats her wings frantically as she flees. Here and now, her breath becomes unsteady and catches in her throat as her heart tries to chase down the awareness that she is not alone. Here and now she dares not move and hopes that her stasis might, and just may-be, a shield against the foreboding creeping its way towards her. The woman's motionless propels her "towards the most frightening [knowing that] this is what makes writing thrilling but painful [she] writes towards what [she] flee[s]" (Cixous, in Derrida, Cixous, Armel, & Thompson, 2006, p. 9).

3.

Cixous (1994, p. xvi) tells us that writing is a "particular urgency, an individual force, a necessity" which is not "economically or politically indebted to all the vileness and compromise [and] not obliged to reproduce the system" (1976, p. 892). Her words urge us to "shrug off the old lies" (Cixous, 1991, p. 40) of the "demon of Coloniality" (1997, p. 262) and suggests that this is what writing will do—writing must no longer be determined by the past and instead must seek to break up, to destroy, and to foresee the un-seeable (Cixous, 1976, p. 875). In 2005 the shrugging, urgent, necessary, and destructive writing that Cixous foretold began. I cannot be sure; but I *am* sure that this is when I first begin to write about decolonisation. That's the word I used then—decolonisation, *not* decoloniality. I say I want to negotiate the challenges and complexities and choreographies of decolonisation and I there and then start moving and dancing through my ethnomusicological world in words. You see, decolonisation in my discipline is a secret, the barest of soft whisperings. I say it is new to me too and that it holds a lot of promise and it is time to begin. I say I do not want to preach. I write about it what it means. I think I know.

The words I use shift from desire to explore to reflect to question to deconstruct to interrogate to contest to disrupt to hope to decolonise. They are deployed for a specific purpose": to tangle up and tangle down what it means to live and work in-between: on the borders, on the edge, across, through and with difference: alongside knowing, being and doing I describe as intersubjective, intercorporeal, and intercultural. I think these words give me a way into, to *inter*. I think and wonder that perhaps there and then I always already knew that by going into would take a dead woman to begin, she would need to *inter* herself. I cite and reference others who I hear speaking a decolonising language—Smith (1999), Poka (2000), Cary (2004), Fox (2004), Mutua and Swadener (2004). A short list, but a list it was. I call out and colour my ethnographic and educative praxis as white. I declare talking about decolonisation in my discipline as messy, dangerous and risky business. I assert a knowingness of the coloniser and fess up to forgetting. I say that the body thinks, knows and feels intimately the relationship between. I contend that the moving and dancing body is a performative and a possibility for relations of difference, for *different* relations of difference. I think and wonder, in the end, that bringing who we are-in-relation and what we might come to know-in-relation back to embodiment is a good place to begin moving and dancing towards decolonisation. I think and wonder now how I thought there and then that this was the beginning.

4.

Decolonisation. A dangerous business. Even more dangerous as it dances towards decoloniality. The word "danger" is used doubly here and becomes double hand in hand with difference. Indeed the word "difference" and the family of words it carries in its folds—differ, different, differently—there are words that come "right up to us so suddenly we don't have time avoid…feeling [their] breath touch us" (1991, p. 7) as soon as we begin to sway and swing decolonially. Difference is a word that turns up everywhere in decolonial talking, chalking and waltz-walking; even when it remains hidden and secreted way in the back of the cupboard. It seems that "everything…in the end [comes] back to this word", difference (Cixous, 1994, p. 42). It does not exist alone, it can always be heard as "twos", "all the couples, the duals, the duos, the differences, all the dyads in the world: each time there's two in the world" (1991, p. 42); "the one and the other both together" (1998, p. 42): reparating and separating to "unlock the door for us that opens onto the other side, if only we are willing to bear it" (1991, p. 9), if only we are willing to "experience the end of the world" (1991, p. 10) as we know it. I think and wonder; is ethnography poised at the ready, set, go to make this move into a different and decolonial danger? Is *auto*-ethnography prepared to experience and bear it? And what of *critical* autoethnography? In her 1994 essay entitled "To live the orange", Cixous highlights that a move towards being two and being in relation is *always already* dangerous. She suggests evocatively that the practice is not an innocent one and asks under what conditions may I "live the orange"?

5.

Hamish and I are sitting at the kitchen counter. It is one of our favourite places to be; sometimes reading one beside the other, sometimes talking one beside the other, and sometimes, like tonight, sitting, talking and reading one beside the other all at once. I am trying to find a way through the inertia that has crept into my writing about decoloniality. Sometimes it seems that I have written in and around this topic so often that there is nothing more to say, nothing left to say and yet so much more to say because we are not there yet. For weeks now, I have been searching for what to say, trying to remember Patti Lather's (1998) insistence that being in a "stuck place" of thinking and wondering is an enabling site for working through doubt and uncertainty. I look down at the paragraphs from self-authored academic papers on decoloniality (Mackinlay, 2015a, 2015b, 2018) that I have cut out and coloured coded in an attempt to piece together my thinking and wondering within the impossibility this task necessarily presents. The highlighted fluorescent yellow, pink and orange pieces of paper are strewn across the bench and now that these once care-fully composed words stand on the edge of deconstruction, I am not sure what to do with them.

We both sit and stare at the scraps of writing, eyes grazing over the letters and words printed on each piece of paper. There is one paragraph that grabs Hamish's attention. The heading reads, "Two. A story about oranges".

"You're writing about fruit?" he asks, one eye-brow raised.

"Mmm?" I look across to see what he is reading. "Oh that…that's some writing about an idea I've drawn from Hélène".

"Some writing! I'd say a *lot* of writing—she's everywhere here", his finger gently taps the places where I have written her name. "Who is this Hélène again?"

"Hélène who?" I echo. "Hélène Cixous! If you look over there on the shelf you'll see some of the books she's written".

Hamish lifts himself up slightly to glance over at the bookcase and nods in recognition of her work.

"So, is *she* the one who likes oranges?"

"Actually Hamish, she *lives* oranges", I wink, trying to keep the suspense that has crept into our conversation going just a little longer.

He rolls his eyes and is no longer buying it.

"Come on Mum, spill. Tell me what oranges have to do with Hélène and living and…", he pauses to read from the piece of paper, "to do with living and politics and ethics and others and your work and…what?" Hamish looks up incredulously. "Living the orange is dangerous too?"

"Well, Cixous uses the orange as a metaphor for the body, a female body that is constructed as other, as forbidden fruit because the knowledge it holds, and the way we might write such feminine knowledge, is different to and disruptive of the patriarchal norm, and it represents a threat".

"So, the fruit is kind of like a feminist intrusion and that's why it's dangerous?" He frowns slightly. "But who is it dangerous *for*?"

6.

"One cannot think well, love well, sleep well" (Woolf, 1929/2001, p. 18) if one has not had a decent cup of coffee in the morning, never mind about the oranges. Virginia's words often play around and through my body, heart and mind as the day begins; some days they are a mantric reminder of the mechanics of writing, other days they are a call to arms of the Ahmedian kind where this woman *will* make and have her way through the world in words; today, they serve as a prompt to begin. With her words and Hamish's question as companions, I find myself once more in a cafe on the other side of the world, sitting down to write about, in and through decoloniality; and "repair some of the damage" (Woolf, 1929/2001, p. 19) that underpins the (un)kind of work I sense I have been doing as an auto/ethnographer-ethnomusicologist.

It's an out of the way little place cornered at the end of a cobbled side street. The farmhouse style chunky benches, artisan fair trade percolations and sweet pastries on the menu welcome me inside. Taking my seat, I hear my favourite song of the moment streaming through the speakers. It's Florence, from Florence + the Machine (2011), the lines of the song "Heartlines" bursting from her lips and overflowing from her lungs: "Just keep following, the heartlines on your hand". My fingers restlessly drum the bench, and my heart, not being able to keep up with the song or the moment, skips every second beat. While I have not yet been condemned to dine on bad intellectual food such as "beef and prunes" in exactly the same way as Virginia, her fictional friend Mary Beton and countless other academic women were in the nineteenth century (Woolf, 1980, p. 18), I am nevertheless helplessly and hopelessly stuck. There are many, so many, "double contradictory memories" of being and belonging "perfectly at home, nowhere" (Cixous, 1997, p. 261) in relation to the work, words and worlds I have shared with my Yanyuwa family that accompany this vain attempt at writing beyond that which I have already written. I smile wryly, thinking and wondering not for the first time that Patti Lather (1998) would be pleased at the state I am in. I send her a silent curse, "my pen protests" and quips an aside, "this writing is nonsense, it says" (Woolf, 1980, p. 175). My hand won't move, stuck as it is in the infinite and vulnerable moment between pen and paper. I imagine Virginia offering words of consolation and cajolement, "It is the oddest feeling", she whispers, [isn't it?', she whispers], "as if a finger stopped the flow of ideas in the brain" (Woolf, 1980, p. 175). I realise with despair that I have nowhere to go in my head that will engage my thinking heart and like many others before and after me, I am paralysed by an inability to write.

Perhaps if I cite and converse with Virginia enough I will at least return to sensation of some kind. Writing and I need to go somewhere today or else I fear I will get nowhere at all—like the white lines on a black road, the black letters on this white page will simply flatline. Damn it! I rode all the way across town on my borrowed bicycle this morning to arrive in this practically perfect café to write. The whole purpose of my two-tyred/tired/tiered vehicular adventure is to sit at this very table, with Virginia as my companion, in the vain hope that together we might make room for a skinny latte to kickstart my heart into, through and by my own hand. But alas, even the most 'new and detestable ideas' (Woolf, 1980, p. 156) escape my page. Looking outside I notice it is clear and blue, full of promise for new letters, new words and new writings that have not yet decided whether they want to enter in the folds of friendship my hand offers them. While the "world [is] swinging around again" (Woolf, 1980, p. 177) outside, here I am inside with my 'mind like a dog going round and around to make itself a bed' (Woolf, 1980, p. 156). Hoping for a fresh wind, I decide that my "skeleton day needs reviving" (Woolf, 1980, p. 248); "time flaps on the mast" (Woolf, 1980, p. 233) and now I must leave the safe and warm cocoon this cafe provides to breathe some flesh of experience onto the bare bones of my awareness (after Holman Jones, 1998, p. 423).

7.

I fell in love with the writing of Cixous and Woolf for many, so many reasons, in different times at different places and yet always enticed by the playful, poetic, performative and political possibilities their words hold for being and becoming autoethnographic. Woolf tell us that writing enables us to "see the heart of the world uncovered for a moment" (Woolf, 1980, p. 153), Cixous insists that writing must take us to all the "low-angle close-ups in the corners, undersides, or edges in the scene" (Hilfrich, 2006, p. 217) of life. I wondered what kind of de/stroying/destroying of ethnographic practice in the colonial matrix might be imagined and performed by entangling Holman Jones notion of autoethnography as writing which puts the "flesh of life on the bones of experience" (1998) with Woolf's idea that the soul slips into stories when no one is looking to blur the boundaries between fiction and fact (Woolf, 1980, p. 62); and further, Cixous' new insurgent *écriture* feminine or 'feminine writing' which insists that in laying herself bare, "her flesh speaks true" (1976, p. 881).

I think and wonder now how I might remain in love with Woolf and Cixous and the autoethnographic possibilies their words hold if I re/turn them around in relationship with colonialism. After all, isn't this what this "book I don't write" is trying to un-forget as it moves—sometimes sidling, sometimes sashaying, and maybe sometimes "choreographilosophising" (Cixous, in Derrida et al., 2006, p. 2)—towards decoloniality?

8.

Hélène Cixous and Virginia Woolf are particular kinds of characters in the worlds of writing, philosophy and feminism. An author of "poetic fiction, chamber theater...criticism, essays...notebooks" (Cixous, 1994, p. xvi), Cixous is most often described in the English speaking world as a French feminist theorist, and associated with the concept *of écriture feminine* or "feminine writing" (Sellers, in Cixous, 1994, p. xxix) in which she seeks to write as a woman in order to empower women. Virginia Woolf is positioned as a modernist writer for the "common reader" (Sellers, 2010, p. xix) who similarly wrote works of fiction and non-fiction. Like Cixous' écriture feminine, texts such as *A room of one's own* (1929/2001), look to complicate the relationship between gender and subjectivity in, through and as writing (Goldman, 2006, p. 97). If the experimental and fluid nature of their writing brings Cixous and Woolf into close proximity; so too does their positioning as white women and their apparent associations with French and British kinds of colonialism respectively. At first glance, I see myself in Cixous and Woolf; there is a white-settler-colonial "sisterhood" of gender and race which binds us to the self-same cause, but the question of their relevancy in this conversation about autoethnography and working with Indigenous Australian peoples lingers uneasily in the air. Why would I continue to look towards the self-same if that kind of looking can only reproduce the *selfsame*? As I come to know both Woolf and Cixous more intimately through their texts, I begin to see that perhaps it is their entanglement with colonialism in, through and as subjectivity, writing and life, which makes the use of their work in this context appropriate, albeit for divergent and almost opposing reasons.

It is little known that while Cixous has spent much of her adult life writing and living in France, "to be French" and "being French" has always been incredibly puzzling and problematic for her. Cixous was born in 1937 in Oran, Algeria, daughter to a French/Spanish/Jewish father and German/Jewish mother. Her childhood was spent in the "Mediterranean atmosphere of a French colony in North Africa" (Penrod, 2003, p. 136). I am at once curious, perplexed and keen to know about the ways in which Cixous lives and breathes herself in and out of coloniality.

I pluck up the courage and ask, "What do you remember about your first encounter with coloniality, with knowing that you were both inside and outside this particular kind of relationship between and in-between self and other?"

She does not reply at once. I watch her face intently, looking for a sign that she too is, and has been, wedged into the kind of stuck ethico-onto-epistemological place I now find myself.

"I learned everything from this first spectacle", Cixous remembers. "I saw how the white (French), superior, plutocratic, civilized world founded its power on the repression of populations who had suddenly become 'invisible', like proletarians, immigrant workers, minorities who are not the 'right' color" (Cixous, in Cixous & Clement, 1986, p. 70).

The right color. The white shop assistant in Casuarina shopping centre turns to ask me if I need assistance. My baba Jemima is the one buying. The white postal worker at Burrulula who refuses to let Jemima pick up the boxes of clothes I have sent her, claiming she needs to pay cash on delivery. The white health worker refuses to administer first aid to Jemima's grandson who has cut his foot on some broken glass. She tells him to come back when he is sober and in the meantime asks me if I need a health check. The white boat club owner who insists that Jemima must pay to sit down for the day by the river if she wants to fish, even though she is sitting down on her traditional country, an ownership she and her people have lawfully been granted. He pays no heed and I am not asked to pay a cent. The wrong color.

"And not the 'right gender'", I whisper.

"Yes", Cixous nods. "Women. Invisible as humans. But, of course, per-ceived as tools—dirty, stupid, lazy, underhanded, etc. Thanks to some annihilating dialectical magic. I saw that the great, noble, 'advanced'; countries establishing themselves by expelling what was 'strange'; excluding it but not dismissing it, enslaving it. A commonplace gesture of history: there have to be two races—the masters and the slaves (Cixous, in Cixous & Clement, 1986, p. 70)".

I listen to Cixous speak about her experiences with coloniality—her Algeriance—and recognise how deeply her identity as a Jewish Franco-Maghrebian, is central to her writing and the ways in which she theorises her approach to difference and the other (Ahluwalia, 2005, p. 149). Algeria, for Cixous, was the "land of the eyes" where the anguish and suffering of the other wrought by the phenomenon of colonialism was everywhere and necessarily inescapable:

> We sent looks at each other, we saw, we couldn't *not* see, we knew and we knew that we knew we knew, we were nude, we were denounced, threatened, we flung taunts, we received glances. It was the land of the other, not of the fellow human being. The other: foretells, forewarns me, forecasts me, alters me, alters me. (Cixous, 1997, p. 270)

Her experiences of being and not being French, of belonging and not belonging to Algeria and France, are intertwined then with the history of French colonialism. Cixous refers to this history as a "double contradictory memory" (1997, p. 261) in which France granted her German family French nationality in 1918 at the end of First World War. "The same France" she writes, "threw us out of French citizenship in 1940 in Algeria and deprived us of all civil rights" (1997, p. 261). For Cixous, on the one hand to say "I am French" is "lie or legal fiction"; and yet on the other, to say "I am not French" a "breach of courtesy" (1997, p. 261). She sits on the borders—neither French, nor German nor Algerian—and it is Cixous's own shifting colonial subjectivity which arguably makes it possible for her to ask once questions of the "single and double":

> Questions of the ethical, politico-cultural, aesthetic, destinal value of this constitution [writing]; questions of the necessity of writing for myself and for others' of the usefulness, the strangeness of forever being here and elsewhere, ever here as elsewhere, elsewhere as here, I and the other, I as other. (Cixous, 1994, p. xv)

Her words speak to the peculiar, uncomfortable and yet dialogic double-ness inherent in-between. She, with and of her texts, sits always on the borders and I wonder about the "the materiality, the locatedness, the worldliness" (Ahluwalia, 2005, p. 141) which lies over and under Cixous' texts that lead her to such an attentiveness towards the ethics and politics of difference. I think and wonder, not for the first time, how Cixous's questioning of her own alterity in, through and as writing which makes Cixous a most necessary companion in this search for an affective and critical writing practice which must "no longer be determined by the past and instead must seek to break up, to destroy, and to foresee the unsee-able" (1976, p. 875).

Virginia Woolf's positioning in this re/turning is at once the same but different to that of Cixous. Her musings about the benefits of being "locked in" or "locked out" of material and intellectual spaces as a woman resonant with Cixous' simultaneous rejection and desire of "French passporosity" (1997, p. 261) and equally with Cixous refusal to be impressed by the "phallic stance" (1976, p. 892) in writing. However, Woolf departs from Cixous in the way in which she engages with her positioning as a white woman and writer of Empire. At first glance, the following passage from *A room of one's own* reveals much about Woolf's entanglement with colonialism and the ways in which much Western feminist discourse constructs its subject through processes of exclusion: "It is one of the great advantages of being a woman that one can pass even a very fine negress without wishing to make an Englishwoman of her" (Woolf, 1929/2001, p. 42). As Emery (1992, p. 217) suggests, this sen-tence simultaneously "constitutes its subject—'woman' and 'one—as exclusively English and white" and "excludes black women from the cat-egory 'woman' and presumes to judge them as 'very fine' in the same breath that it criticizes masculine imperialist habits of thought". I can distinctly remember reading this line in *A room of one's own* for the first time and recall the affective and material effect brought by their senti-ment—sour bile rising to mix uncomfortably with shame, complicity and guilt, for after all, are not Virginia and women like me somehow the selfsame? As Marcus notes in relation to this sentence, "measuring the degrees of irony that raise the temperature of the debate about gender and colonialism...cannot relieve it from the burden of racism...however sharp the social pain the passage produces in the reader, we cannot make this particular subaltern speak" (2004, p. 24). White power, race privilege, an objectifying gaze and colonial possessive logic reek and ooze from this combination of letters and words; I pause for a moment, no longer sure of what, how and why to read Woolf, and whether to continue my writing conversation with her. I think and wonder too what my Yanyuwa family would think and feel about me using the work of Woolf. Would they see her, and by extension me, as another kind of colonial predator? How does using Woolf's work implicate and tie us together in imperialist and colonial matrix of which I/she/we/were/are inextricably implicated and embedded within? How useful is her work for critically re-thinking autoethnography as moving and dancing towards decoloniality while we remain inside the white, supremacist, imperialist, capitalist *and* patriarchal (after hooks ref) academic strictures and structures of which we are a part? How useful is Woolf's work for re-imagining the kinds of strategies that I, and others like me, must use in our work as critical autoethnographers for taking account of coloniality and thereby being accountable to the ethico-onto-epistemological response-abilities these questions call into our knowing, being, doing and writing towards deoloniality?

I turn to the work of Emery (1992), Marcus (2004), Goldman (2006) and Carr (2010) to better understand the implications and relationships with imperialism, which seem to be embedded in Woolf's now infamous sentence. Marcus (2004, p. 28) suggests that the writings and political activities of Woolf's own family on racial freedom—her great grandfather James Stephen campaigned for the anti-slavery movement in England during the mid-1800s and her husband Leonard Woolf wrote extensively about form an anticolonial perspective on Empire and commerce in Africa—provided a ready-made platform for her to promote the autonomy of women. While Woolf may have felt nervous "about sisterhood under the skin" (Marcus, 2004, p. 29), she comfortably used "her great grandfather's antislavery arguments and metaphors to articulate feminist claims for freedom and citizenship without relating racial subjectivity to gender" (Marcus, 2004, p. 29). Much of Woolf's work (e.g., The waves 1931/2000, Three guineas, 1938) exhibits an anti-imperialist critique of Empire and a direct linking of imperialism with patriarchy (Carr, 2010,

p. 201). It swings and see-saws between lending "subjectivity to Englishwomen, who now may have desires of their own different from those of Englishmen" and "repeating the colonialist construction of womanhood as an identity created in the positioning of a 'negress' who can be gazed upon and judged by an 'Englishwoman'" (Emery, 1992, p. 218). Concerned with the master-narratives of her culture (Carr, 2010, p. 209), Woolf could see how deeply her contemporaries' ways of living in and viewing the world were formed and embedded in colonialism, but as Carr (2010, p. 199) questions, "how free is she herself from imperialist assumptions?...How far could she manage to escape the racist attitudes she learnt in her earliest years?" This question prompts me to ask another—how far can I succeed, as white settler colonial woman, to escape the colonial matrix (after Mignolo, 2011), which permeates so much of my own being, doing and knowing? For now however, this "very fine" specimen upon which Woolf's narrator gazes remains the "Angel in the house" (Woolf, 2008); hovering, watching, waiting for another chance to engage and entangle itself in the dangerous moment of writing in and out of the borders of race, colonialism and autoethnography.

9.

The heavy bench scrapes noisily on the wooden floor as I stand up. I am desperate to be on the move now that I have decided to leave this stagnant and stuck place of not-writing and "make a great try for it" (Woolf, 1980, p. 240). I pause just for a second, only a moment, as my hand brushes the cover of Virginia Woolf's (1929/2001) *A room of one's own*, sitting at the bottom of my bag. She is in fine company there with copies of Hélène Cixous' "The laugh of the Medusa" (1976), *Coming to writing* (1991), and "My Algeriance" (1997). I imagine the material impossibility of such an encounter, women moving backwards and forwards, flashing and dashing between one, between two, between "writing, dreaming, delivering; [and] being [their] own daughter[s] of each day" (Cixous, 1991, p. 6). A grey cloud passes over as I unlock my bicycle from an old oak tree, casting shadows that warn me not to disrupt but simply give in and let myself be "swept along by what the great ones have said and [to be content to] remain partially submerged by them" (Greene, 1994, p. 109). I shiver and look over my shoulder; is that the great one-eyed Father that Haraway speaks of I can see skulking around the corner?

The books and papers in my bag shuffle and shift. Cixous's frustration screams from the depths, "Woman be unafraid! (1976, p. 890) The woman who allows herself to be threatened by the big dick, who's still impressed by the commotion of the phallic stance, who still leads a loyal master to the beat of the drum", her voice reaches fever pitch, "that's the woman of yesterday!" (1976, pp. 891–892). The heartlines in my hand are throbbing, pushing urgently and violently at the translucent skin, ready to blow up and splatter the life-blood of writing everywhere. I push off from the kerb, and my body-as-text, carried as it is by a bicycle, takes into its own heartlines of flight.

10.

What are the secrets of me that wait just behind the introduction to this autoethnographic piece? What secrets of my critical autoethnographic life as a feminist-educator-ethnographer-white-settler-colonial-woman-are poised to pounce and take you and me backwards and forwards to such places of un-forgetting? How much will I reveal and how much will I conceal about the kinds of ethico-onto-epistemological heart-thinking which forms the letters, words and paragraphs of this chapter? Should I tell you, for example, that the poetic writing which comes next are lines and phrases which I wrote, many years ago in my ethnographic writing? No, perhaps, that should remain secret—it is writing of which I do not wish to be reminded, dripping as it is with the power and privilege of coloniality. I do not wish you as the reader to be reminded of where to find them so I have secreted away the references. Indeed, much of the writing here is usually secreted away, and yet I have already given the secret away because now it is "known and hidden, impossible to reveal because the revelation would bring about the destruction of the secret thing, and also of life" (Cixous, in Derrida et al., 2006, p. 11). Perhaps, learning to live, work write and love in this way, in the folds of friendship with secrets, is the most powerful strategy we have as critical autoethnographers.

Now that I have begun secret-ing and un-forgetting, there is no stopping. The bicycle of language that I am riding past you is an ode to and in mimicry of the writing of Hélène Cixous and Virginia Woolf. Fragments of their words became further fragmented as they enter into conversation with mine as if we were old friends. Fragmentations of old ethnographic words once mine and written a long time ago now find themselves the objects of the subjects own dialogue. The non-English language included here is Yanyuwa, the language of my family. It is not translated as a statement of philosophical and political refusal in regards to what Western knowledge production and coloniality wants, that is, to know, thus possess, and therefore control the colonized. This act of non-translation and what I hope moves toward non-violence by a non-Indigenous woman of Yanyuwa language is intended to unsettle, to challenge and to disrupt the binaries—the status quo politics of difference mentioned earlier—and begin a process of delinking from coloniality. I willingly refuse to open this particular door of colonial possession and trust that you as reader will be content to stand outside. For in some ways, won't that serve to take you further in? I am forever in motion, flying, writing, moaning, singing, gesturing, and daring (after Cixous, 1991, p. 44). My bicycle takes me through moments of being in time, out of time, timeless, time-lacking, time-beholden; a partner in crime with the thief that creeps towards you in broad daylight without shame, cheeky and showing no mercy, she lifts letters and language to lay his own claim. I am soaring at full speed into yesterday, watching my heartless handwriting take me deep into a memory from which I fear I might yet and perhaps never awake. Letter by line by language I am swept away in the fluidity of this poetic becoming.

11.

   Yu! Ngarna a-wunhaka, a-mangaji yinda a-balirra baji barra
   The group of Aboriginal people.
   They call themselves Yanyuwa.
   They live in the township of Burrulula in the Northern Territory of Australia.
   Map 1 shows Burrulula situated approximately 970 km south east of Darwin and 80 km inland from the Gulf of Carpentaria.
   These are strongly reflected and notable facts.
   Recorded and thus affirmed, they may be said to serve and to corroborate.
   This type of examination elucidates.
   The significant role they play.
   The results of this combined linguistic and musical analysis.
   It is important to understand.

Kurda! Yinda a-murdu wunhaka, a-mangaji a-balirra ambirrjanjarra a-linginmantharra
They must stand in particular kinds of relation.
The relationship is threefold.
Women play too.
Under the increased pressures of assimilation.
Worldly escapades thinly veil.
A greater understanding.
See Map 2. Prior to contact with Europeans.
They are more frequently encountered.
As a marker of their social and spiritual identity.
Primarily vocal, paired, most necessary companions.

A-mangaji a-warriya a-mijiji! Nda-wuthu wunhaka?
The dual role I have to play.
Sister and searcher.
Seeing to, showing to, talking to, singing to, working to,
Meaning to, making to, growing to, writing down.
I have been to Burrulula many times.
This performance ethnography hopes to.
Present the business of representation.
As close as I can come.
To Yanyuwa people.
Inextricably bound up with.
Seeing to, showing to, talking to, singing to, working to,
Meaning to, making to, growing to, writing down.

Jurda, jirda ngalki! Ngalhi a-balirra wunhaka?
Is anybody listening?
For our's mothers song we sing music for dreaming.
Maintaining grandmothers law is a case study of the mermaid song.
Memories in the landscape blurring boundaries.
Many songs, many voices and many dialogues.
To be two, the personal is political.
Making the journey in.
Advocacy and applied stringing together.
moving and dancing towards.
Reading race, culture and gender,

research as sisterhood as relationship.
on Yanyuwa terms.
Engaging our thinking hearts.
PEARLS not problems.
In memory of music research.
We're not afraid.
Unknown and unknowing possibilities.
Decolonisation unto.
The whispering.

Yu! Mingkin wunhaka! Ngalhi barra?
You seeing me seeing you.
Growing up a young white woman.
Without invitation but always already in relationship.
Your husband, our son.
Your sons our grandchildren.
For one score years and a little bit more.
Interpreting, smiling, grimacing, appeasing, discomforting.
Writing words without worlds not mine.
Trying to write in-dulgent, confessional, ethnographic truths.
Giddy and soaring with the good writing.
Working towards social justice,
translating research into something better.
Because that's what the words said.

Yalayka wunhaka! Yalayka! Kurdardi a-barratha, bawuji barra!
Pen flying, fervent, fighting against the futility.
The words are not right yet.
Still performing the same right/rite they have always done.
Empty words, two-faced words, white words you might say.
Words that didn't tell a good enough story.
The gap widens, mind it, step over it and close it.
With a passion for forgetting.
Spots of racism on blankets of colonialism.
Smudges of ignorance and stupidity.
Old blemishes and new stains.
Screams curdle in blood slaughters.
now just as they did then.

Other kinds of words need to be found.
For whiteness does not play well with others.

Kirna balirra, ngarna a-wunahka. Yinda a-nungarrima, a-kundiyarra,
a-Yakibijirna—inne a-wunhaka? Kirna balirra.
Words replete with relationship and being in relation
Words at once curious and furious
Cheekily refusing easy endings
Brave enough to ban boring beginnings
Meddlesome enough to mix it up
Mess around in the middle ground
Going straight to the heart of the matter
For it has its reasons, feeling, with
No thought or care for return to
Using white power and privilege
To cross over under the guise of research
A woman about to make herself radically vulnerable
As the heartlines in her hand become her
And if it doesn't break your heart
It just isn't worth doing anymore. (after Behar, 1996)

12.

She tossed and turned, trying to find the comfort that would return her
to the deep nothing of her grey sleep. It was safe and warm there in her
colonial bed and she was in no mind to arise just yet. The digital clock on
the dresser signalled a time and place where her futurity as white settler
colonial woman was secure. She laid stone still, her dull eyes focussed on
the soft white light of the display, certain in its capacity to lull her back.
Wide open, she watched and waited. The seconds became minutes
became hours became more and the restlessness in her mind crept into
her feet, entangling her heart and legs in white cotton sheets. She was
haunted and hunted by the words and worlds she had written which
scrolled like film credits down in front of her of eyes.

The linen wound and pulled tightly, so much so that soon she felt
completely trapped in the colonial matrix wrapped around her. She
worked her body this way and that, trying to desperately to escape the
black words and worlds written on white in their relentless pursuit. But

she soon became frustrated and uneasy as her literary moves towards otherwise only served to bind her more tightly in her complicity to oblige and reproduce the system. She had tried to un/entangle her "white settler feminist colonial, teacher of Indigenous Australian studies and education, and mother and wife in an Aboriginal family" autoethnographic writing from colonialism before but had felt like an endangered purple, red and yellow butterfly in the rainforest desperately beating its wings against the drab and relentless forces of domination. The credits continued to roll.

The truth was, she was caught and yet she knew that she had to do "something other than the return of the same old" (Ellsworth, 1997, p. 125) to turn this "stuck place" around (Lather, 1998). Lying in a room of her own, she realised that it was up to her decide whether in fact she was locked in or locked out and with this thought, the second wave words of "insister" Hélène Cixous, rushed in to overlap and become one with a third.

"Woman must put herself into the text—as into the world and into history—by her own movement" (Cixous, 1976, p. 875), she whispered.

"Writing", she declared, "a way of leaving no space for death, of pushing back forgetfulness, of never letting oneself be surprised by the abyss. Of never becoming resigned, consoled; never turning over in bed to face the wall and drift asleep again as if nothing had happened; as if nothing could happen" (Cixous, 1991, p. 3).

"It's time to wake from the dead", she shouted, "your writing must become a different kind of 'rite/right'; one that does not seek to 'master', but rather "reminds people that they once wept for love, and trembled with desires, and that they were then very close to the life that they claim they've been seeking while constantly moving further away" (Cixous, 1991, p. 57).

"Shrug off the old lies", she screamed, "Dare what you don't dare... rejoice, rejoice in the terror, follow it where you're afraid to go...take the plunge" (1991, p. 40).

She was desperate to run her writing and make her escape from this dis-cursive/cursed place of pen-man-ship. With one final struggle, she wrenched herself free and stepped outside.

1J.

The purple, yellow and red runners she wore dared to interrupt the grey thoroughfare of truth she found herself in. But the street with no name, no name that mattered to her, made no sound in reply. She shivered as the vanishing night placed cold fingers uninvited on the back of her neck and whispered an age-old warning. She glanced quickly over her shoulder; she seemed to be doing that a lot lately, and for a moment she was sure she saw a/not/her lurking in the shadows, watching, waiting, wanting, and was relieved to find herself alone. Her feet sensed the urgency she held to leave this boulevard of the broken and carried her quickly in-between to her becoming. In the distance she heard the sounds of the world waking up and they wrapped around her in a blanket of familiarity. The hum of the highway below her persisted and kept the cotton wool of daily life firmly lodged. Down the road and a couple of houses away, a rooster resisted his erasure and sang his siren's call. A woman in the house on the hill sighed as she ground the coffee for the cup that would revive her weary soul and the marriage that entrapped her. The cries of a newborn baby pierced the mask of inner suburban serenity and rendered the deadness of the day begun.

Familiarity wrenched its warmth from around her shoulders and in truth she was glad to be rid of it. A mantra played around and around in the cool spot it left behind and pushed her forward. "Un-forget regret rue the blue day dream sleep repeat retreat back down step ladder rungs writings un-forget regret rue the blue day dream sleep repeat retreat back down step ladder rungs writings un-forget". The words ran through her mind like rolling waves, breaking teasingly on the sand at first, then smashing deliciously on the rocks. She was on her way to danger and she loved the feeling of freedom it heralded. She began to run the paths to ruin, working them ferociously, the devil may care, and she dared to anyway. Now and then those who desired to consume, copy or cull her moved to block her course but she had seen their kind before and was not impressed. With blue lips she simply lifted her pen in hand and blew them away. She was unstoppable. She did not bend, she did not break but she did bleed words a plenty, all over her purple, yellow and red runners and the page in front of her. The life blood continued to pool and grow, leaking through the borders, leaving the boys and their ban/d-wagon behind. She watched and become entangled hopeless(-less)fully in the pleasure and pain of the moment. She saw clearly then that danger is a woman writing. The woman becomes the danger in writing. In writing the woman finds the danger. In danger the writing finds the woman and she descended gladly down into its depths to begin again.

14.

The woman in the vertical suit sat in her high-backed blue-flecked swivel chair and regarded me coolly, her slate laced eyes not blinking nor giving anything. In her right hand she held a slim silver fountain pen. Later she would use this weapon of black ink to make her mark of domination on a white page, but for now it tapped out a steady beat on the clean laminate desk. It marched to the beat of her own drum, and like the boots of soldiers on concrete paths, called others to join her. The tapping was tick-tock timed to the clock like a countdown to missile launch, and with each passing second a rash began to blotch and creep its way from her chest to her cheeks. I watched it scrambling and scrawling an age-old rage that reeked in refusal and race/d across her body. I struggled to control an urge to itch and squirm, but the woman in the vertical suit continued to sit unnervingly still.

"Let me just explain to you Liz…this whole business of intercultural engagement is dangerous business. Non-Indigenous people like you, with your publicly performed personal-political-pedagogical palaver, proclaiming to work with and for Indigenous people, are dangerous. Loose cannons who spend and waste precious time talking and being-in-relation with Indigenous people, then fire bullets and barrages of anti-colonial-de-colonial research agendas, aims and outcomes into the centre where and when the war should already have been won!"

She smiled then, and I could almost be fooled into thinking she was sympathetic had her grimace not been framed within pursed lips of steel.

"You see, you need to realise that it's a fight for knowledge at all costs, waged on a battle ground where words like relationship, ethics and love are our prime targets and must be obliterated. They don't serve me, nor those of my kind, well. We will continue to use the selfsame dichotomous and direct commands to get in and get out as quickly as we can to get the job done. You have to understand Liz…".

Her voice droned on. But it was too late; I had heard all that I could stand. Just when I was quite sure I was going to die from the brutal diatribe cloaked as it was in blah blah blahness, my mobile mercifully rang from the depths of my hobo bag. It shrieked and echoed an irritation towards the woman in the vertical suit that I could barely contain.

I smiled apologetically, "Do you mind if get that? It might be the school about my children…"

The woman in the vertical suit threw her hands up in the air. "If I had a dollar for every time a female academic asks to be excused because she chose to breed and feed instead of read, I'd be a…"

I tried to ignore her words that had become the wrong kind of whine and scrambled around in my bag. I found my phone buried at the bottom but it was not a number I did not recognise.

"Hello? Liz speaking". There was a pause. "Who is this?"

A thick French accent answered. "Dear Liz, 'There is a memory in our forgetfulness'" and I recognised Hélène's voice at once.

"And [Indigenous people]? Your autoethnograhic work? What are you doing?" She paused. "You are forgetting?"

I was not quite sure what she meant and so I said nothing, waiting for Hélène to "put the word in [her] ear" (Cixous, 1994, p. 86) as I knew I would.

"Can you smell that?" Hélène asked, "The perfume of those oranges?"

I looked around the stark office and was surprised to see a farmhouse style wooden fruit bowl, distressed in white paint, tucked away on a corner book shelf holding three fresh oranges. I took a moment to smell and breathe in the sweet aroma of ripe citrus fruit.

"Yes", Hélène whispered, "I can sense that you too have entered into this moment to live the orange—and after all, is that not why I have called?"

I glanced across and saw that the woman in the vertical suit, was now preoccupied with checking messages and email on her iPhone.

"Ah yes, Vivre l'orange", I said softly. "I've looked at this essay of yours countless times Hélène and after each reading I feel like I've been…'eating the forbidden fruit' (Cixous, 1993, p. 21) and consuming with each mouthful the political and ethical dimensions of my academic life. The concept of 'living the orange' asks uncomfortable questions about who I am in relation to others, who I/we/they might be in the process of becoming in relation to others through my/our/their autoethnograhic work and what happens in that material yet intercultural, intercorporeal, intersubjective *and* de/colonial moment of being in-between".

Hélène's voice dropped and closed the distance between us. "It sounds like you are full to overflowing with the taste of it and I wonder, why is this so important to you Liz?"

"For me it's the 'r' word—response-ability. What response-ability do we hold in that moment of de/colonial encounter for responding in a profoundly loving, ethical and non-violent way to the materiality of the other?"

"Yes, 'the love of the orange is political too' (Cixous, 1994, p. 90), there is no epistemological, ontological, methodological or pedagogical innocence to be found there" Hélène added. "Indeed, it is replete with many dangers; 'dangers of error, of falseness, of death…of complicity… of blindness, of injustice, of hypocrisy. That we fear and that we seek. For we fear the greatest danger which is forgetting to fear' (Cixous, 1994, p. 90)".

I frowned and shook my head. "But what now Hélène? How do I/ they/we begin to un-forget the dangers?"

"I ask you to not flee the question" she replied quickly, "hold the orange in your hand and 'change from feet to blood'" (Cixous, 1991, p. 3).

"I beg your pardon?" I asked.

"If you hold, as I do, that decoloniality praxis is about a response-able ethico-onto-epistemology to, with, in and through in autoethnographic work—and here I mean critical autoethnographic work—then the orange is a beginning", her voice is patient and kind. "Starting out from the orange all voyages are possible. Become, 'freely, a dangerous woman. In danger of writing' (Cixous, 1994, p. 90)".

There was a moment of silence and then I heard a soft click as Hélène replaced the handset in its cradle. I sat for just a moment, "quite far from the peel of the world, in truth" (Cixous, 1994, p. 88) to collect my thoughts but soon found that I was alive and humming orange all over.

"I'm terribly sorry", I said hurriedly to the woman in the vertical suit. "I have to go!" I had places to go, people to see, oranges to behold.

"Yes, yes, I heard", the woman in the vertical suit didn't even bother took up from her mobile screen. "Something strange about fruit, and it's not even citrus season".

I grabbed my bag and raced out of the door into the "storm of the world" (Cixous, 1994, p. 89) that is being, doing, knowing and writing decoloniality in critical autoethnographic praxis.

15.

Her heart pounded, keeping time with her purple, red and yellow encased feet as they moved in tandem with her hands across the page. One step became one word became one sentence became one hundred metres became one paragraph became one kilometre. Flashes of yellow mixed with splashes of red as the woman's beloved purple runners relentlessly pushed her forward and forever downwards to the danger she declared loudly and proudly in her prose. Streams of sweat ran down the sides of her face, pooling at the end of her elbows to drip a transient line on the grey concrete. The tiny beads of perspiration meandered their way from the pavement to the page and breathed a sigh of relief, as they become one with a language and way of knowing that readily embraced them like family. The woman lifted her arms high in the air as she ran and relished the cooling kiss the breeze placed on her armpits. She closed her eyes and simply let her legs carry her. Racing and flying down the hill she knew for certain that she had come back from always and found freedom in the wind.

Flying and racing, racing and flying, she was seduced by the methodical way her feet and hands and words and writing became one by her own dangerous movement. A woman outside herself she watched in fascination as all that her writing could hold grew deeper and wider. The heartlines in her hand stretched skin, pulled muscles and created a boundless thirst for wisdom born of pain. The woman reached the bottom of the hill, and without warning, she sensed that her descent had now plateaued along the flat lines her own two hands had created. With despair she saw then that she had taken a wrong turn and found herself nearing a dead end. The street around her sounded a stony silence. The woman's mouth was dry, each breath a coarse file that rasped cruelly across the back of her throat. She tried to lift her pen, but where once she flew, she now found herself weighted down with cast iron chains. Glancing down at her feet, the woman was not surprised to see them now blood-stained, the brilliance of yellow, red and purple becoming brown and a taunting memory of liberation lost. She tripped and fell heavily to the ground, the flesh on her knees ripped savagely on the loose gravel. The woman winced as she rolled over and assessed the collateral damage this particular flight of danger had inflicted upon her. The smell of her bodily secretions mingled with grit and dirt, and her stomach heaved abhorrence in response. She sat there for some time, watching and waiting for her hands, heart and feet to become one again.

16.

I find myself a long way from the beginning, standing on the edge of an academic playground. Writing holds out her hand and beckons me to step in. Her fingertips are soft as they touch mine, the rough callouses of her palm scratch a reminder that the heartlines a hand holds are hard fought and won; battle scars put there by words screaming their outrage at the very thought of becoming life on the page. Her hand grips mine tightly now and the pulsating of blood pumping at her wrist connects with my own heartbeat. A gentle rocking backwards and forwards between us. Inwards and outwards, our clasped hands begin to keep time with our steady life rhythms. We look at one another and smile, delighted in the company we keep and not wanting to let go of that moment of being in relation. Faster our hands swing. Writing begins to giggle as she skips across the page towards the inevitable full stop. Letter after letter, word after word, together once more we are flying, soaring and swinging high into the air in the playground. I realise then that I am not alone. Writing is sitting on the swing beside me, the wind in the air caressing her face and soothing those rough spots on her hand. Backwards and forwards, inwards and outwards we swing, watching the one becoming the two becoming the one again, becoming more than two.

Out of the corner of my eye I notice that a woman has joined us and is sitting quietly on the end of the seesaw. Not moving, but simply watching me watching her. I look over at Writing to see if she has noticed her arrival, but Writing is busy dodging this way and that, her face turned up to the sky relishing the unimpeded view, which accompanies the rays and rushes of freedom that her body in motion brings. I sneak a closer look at the woman on the seesaw. A smile plays about her face, almost as though she can read each thought as it waves through my mind. A first and a second. My cheeks flush red and I quickly turn away and focus on the movement of my legs, backwards and forwards, steadying myself in their familiarity. When I look up, another woman has arrived in the playground. She is sitting on the other end of the seesaw and the two women improvise a singsong piece as they gently rock up and down between the generations. I silently will the squeaking swing to find a quiet space, entranced as I am by the words and phrases that flow freely from their mouths.

Hélène's head tilts back and drinks in the sun, "[Aah] Yes, and here I am, 'my writing watches, eyes closed' (Cixous, 1991, p. 3)".

Virginia too is soaking in the warm shards slicing through the chill autumn air. She speaks softly, not wanting to disturb this particular moment of being.

"'Now and again I feel my mind takes shape. Like a cloud with the sun on it, as some idea, plan or image wells up, but they travel on, over the horizon, like clouds, and I wait peacefully for another to form, or nothing—it matters not which' (Woolf, 1980, p. 248)".

"'Wouldn't you have first needed the right reasons to write'?" asks Hélène, curiosity and concern a shadow across her face. "The reasons, mysterious to me, that give you the right to write?" (1991, p. 7)".

Virginia pauses and then declares triumphantly, "'For once truth does not escape me…And I can tell you quite openly [Hélène] I get nearer feelings in writing—I think: graze the bone, enjoy the expression' (Woolf, 1980, p. 239)".

But Hélène is not satisfied, "'But write? With what right?' (1991, p. 12) After all, I read them—other texts—that people like her wrote".

My heartlines begin to stutter and stammer in all the wrong places as I realize with horror that Hélène is talking about me.

"*She*", Hélène purses her lips in my direction, "*She* writes without any right, without permission, without their knowledge" (1991, p. 12). I would urge you "not to flee the question" (Cixous, 1994, p. 86)'.

Virginia's face flushes, her body and mind tingling with the "vitality" (1980, p. 200) of their talk.

"In writing 'I mean to eliminate all waste, deadness, superfluity: to give the moment whole; whatever it includes. Say that the moment is a combination of thought; sensation; the voice of the sea. Waste[r], deadness, come from the inclusion of things that don't belong in this moment: [such writing]…is false, unreal, merely conventional' (1980, p. 209)".

"Yes", Hélène agrees. "Writing must be, 'a way of leaving no space for death, of pushing back forgetfulness, of never letting oneself be surprised by the abyss. Of never becoming resigned, consoled; never turning over in bed to face the wall and drift asleep again as if nothing had happened; as if nothing could happen' (1991, p. 3)".

"'And yet, the only exciting life is the imaginary one' (1980, p. 181)', offers Virginia. "[I'm] 'like a voyager who touches another planet with the tip of [her] toe, upon scenes which would have gone on, have always gone on, will go on, unrecorded, save for this chance glimpse. Then it seems to me that I am allowed to see the heart of the world uncovered for a moment' (Woolf, 1980, p. 153)".

Hélène immediately recognises the sentiment of Virginia's words. "'You don't seek to master. To demonstrate, explain, grasp. And then to lock away in a strongbox. To pocket a part of the riches of the world. Rather to transmit: to make things loved by making them known. You, in your turn, want to affect, you want to wake the dead, you want to remind people that they once wept for love, and trembled with desires, and that they were then very close to the life that they claim they've been seeking while constantly moving further away" (1991, p. 57)".

"Yes, now that you mention it, I think 'how unpleasant it is to be locked out; and [yet] how it is worse perhaps to be locked in' (1929/2001, p. 21)", Virginia adds, deep now as she is in thought. There is a heavy silence before she speaks again. 'I feel this history beginning to rage within, interrupting, breaking in between, just as "the soul slips in' (1980, p. 62)".

'This is 'the work of un-forgetting, of un-silencing, of unearthing, of un-blinding oneself, and of un-deafening oneself' (1994, p. 83), Hélène replies, her voice so quiet it is but a suggestion on the wind. "'Loving, saving, naming what would be erased and annihilated is political in an immediate sense'" (Cixous, 1994, p. 83)'.

"Perhaps [then Hélène] 'I can say something quite straight out; and at length; and need not always [be] casting a line to make my [Writing] the right shape' (Woolf, 1980, p. 285)".

"Dear Virginia, you must hold onto writing, 'Writing prevents the questions that attacks life from coming up' (1991, p. 6). In writing 'our blood flows and we extend ourselves without ever reaching an end; we never hold back our thoughts, our signs, our writing; and we're not afraid of lacking' (1976, p. 878)!"

17.

A shadow fell across her face and brought the woman back to the present. The man stood in front of her, legs wide apart, his crotch but a few inches from her face. He reeked of piss and patriarchy. She stood up and tried not to show her panic.

"Well, well, well", he sneered, "Little girl lost and nowhere left to run! Where you gonna' run to darlin' in this big colonial city?"

She kept her eyes and head down.

He spoke quietly but the woman recognized the violent misogyny it masked—she had met his kind before and it filled her with dread.

"No one here but you and me, and you should know by now darlin', I own this past and present—fact, far as I can tell, I own you as well".

He circled around her like a great white shark, a deep-seated desire for female flesh and blood fuelling his desire. His unshaven cheek scraped against her ear and his sour breath curdled down her neck, taking with it any hope she might have had about the promise of running and writing into danger.

"So, nothin' left for you to do but surrender your pen, wipe away those words, and shut your pretty mouth! You know you want it—you've been askin' for it for years—all that feminist writing when you're just a fucking slut. Playing in the ivory tower with the big boys, what did you think would happen? Did you really think you could keep on just keep on just giving me the decolonial-ethico-onto-epistemological finger and I wouldn't notice?"

The man grabbed her shoulders and spun her roughly her around to face him.

"Lie back you bitch and think of England—that's what this country is built on. I'll show you the power of the c-word once and for all!" He lunged forward and tried to push her to the ground.

In that moment time stood still. The woman saw him for what he was—a man and machine defined, driven and destined by the colonial matrix and determined to drag her down with him at all costs. And that was enough for her to do otherwise than surrender. She would no longer be the shadow, "in the shadow he throws on her; the shadow she is" (Cixous & Clement, 1986, p. 67). It was time for her woman to come back from always (Cixous, 1976, p. 878), to resist death, proclaim deco-loniality and make trouble (Cixous, 1976, p. 876). Her voice joined those of her Yanyuwa family and she opened her mouth to sing.

Ngarna Yanyuwa a-ngabiyarra
Ngarna Yanyuwa a-ngabiyarra
Ngarna Yanyuwa, jibiya wali-angku
Ngarna Yanyuwa

The heartlines in her hand began to pulse and her beloved kundiyarra urged her forward.

Yu! Ngarna a-wunhaka, a-mangaji yinda a-balirra baji barra
Jina-bunalkarra ardu, nya-ladalada, jina wardi

Hélène Cixous' voice returned and joined those of her Yanyuwa family.

"Listen to your kundiyarra, your baba, listen!", she said. "Don't be indebted to all the vileness and compromise, refuse to be impressed by the commotion of the phallic stance (1976, p. 892), break the codes that negate you, and with harrowing explosions, bring on the revolution! (1976, p. 879) Become at will the take and the initiator, [in your] own right, in every symbolic system, in every political process (1976, p. 880)".

Yinda barra, yinda a-Yanyuwa ngabiyarra, kurdardi a-mijiji.
Yinda a-linginmantharra a-Yakibirjirna; nda-marruwarra, nda-baba, nda-kujaka, nda-kukurdi, nda-nagbuji, yu, nda-wunhaka.

Hélène nodded her head in agreement as she listened to the Yanywua women speak. "You are forever being the single and the double, forever being here and elsewhere, over here as elsewhere, elsewhere as here, I and the other, I as other" (1994, p. xv). She paused, "You found yourself in the land of the other, not of the fellow human being. The other: foretells, warns me, forecasts me, alters me, alters me" (1997, p. 270). "This is the moment of your passance (passing by) and arrivance (movement)—your Yanyuwance. You must never settle in (1997, p. 270), no longer be forced by the demon of Coloniality to play the play with a false identity (1997,

p. 262) and instead you must seek to break up, to destroy, and to foresee the un-seeable (Cixous, 1976, p. 875). From now on, who can say no to us?" (Cixous, 1991, p. 42).

> Yalayka wunhaka! Yalayka! Kurdardi a-barratha, bawuji barra!
> Yinda-jurnduma kulu kiwa-nba narra nungka a-wunhaka. Yinda a-ramanthamarra, kirna balirra!

The woman needed no more encouragement. The heartlines in her hand throbbed, she was ready to blow up and splatter the life-blood of her writing everywhere.

18.

By the time the woman had finished, the sun was high in the sky and she felt truly alive. Her purple, red and yellow runners sparkled with the vibrancy of life which "borders on death; right up against [that which she vowed] to write" (Cixous, 1991, p. 5). She wiped her hands on her jeans and looked at the disappearing spectre of the man sprawled on the ground in front of her. With each word she wrote, she saw him slowly fading away. Would she ever be completely rid of him? Of this the woman was not sure. The effects of him and his past would remain in the present, but she refused to "strengthen him/them by repeating them" (1976, p. 875). She would no longer fear being a woman, being a white settler colonial woman, being in her Yanyuwance, arriving over and over again to never stand still (1976, p. 893). She would no longer fear any risk and instead take thrill in her constant becoming writer, written, and writing. Through the same decolonial openings and cracks that are her "danger, [she would] come out of herself to go" (Cixous, 1991, p. 42) in writing. To writing then in danger. To then in(en)danger writing. Writing then in to danger. Danger then in to writing. Danger into then writing. Then in to danger writing. Then to danger in writing. Then writing in to danger. She did not care which way one turned it, she was on her way to becoming a dangerous woman writing (Cixous, 1991, p. 90).

19.

The question from Hélène Cixous hangs tantalisingly in the air, like the sweet fragrance of ripe fruit on an orange tree—and for now there it shall remain—an unfinished conversation with Virginia Woolf in the academic playground and me as critical autoethnographer flashing and crashing my bicycle this way and that with Writing, who is standing on the edge with decoloniality. As much as you may want it, I am going to refuse a neat ending because ultimately, I know I shall fail "what I understand is the first duty of a writer—to hand you…a nugget of pure truth wrapped up between the pages of your notebooks to keep on the mantelpiece forever" (Woolf, 1929/2001, p. 2). Writing as heartlines, the letters, words and phrases which, through their own flesh and blood, breathe life into the decolonial possibility for living the discomfort of researching and being-in-relation as a white settler colonial woman. Worn on sleeves and written in white ink as she sits in a room of her own, they belong to the undutiful among us—daughters or otherwise—who delight in the ethico-onto-epistemological disturbances and diffractions we might create in the decolonial moment of being Writing as heartlines. Personal becomes political becomes pedagogical becomes performative becomes thinking-full, theory-full, becomes hand and heart-full to overflowing as Writing watches and weaves her way outwards, inwards (Ellis, 2004), back and forth in time at the self and the social. Writing as heartlines is a beautiful woman laughing, dancing and rejoicing like the Medusa in the power she holds for embodied, emotioned and ethical ways of thinking, being and doing critical *and* decolonial autoethnography.

The question from Hélène Cixous is replete with danger, holding on the one hand the potential decoloniality as critical autoethnography holds to bring into being an inbetweenness of self and other which is at once transgressive, innovative, and empowering. On the other hand, however, it is the very inbetweenness which lays bare the possibility for power and privilege to be mis/used/represented to perpetuate and reproduce dominance of self in relation to other. The playful, poetic and political nature of Hélène Cixous's work is a constant reminder that the language, knowledge and performativities I hold as a white settler colonial woman are powerful. Her writings, alongside those of Virginia Woolf call me in Cixousian terms, to un-forget and act on the sense of response-ability I have to come clean. To own up, to use my white race power and privilege to shake, rattle and roll our autoethnographic research and writing practice into a more ethical way of attending to our complicity in the wound up, bound up colonial past and present of this moment.

The question from Hélène Cixous is more than that though—it is also attending in writing to the ways in which our words-as-worlds-as-works engage in a performance and perpetuation of dominance—white suprema-cist imperial capitalist patriarchy bell hooks would call it—and forever seek-ing to be wide awake to the incompleteness and possibility of that which is not here yet. To re/turn to Cixous' concept of living the orange, to enact decoloniality in critical autoethnography is to ask questions about the moral obligations we hold to work in a manner which works *against* the epistemo-logical violence of taking from the other, disrupting the dominance which makes such appropriation possible, and imagining a critical autoethnogra-phy which beats as it writes and rights to a different *kind* of heartline.

But do not be fooled, a heartline is like any other—it can break and be tossed ruthlessly aside by others, once, twice and many times over but Writing is not afraid; she knows from her heart to her hand, that "censor the body and you censor breath and speech at the same time…your body must be heard" (Cixous, 1976, p. 880). Indeed Writing-as-heartlines demands a response and will continue to speak where some would prefer silence. In the rubbish bin by her desk sits her white naiveté. Writing as heartlines stepped away from the popularity race in academia because she knows that in a world where everything is manufactured and photo-shopped according to the colonial matrix, not everyone likes, respects, understands or thinks she has a place but she stays the course. There is too much at stake to give up now, and besides, that would be the easy way out. Writing wants the heartline to beat long and strong after the sun goes down, the cold sets in and this autumn day ends, to carry you across the threshold from mere disinterested critique into a space where empathy, compassion and mindful caring emerge as necessary recognition and a vital response to the somewhere we find ourselves in between. Is that not what you thought Writing-as-heartlines-as-decoloniality-as-critical autoethnography will do?

References

Ahluwalia, P. (2005). Out of Africa: Post-structuralism's colonial roots. *Postcolonial Studies, 8*(2), 137–154.

Behar, R. (1996). *The vulnerable observer*. Boston, MA: Beacon Press.

Carr, H. (2010). Virginia Woolf, empire and race. In S. Sellers (Ed.), *The Cambridge companion to Virginia Woolf* (2nd ed., pp. 197–213). Cambridge: Cambridge University Press.

Cary, L. (2004). Always already colonizer/colonized: White Australian wanderings. In K. Mutua & B. Swadener (Eds.), *Decolonizing research in cross-cultural contexts: Critical personal narratives* (pp. 69–83). Albany, NY: New York University Press.

Cixous, H. (1976). The laugh of the Medusa (K. Cohen & P. Cohen, Trans.). *Signs, 1*(4), 875–893.

Cixous, H. (1991). *Coming to writing and other essays* (S. Suleiman, Ed., S. Cornell, Trans.). Cambridge, MA: Harvard University Press.

Cixous, H. (1993). *Three steps on the ladder of writing* (S. Cornell & S. Sellers, Trans.). New York, NY: Columbia University Press.

Cixous, H. (1994). *The Hélène Cixous reader* (S. Sellers, Ed.). London: Routledge.

Cixous, H. (1997). My Algeriance: In other words, to depart not to arrive from Algeria. *Triquarterly, 100*, 259–279.

Cixous, H., & Clement, C. (1986). *The newly born woman* (Theory and history of literature) (Vol. 24). Minneapolis, MN: University of Minnesota Press.

Cixous, H., & MacGillivray, C. (1998). *First days of the year* (Emergent literatures). Minneapolis, MN: University of Minnesota Press.

Derrida, J., Cixous, H., Armel, A., & Thompson, A. (2006). From the word to life: A dialogue between Jacques Derrida and Hélène Cixous. *New Literary History, 37*(1), 1–13.

Ellis, C. (2004). *The ethnographic I: A methodological novel about autoethnography* (Ethnographic alternatives book series) (Vol. 13). Walnut Creek, CA: AltaMira Press.

Ellsworth, E. (1997). *Teaching positions: Difference, pedagogy and the power of address*. New York, NY: Teachers College Press.

Emery, M. L. (1992). "Robbed of meaning": The work at the centre of to the lighthouse. *Modern Fiction Studies, 38*(1), 217–234.

Florence + The Machine. (2011). Heartlines. On *Ceremonials* [CD]. London: Island.

Fox, C. (2004). Tensions in the decolonisation process: Disrupting preconceptions of postcolonial education in the Lao People's Democratic Republic. In A. Hickling-Hudson, J. Matthews, & A. Woods (Eds.), *Disrupting preconceptions: Postcolonialism and education* (pp. 91–106). Flaxton, QLD: Post Pressed.

Goldman, J. (2006). *The Cambridge introduction to Virginia Woolf*. Cambridge: Cambridge University Press.

Greene, M. (1994). Postmodernism and the crisis of representation. *English Education, 26*(4), 206–219.

Hilfrich, C. (2006). The self is a people: Autoethnographic poetics in Hélène Cixous's fictions. *New Literary History, 37*(1), 217–235.

Holman Jones, S. (1998). Turning the kaleidoscope, re-visioning an ethnography. *Qualitative Inquiry, 4*(3), 421–441.

Lather, P. (1998). Critical pedagogy and its complicities: A praxis of stuck places. *Education Theory, 48*(4), 487–497.

Mackinlay, E. (2015a). In danger of relation, in danger of performance, in danger of research: An ethical conversation with Hélène Cixous about writing, creativity and intercultural arts praxis. In P. Burnard, E. Mackinlay, & K. Powell (Eds.), *The Routledge international handbook of intercultural arts*. London: Routledge.

Mackinlay, E. (2015b). In danger of writing: Performing the poetics and politics of autoethnography with Hélène Cixous and Virginia Woolf. *Qualitative Research Journal, 15*(2), 189–201.

Mackinlay, E. (2018). Shrug off the old lies: Writing decoloniality in and through critical autoethnograhy with Hélène Cixous. In S. Holman Jones & M. Pruyn (Eds.), *Creative selves/creative cultures: Critical autoethnography, performance and pedagogy* (pp. 169–182). Basingstoke: Palgrave Macmillan.

Marcus, J. (2004). *Hearts of darkness: White women write race*. New Brunswick, NJ: Rutgers University Press.

Mignolo, W. (2011). Epistemic disobedience and the decolonial option: A manifesto. *Transmodernity, 1*(2), 44–66.

Mutua, K., & Swadener, B. (2004). Introduction. In K. Mutua & B. Swadener (Eds.), *Decolonizing research in crosscultural contexts: Critical personal narratives* (pp. 1–26). Albany, NY: State University of New York Press.

Penrod, L. (2003). Algeriance, exile, and Hélène Cixous. *College Literature, 30*(1), 135–145.

Poka, L. (2000). Processes of decolonization. In M. Battiste (Ed.), *Reclaiming Indigenous voice and vision* (pp. 150–160). Vancouver, BC: University of British Columbia.

Sellers, S. (Ed.). (2010). *The Cambridge companion to Virginia Woolf* (2nd ed.). Cambridge: Cambridge University Press.

Smith, L. T. H. (1999). *Decolonizing methodologies: Research and Indigenous peoples*. New York, NY: Zed Books.

Woolf, V. (1929/2001). *A room of one's own*. New York, NY: Harcourt, Brace, Jovanovich.

Woolf, V. (1980). *The diary of Virginia Woolf, Volume III: 1925–1930* (A. E. Bell, Ed.). London: Hogarth Press.

Woolf, V. (2008). *Virginia Woolf: Selected essays* (D. Bradshaw, Ed.). Oxford: Oxford University Press.

Woolf, V. (2015). *The waves* (New ed., Oxford world's classics). Oxford: Oxford University Press.

9

Critical Autoethnography, to Trouble with Words

Always the last chapter slips out of my hands. One gets bored. One whips oneself up. I still hope for a fresh wind, & don't very much bother, except that I miss the fun, which was so tremendously lively all October, November & December. I have my doubts if it is not empty; & too fantastic to write at length.
Woolf (1980, p. 175)
How am I to begin it? And what is to be? I feel no great impulse; no fever, only a great pressure of difficulty. Why write it then? Why write at all? Every morning I write a little sketch to amuse myself. I am not saying, I might say, that these sketches have any relevance. I am not trying to tell a story. Yet perhaps it might done in that way.
Woolf (1980, p. 229)

1.

There is always one chapter which causes all manner of trouble, and this chapter, Chap. 9, is it. *This* is my troubled chapter. It has troubled me right from the beginning, because I didn't know where, how, why or what to begin. This chapter was intended to be *the* defining chapter on critical autoethnography, because this *kind* of book needs a definition. And yet,

© The Author(s) 2019
E. Mackinlay, *Critical Writing for Embodied Approaches*,
https://doi.org/10.1007/978-3-030-04669-9_9

if Stewart (2013, p. 660) is right, then most of what I write here about critical autoethnography, readers already know. As soon as I sat down to write this chapter then, the *defining* chapter, I knew I was in trouble. These neo-liberal, neo-colonial, neo-positivist times are troubled times, "dark times" as Hannah Arendt (1983) would say, and such moments require deliberately will-full and troubling acts of speech-as-writing which ask us to pause for a moment, care-fully and thought-fully, to think and wonder about the question posed by Cixous' work, that is, who I *are* and who I are *as* critical autoethnographer? Sitting behind such thinking and wondering about being, knowing and doing critical auto-ethnography there is a hidden assumption that some *kind* of definition will be provided. Is that not what you are looking and hoping for, that I will uphold my responsibility (note, *not* response-ability) and *define* criti-cal autoethnography?

"Psst", whispers Robin Boylorn (2018, p. 233), "[You] 'We don't owe anybody explanations, extensions, sequels or epilogues' on the autoeth-nographic stories you we share".

"Listen to her, she's right you know," I imagine Virginia Woolf mur-muring in reply, "'A thousand pens are ready to suggest what you *should* do' (1929/2001, p. 113)".

Carolyn Ellis' hand on my shoulder presents a gentle interruption, "I have been an ethnographer all my life, and an *auto*ethnographer for a quarter of a century—myself and the community of autoethnographers of which we are a part have no 'desire to police the use of term "autoeth-nography"'" (in Bochner & Ellis, 2014, p. 63). "The question is, what is it that you *will* to do in relation to and with the trouble of defining criti-cal autoethnography?"

I am tempted to paraphrase the opening paragraph of *A room of one's own* as a-way to move through and within this definitional, citiational and "compositional complicity" (Stewart, 2013, p. 661). If I were to do this, you would ask, in mimicry of Virginia Woolf, "We asked you to write a book about autoethnography—what has that go to do with being critical?" And I would, at first, attempt a simple answer, one that respect-fully cites the ground-breaking work of Carolyn Ellis and Arthur Bochner, makes reference to the equally trailblazing writings of Laurel Richardson, pays homage to the inspiration provided by Stacy Holman Jones and Anne Harris standing steadfast and strong at the posts and beyond, and in rational and logical academic language dutifully quotes the words of others on the alternative qualitative research team such as Tony Adams, Jonathan Wyatt and Norman Denzin. Without these thought-full and care-full and insight-full people who have come before me, and who I am privileged to work alongside, I would not be able work with and in the kind of words and worlds of autoethnography that I do. Reading and referring and referencing their work seems like the most respectful and relevant thing to do; and yet, I am yet to resolve which rite is the right way to write.

Truth be told, when I begin to consider to write and define critical autoethnography in this way, I realise not a moment too soon that I am already in trouble because this approach has one, two and maybe more fatal drawbacks. Not only do I *not* know how much you already know about critical autoethnography, I would be surrendering to the status quo of obedient and appropriate citational scholarship expected from a book like this. *And* that acquiescence to the orthodox, the proper, the *more* appropriate would be an act of numbing myself, as de la Garza (2014, p. 220) suggests, to an ethics of living, researching and writing grounded in my embodied experiences of life.

And by extension then, I would become submissive all over again to phallocentric and masculinist approaches to academic writing.

And therefore, by repeating and returning to the selfsame, I would be reneging on my pledge to only cite the words of women.

And I sense and feel from the flesh on the bones of this body to the bones that flesh out this body of writing and the body that writes, that I will-fully never be able to come to a definitive conclusion. I will-fully will would never be able to provide a "nugget of pure truth to wrap up between the pages of your notebook and keep on the mantel-piece forever" (Woolf, 1929/2001, p. 4) and nor should I want to because that is not the *kind* of definition I would like to provide at all.

If autoethnography is telling stories of lived social experience through the self and back to the social in a constant state of re/turn; if *critical* autoethnography is telling stories about theory and theorising through the autoethnographic stories we tell, then the *kind*-est thing I can do is show and *not* tell you how I have come to understand who I are as critical autoethnographer in and out and all manner in-between of daily life. As I write this, I remember reading Holman Jones reflections on storytelling in autoethnography as a "relational accomplishment", as a way to "write us into and out of being" as selves and in relation to others (Holman Jones, in Ellis, Holman Jones, & Adams, 2013, p. 19). Perhaps then, if I make "use of all of the liberties and licences of a novelist" (Woolf, 1929/2001, p. 4) and use storytelling as a way to reveal "meaning without committing the error of defining it" (Arendt, 1983, p. 147) this *kind* of discussion of critical autoethnography sidesteps classification and instead becomes one which attempts to show concern, compassion and care to those inside and outside these words and worlds. This *kind* of writing is precarious business—if I have learnt anything about coming to critical autoethnographic writing in this way, the personal, relational and ethical dangers are familiar and necessary friends and chosen, as Holman Jones suggests (2013, p. 19) in loving solidarity in order to be *who I are*. This is "not the kind of thing you expect in a talk or an article", writes Stewart (2013, p. 659), instead, she reminds us that this *kind* of "autoethnography can be a way of doing something different with theory and its relation to experience". I resolve that this is what I will-fully do: shirk my responsibility in favour of response-able trouble making with words and "develop in your presence as [will]fully and freely as I can" (Woolf, 1929/2001, p. 4) an endurance and attunement (Stewart, 2013, p. 661) to the small and large tugs of experience so that you may be able to listen "not entirely to what [is] being said, but to the murmur or current [of meaning] behind" (Woolf, 1929/2001, p. 12) each and every-one.

2.

The first time I used the word autoethnography I knew I was in ever so much trouble. The taste of the word flowing in and around my mouth was ever so sweet; ever so softly and ever so care-fully it allowed its unusual flavour to mix and mingle with the tang of an/other I was already familiar with. I knew one mouthful would never be enough and I would have to go back for more, to taste, retaste and taste again. Something that tasted like *that* could only mean trouble and the trouble is, how might critical autoethnography be defined?

Ethnography.
Autoethnography.
Evocative autoethnography.
Analytic autoethnography.
Interpretive autoethnography.
Collaborative autoethnography.
Critical autoethnography.

I think and wonder about these words that over time have arrived next to and continue to attach themselves to the word autoethnography as in and of itself it lives, breathes and grows wings, flitting and fleeting between there and then and here and now. The word autoethnography doesn't appear in my grandfather's dictionary; I raise my eyebrows, thinking and wondering why I might be surprised that. Seventy years ago, autoethnography was not a word that people inside or outside academia used. As a way of doing ethnography, autoethnography, auto-ethnography and/or auto/ethnography belongs out of the past and in with the posts. I think and wonder whether the latest web-based edition of the Merriam Webster might include the word autoethnography. I enter my subscription to the Unabridged Dictionary login online and type A-U-T-O-E-T-H-N-O-G-R-A-P-H-Y in the search bar. I watch and wait. After a few seconds, the following message appears in a pop-up box: "The word you've entered isn't in the Unabridged Dictionary. Click on a spelling suggestion below or trying again using the search bar above". I scroll down but there are no spelling suggestions below. I type the word again the search bar above as directed but the same message appears. I tap my fingers on my desk, thinking and wondering what to do next.

3.

"Remember the moment when you realised that you could write autoethnography as loving work you love?" asks Stacy quietly, gently, and with strength, as the inaugural critical autoethnography conference begins. Some people around me softly snap their fingers, a rhythmic sign of appreciation for the lilting lyrics which have taken the place of business as academic prose. I settle myself into my chair; position my notebook precariously on my lap and rest my mind and body back to relish in the affective ride her words promise.

"Remember when you came to the realisation that what you love about autoethnography is the way is opens up the possibility of theory as story, that theory tells a story of the everyday and story tells theory through and with the everyday?" She continues.

"Remember when you became aware that critical to living and loving theory-as-story-as-theory in autoethnography was exactly that, a praxis of criticality where a material, ethical, and embodied creation of knowing are the life-blood of our work?" Stacy pauses.

"In this space of remembrance—if you like, this place of un-forgetting as critical autoethographers", she suggests, "there lies in wait a disturbance of the taken for granted, an unsettling of the ordinary, a movement of revolutionary proportions which pushes towards a future which is not yet here".

Her words echo in my head as my heart rushes madly a-head in thought. Every ounce of my flesh is tingling, and the weight of my bones becomes almost unbearable as I connect with the longing for more in our work as autoethnographers that Stacy speaks of. I look around the room and see the same kind of yearning reflected on the faces of people there with me. I wonder, does their ache for more come from the same place as mine? For so long, longer than I can un-forget, I have longed for more and what to do with that longing is a question that lingers long into the days and nights. Ruth Behar's (1996) provocation has become a mantra that has me caught and captured, "If you are not doing an ethnography which breaks your heart, why do it at all?" A move towards the critical seems like the only movement, the only kind of movement that might be able—response-able enough even—to respond to the longing such heart break brings and begin anew the bothering. Disruption, upset, trouble; yes, trouble. Being response-able to such longing is replete with trouble.

I reposition myself in my chair, readjust the precarity of the notebook balanced on my lap, and not feeling quite comfortable, lean back to listen to the final words of the inaugural critical authoethnography conference.

"It is time for autoethnography to be troubled by criticality", says Sally. I hear her words as a call to arms and raise my fist high in the air.

"Troubling the auto is troubling the self", she speaks a little louder.

"Yeah!" The audience replies in unison.

"Troubling the ethno is troubling the description", Sally shouts.

"Yeah yeah!" We are with her, our voices rising to the occasion.

"Troubling the graphy is troubling the writing", Sally's voice has reached fever pitch. The room shakes as we holler our agreement.

"Are you with me?" She begs the question.

"Yeah!"

"I can't hear you!" She screams. "I said, are you with me?"

"Yeah, yeah yeah!!!" Our feet stamp the ground and our voices thunder.

"Well", she drawls with a cheeky grin, "What do we want?"

"Trouble!"

"What do we want?" She roars again.

"Trouble!"

"When do we want it?"

"Now!"

And with this, the trouble of critical autoethnography begins.

4.

It's hard to say *exactly* when it all started, when the *trouble* really began—when I became the *troubable* one, the one *causing trouble*; the *trouble-maker*. Or perhaps I had always been *in trouble* because I was the one charged with naming *the trouble*, therefore accused of causing *the trouble* and once thereby labelled *troubled*; found myself sitting precariously on the edge of individual and collective *troubles* that placed me in a great deal of *trouble*. My body slips its way into a recently purchased previously loved blue and white checked sun dress, and my toes wriggle theirs into my favourite pair of silver sandals. I look at my image in the mirror and see that for now, I have very carefully secreted the trouble I am about to re/present a-way. I smile, for truth be told, I have never been the best secret-er of secrets and un-forgetting the secrets of *troubling* is a secret I have held for a long time.

Today marks the first day I will use the word autoethnography in my academic work. Not just *use* the word, but speak it, name it, claim it and unshame it—a secret no longer. There are other secret words I am going to take great delight in secret-ing too; others which seem to cause trouble on good measure alongside autoethnography. I am speaking on a panel today called, "History and workings of applied ethnomusicology" at a similarly themed conference in Hanoi at the Vietnamese Institute for Musicology. My paper is titled, "From big women, bigger things grow: Talking about an ethnomusicology of the heart and its potential as applied and decolonising work in Indigenous Australia" and all the signs of trouble are there: women, heart, talk and decolonising are words which in and of themselves have always troubled disciplines like ethnography and ethnomusicology. I scan the printed programme I have in my hand once more, searching for others in my tribe of troublemakers who might be living and loving the same kind of language as me and present at this gathering. There are only three papers scheduled in this conference program which refer explicitly to women. I quickly scan the abstracts for any sign that someone else is speaking feminist language but there are no sisterly voices there. "Emotion" is lacking in all of the words about experience, "talk" is replaced with terms like "experiment", "respond", and "strategy", and any reference to the "c" word colonialism or its offensive opposite "decoloniality" is completely absent from the other papers on the program. I sigh; I guess I really *am* in trouble and for a fleeting moment I think and wonder whether it's *worth* the trouble. Before it's too late I catch the clever and colluding feelings of doubt and despair which have waded in uninvited and choose instead to un-forget the response-ability I have in this moment to do difference differently.

I carefully place a strand of long red beads around my neck, made for me by baba Jemima, as a gesture of that critical commitment. It does not matter to me whether others know or don't know this; it is not a matter *for* them *to* know but one which matters to me. The bright smooth red beads are seeds from the tree *Erythrina vespertilio*, more often called the "bean tree". It is a native tree which grows far, wide and well across the north east of Australia and the seeds are a popular item in jewellery making. Baba Jemima gifted me this necklace a long time ago and even still it holds the faint smell of dry season burning and tiny traces of traces of red dirt occasionally make their mark on my skin. I feel her presence with me as the beads gently sway in and across time with me; a present/ce of shared relationship, sisterhood and something, perhaps something more that yet I am to word.

My decision to wear the beads is deliberate; I intend them to perform a particular kind and set of diffractive body politics where women's ways of knowing matter and the matter of women's knowing matters. My decision is all that and more; it is deliberately willful. I *know* that the feminist and decolonial and *critical* language my red seed necklace speaks is an interruption to the loud and dominant voices of coloniality which are slowly but surely flexing their muscles to squeeze the fight out of me and my kind. I *know* that placing myself in this room at this conference as an openly white-settler-de/colonial-feminist-ethnomusicologist-activist speaking a particular kind of critical autoethnographic language *will* create tension, unease and perhaps even kill the joy that others attending this conference hold (Ahmed, 2010, p. 2). I *know* that I am making a willful choice to place myself *in trouble* for as Ahmed holds, such a willful body is to be "compelled to live (and even die) in proximity to this category" (Ahmed, 2011, p. 240). Today I *know* I would not become the background (Ahmed, 2011, p. 245) and instead resolve to be the "the willful character…the one [who] 'stands out'" (Ahmed, 2011, p. 245), by naming the trouble, even if it meant that I would, by necessity, be read as the source of *all* of the trouble to come.

5.

I am tired from my trip, but I do not want to waste a moment; the city outside awaits. I can hear it humming deep and low in synchronicity with the thick dense and tepid air that encloses it. Stepping outside my hotel room, the street is like nothing I have encountered before. The pungent aromas of coffee, coconut and coriander eddy and swirl around me as I walk. I close my eyes so that I might drink them all in and soon become intoxicated.

"Oh! I'm sorry!" I exclaims, as I stumble into an elderly woman bent over double as she balances a bamboo yoke on her shoulders.

I reach forward to take hold of the woman's arm in a gesture to steady us both. Inside each small wooden pale on either end of the pole are thick slices of freshly cut pineapple. As the woman straightens herself tall, she catches my eye.

"You're a very pretty lady—your dress is very pretty".

I glance down at my outfit and smile. It's a blue and white checked sundress I bought from the second-hand shop especially for this trip; light cotton with breezy straps and a thrifty bargain.

"Thank you!" I say to the woman. "Is that pineapple you have for sale?"

The woman nods. "Would you like to buy? 15,000 dong".

I can already taste the cool sweetness of the fruit on my lips and eagerly hands over the money. The elderly woman nods a quick goodbye and walks towards another tourist in her town.

"You're very handsome man", she says to him, "For you this pineapple only 20,000 dong".

With pineapple juice dripping down my fingers, I grin at the elderly woman's business acumen and hold my arms out wide to embrace this moment and continue my thinking and wondering into the centre of the city.

With every step across each crack in every pavement along each avenue there is a new sensory adventure, almost assaultive, to be had. Motorcycles and scooters of all shapes and sizes carrying all manner of human and non-human cargo make all kinds of beeps and blares as they slowly grind their away along the crowded corridors. I stand mesmerised on the side of the footpath at the osmotic traffic in front of me, waiting for a break in the chaotic but seemingly organised movement so that I might cross the road to sit down in the park. A motorcycle carrying a family of five crawls past, so close I feel the breeze created in their wake. Two children are cradled comfortably at the front of the bike and are capably steered by their father in the middle while their mother and grandmother point and shout instructions from a dual dolly seat at the back. They are soon overtaken by a young man dressed in black leather on a much faster model transporting a full-size refrigerator. He honks noisily at an old man on a rusted and smoking scooter meandering in front of him with a load of fat squealing pigs on board. After a while I realise that there is never going to be a right time to get to the other side of the street. All I can hope is that my body will be at once allowed and absorbed into the flow of oncoming traffic.

6.

The business man sits on a bench in the shade. It is the favourite part of his day; the moment when he gets to step away from his solitary and cold office into the warmth and companionship of the busy city street. He is allowed a thirty-minute lunch break and he has it timed to perfection. It takes him five minutes to walk down two flights of stairs and two blocks to the park. He quickly scans the available seating and is relieved that the bench he has come to think of as his bench is unoccupied. The business man sits down without fuss and eats the lunch his wife has made for him. Each day he brings the tightly wrapped chicken rice paper rolls to his mouth in the hope the taste of love will linger on his tongue, but all that remains after he has finished is the bland smack of duty. He sighs deeply and lights up his cigarette. The business man has ten minutes before he must make the return five-minute walk back to his office and he plans to savour every second.

His bench is placed at the front of the park, right in the centre, and he cherishes the position it puts him in. From this spot he is in a prime location for people watching. Over time he convinces himself that there is nothing nosey, voyeuristic or lewd about the way he looks; he is nothing more or less than curious. He finds a certain peace in imagining other possible ways to be and do in the world as he watches people pass by. The business man scans the vista in front of him. He sees an elderly woman balancing a bamboo yoke across her shoulders. He cannot see what is inside the wooden pails, but he knows it is pineapple. The business man has been coming to eat his lunch at the exact same time in the exact same place while working the exact same job for exactly 12 years, and he has watched the exact same elderly woman walk the exact same path in exactly the same way each and every day. The business man and the elderly woman have never spoken a word to one another from their opposite sides of the street worlds apart but now their eyes meet in silent acknowledgement. His gaze comes to rest upon a woman in a blue and white checked sundress standing opposite him across the road from the park. The pretty woman is alone, and he wonders why. He observes her as she turns her head this way and that up and down the street. The business man nods his head in quiet approval; he can see she is waiting for the right time to cross. He takes another drag on his cigarette and chokes as he sees the pretty woman in the blue and white checked dress step out onto the road into the traffic.

7.

The little girl holds on tightly to the handle bars at the front of the motor-cycle as they make the short journey across the city to take her mother and grandmother to work in the quilting factory. She has been sitting nestled in front of her brother on their family bike for as long as she can remember. Her body is the first in line and moves instinctively; leaning forward, now backwards, then side to side, as the bike speeds up and slows down. It is lunch time and the city streets are packed with others just like her family, each and every one on their way to elsewhere. Today they are not travelling fast but the little girl loves the tufts of soft air that caress her face as they weave and wind through the traffic. In fact, she enjoys it more when they are riding slowly, it gives her more time to take notice of what's going on in and around the streets. She waves to the elderly woman carrying the pineapples for sale as they pass her by. "Chào chi Cᴧong!", the little girl sings out. The elderly woman lifts her face from the ground ever so slightly and raises one hand in the air. The little girl stops breathing just for a moment, hoping that the bamboo yoke does not begin to tip and cause the elderly woman to stumble. She breathes out as the pole and the elderly woman remain steadfast and the little girl thinks and wonders, not for the first time, how someone so old could be so strong.

She turns to her left and notices her friend Mr Watson sitting on a park bench smoking a cigarette. Mr Watson lives in the flat upstairs from her and she knows Mr Watson is a business man because he leaves the house very early each morning wearing his navy suit. Mr Watson does not smile a lot and she thinks and wonders how someone who dresses and looks that serious must be a very smart man and he must be very good at his job if his boss allows to him eat lunch in the park each day. The little girl turns to her right and sees someone new on the street. A Western woman wearing a blue and white checked sundress is standing half way between Ninth and Hannepin across the road from the park. She looks very pretty, the little girls thinks and wonders, but why is she alone? The stoplight in front of them turns red and the little girl is pleased; she can take her time to watch the sweet looking woman in the strappy dress. She stares at her intently for a few moments and gently slaps her leg with her palm. The little girl recognises the loss and confusion clouding her face, it is an all too familiar a scene; the woman is trying to cross the road and the little girl sends her a silent blessing of luck. The light ahead turns green. The little girl leans to the left of the bike and turns her head backward to take one final look at the prettily dressed woman just in time to see her body thrown into the air as she steps out onto the road and into the path of a large scooter.

8.

The young man looks down anxiously at his watch. He is going to be late. Again. For his tutorial. He wonders sometimes why he still bothers to put in the effort to maintain his studies and whether in the end his university degree will be worth the long trek across the city each day. The traffic is hectic and normally he revels in the hum but today he feels completely trapped in the swarm of bikes which surround him. He is never going to get out of this jam, he is never going to get out of this place. He sighs and looks around him. The streets look the same as they did yesterday. And the day before that. And the day before that. He remembers as a child he thought the avenues and alley ways of his home town were full of mystery, and he his heart aches to feel that magic again. The sights, the sounds, the smells, the secrecy. "Xin chao Pham Van Bianh!" It is Nguyen CΛong, the elderly pineapple seller, calling to him from the other side of the road. The young man nods a brief acknowledgement to this old family friend. She has been walking along here since he was a little boy, carrying the same bamboo yoke, balancing the same wooden pales, taking the same path, along the same streets day in and day out without pause. He wonders, not for the first time, how everything in his life became so predictable and mundane. He shakes his head; his parents must have been prophetic, even his name means piecemeal and average.

His bike comes to a standstill and the young man looks around, yearning for an interruption. He is not surprised to see the business man is sitting on the park bench smoking a cigarette. He is there every day at the same time on the same seat wearing the same navy suit. The business man stares back at him in cool recognition. Neither know one another and yet there is a sense of familiarity that settles in the distance between them.

The young man sighs again as a family of five on a large scooter weave their way between him and the bikes that surround them. He never wants to be that man, completely responsible for the well-being of the two children perched at the front of their bike and the two women—he presumes one his wife and the other his mother—sitting straddled behind him. The scooter with the family of five represents a whole new layer of routine and regularity he is desperate to escape. The motorbike he is riding is larger than theirs, more powerful by far and he is confident that it will take him away to where he needs to be. The young man puts his head down and revs the engine. The motorbike surges forward and collides with a woman in a blue and white checked sundress who has stepped out onto the road in front of him. The young man feels the friction of rubber against skin as the front wheel makes contact with her body. He watches in horror as the impact sends the woman high into the air and he feels himself beginning to dry retch as he hears the dull thud of her body as it hits the concrete.

9.

From the opposite corner, a group of three academics have been watching the pretty young woman in the blue and white checked sundress with a great deal of interest. They are not so concerned with how she is going to cross the road but her presence. You see, they think they know her. They think they have seen her before—at other conferences related to ethnography, musicology and ethnomusicology. They think they are on the same intellectual circuit and yet there is something about her that they don't quite recognise because, they think, she is not, never has been and never will be invited into their group. They nod amongst each with certainty; we know this woman, but she is not one of us. But not being able to name her infuriates them. Unknown things cannot remain that way; they all agree that she must be labelled so that she can be known, controlled and catalogued away as irrelevant, a-part from them. They think amongst one another for a while, trying to remember in preference to un-forgetting.

The eldest among them, a distinguished silverback, cries, out suddenly. "A-ha! I've got it! It's *her*, I remember her from the conference last year". His head is bobbing up and down and small drops of spittle fly from his mouth.

The others look back at him in puzzlement and step back to void the spray. He startles Mr Watson the business man sitting on the park bench and the precarious pineapples carried by Nguyen CΛong falter at the sound.

"Don't you remember? She's the one who stood tall like a ballet dancer; hair in a bun, feet balancing her back straight, sheer stockings and a little black dress. She *performed* her paper; it wasn't a standard conference presentation at all—it was a *performance*".

The others are still unsure.

The silverback shakes his head, incredulous. "As soon as she began you could cut the tension in the room with a knife. For Pete's sake, she used the word 'I' and the two 'f' words—and I swear she looked me straight in the eye every time. *No-one* was comfortable listening and watching her speak. I mean, who does that?"

A light of recognition switches on. The others now know who they are talking about. Looking at the silverback in a manner mixed up with lust, logic and longing, one of the younger female academics among the group jumps in.

"Yes, I remember! I was Chair of that session", her words are overly animated, and she practically bows before him.

"At the end of her paper I asked if there were any questions and I'm pretty sure I heard a pin drop somewhere at the back of the room. I had no idea what to do".

There was a middle-aged man standing slightly a-part from the group who had been silent up until now. He clears his throat. "Well, you could have done your duty as chair and asked a question to get the conversation going".

The others stand and stare aghast. There is a slight accusatory tone to his words and they do not like it; not one little bit. He shrugs his shoulders and returns to his place of quiet.

"Me ask a question?" The younger female guffaws and giggles. She sounds like a horse. "Don't be ridiculous! I know my job as chair and I *might* have been able to ask something, anything but there was *nothing* academic about what she did. All that crap about theory as story and story as theory and where does she get off thinking that auto-ethnography is the only honest and heartfelt thing for us to do in our field?" She flings her hands in the air in exasperation. "Forget it, I don't even know why she bothered to come back again this year", she wags her finger in the air. "There's no room here for her".

The silverback reaches over and gently touches her back. "Absolutely right sweetie, she needs to watch her step".

They all turn to look at the pretty young woman in the blue and white checked sundress once more and gasp. She is no longer standing across from them but lying on the road, not moving. Bits and pieces of a large scooter lay on the ground around her and a young man is desperately pumping his hands on her chest in search of a heartbeat. A crowd of people have gathered around her and the traffic has stopped.

The silverback stares, disturbed by the pretty young woman in the blue and white checked sundress lying on the road *and* the disturbance she has created. He murmurs softly, "I guess I was right, she really *should* have minded which way she was walking, shouldn't she?"

"Well, at least she won't be getting in *our* way any time soon", the young woman's eyes glow green with satisfaction. Without a second glance she begins to steer herself and her companions away from the scene. The middle-aged man has not moved.

"What are you waiting for?" She asks him. "Come on, we're going to be late for our session".

The middle-aged man shakes his head. "No", he pauses. "We can't just leave her".

The young woman rolls her green eyes impatiently. "Look, there are others here, they'll take care of her".

The middle-aged man looks at her in disbelief and his heart pounds loudly. In that moment he sees that the pretty young woman in the blue and white checked is indeed a-not/her, outside from the inside and far far away elsewhere, and he has a choice to make.

He shakes his head again. "No, not this time…NO! I'm not coming with you—this time I'm done".

The silverback and the young woman look at one another, knowingly. "Suit yourself", the elderly academic says with finality and gives him a look which suggests that maybe, just maybe the middle-aged man has made an irreparable error of judgment.

The middle-aged man watches the pair walk away from him and then turns back to the pretty young woman in the blue and white checked sundress lying lifeless on the road. He remembers fragments of words he thinks he had heard her say at last year's conference. They moved him then and they move him now. "It takes a dead woman to begin", she had said. "Into danger then we must go", she had said. The middle-aged man wastes not a moment longer and runs across the road towards her. He pushes the young man roughly out of the way and lays his body down, so close next to her. He wraps his arms tightly around her and whispers in her ear, "I insist-er you to un-forget; return to this body, return to this woman who has been confiscated from you. Write yourself, your body must be heard (after Cixous, 1976, p. 880)".

10.

I watch myself in this moment of lying still on the road and see a dead woman in crisis. And still, even still, the self-same crisis of the self-same dead woman fetches and holds me there and here. Crisis brings and keeps me sitting still in the moment of writing the book-that I-do-not-write thinking and wondering about being dead and being both; that is, the crisis that is the dead woman, the crisis that is the book, and the book that is the crisis of the dead woman. I am in no mind to shake, sift and situate them a-part from one another and find it curious to think and wonder about them in this way. Thinking and wondering about the book-I-as-dead-woman-I-do-not-write which wants to speak, move, and turn words critically as autoethnography brings me to crisis. Without crisis I would not be in this moment of thinking and wondering critically; together they inhale and exhale on the edge that is the life of this story, breathing in and breathing out the instant at which this story begins to live. The dead woman is no longer still. Crisis takes and saves me in difficulty and danger, poised to face disaster, and always already experiencing dis-ease; a critical response affects and attends to crisis in a way that nothing else might, not even arrival. This critical autoethnography is perhaps no different than any other critical auto-ethnographic text. It is written from a place of personal-political-peda-gogical-philosophical crisis where writing about the crisis became critical.

Crisis number one. How to define critical. No matter how hard I try, this crisis keeps on re/turning. I thought I had put this particular crisis of definition to rest at the beginning of this chapter but here it is, again, so strong is the pull of this seemingly central and essential task to "proper" and "appropriate" academic writing. A wry smile crosses my face as I remember a similar crisis faced by Virginia Woolf as she pursued the truth in words written about the worlds of women. Her solution to the crisis of representation impasse: a notebook, a pencil, and "claws of steel and beak of brass" (1929/2001, p. 27).

Crisis number two. How to define critical autoethnography.

Crisis number three. How to define critical autoethnography and then write it.

Crisis number four. How to define critical autoethnography and then write it in a way which in and of itself lays bare the crisis.

Crisis number five. How to define critical autoethnography and then write it in a way which in and of itself lays bare the crisis in a manner which is critical.

Crisis number six. How to define critical autoethnography and then write it in a way which in and of itself lays bare the crisis in a manner which is critical because this w/riting might move close, *so close*.

Crisis number seven. Thinking and wondering that the crisis is not one, but two and in coming together, moving far beyond and yet closer to.

Seven crises so far which bring and keep me here on the critical edge of writing autoethnography in the book-I-do-not-write. I cast my eyes over the list of crises and realise it is not yet finished; it too is still in draft, waiting and watching for that which remains to arrive; for the moment of *arrivance* as Cixous (1997) would call it. Arrivance spares arrival; arriv-ance is movement, arrivance does not stand still, arrivance insists on unfinishing. I think and wonder about the ethical necessity that sits with writing in arrivance; and that perhaps, this is exactly what critically writing in-as-through crisis will do. I think and wonder how arrival is an ending and how the arrival of crisis is not the place where I want to end writing critical autoethnography. I think and wonder how crisis *arrivance* in writing is always already a beginning towards criticality.

Crisis number eight. A chapter outline which no longer fits the book-I-do-not-write.

Crisis number nine. A chapter outline which no longer fits the book-I-do-not-write because the book-I-do-not-write is no longer that book.

Crisis number ten. What exactly is the book-I-do-not-write?

Crisis number eleven. And if I can't say what it is, then how can it be written?

11.

Siting and wondering about writing about critical autoethnography in the book-I-do-not-write I think and wonder about marmalade sandwiches. When I was a little girl, one of my favourite story book characters was a bear called Paddington. Paddington, who featured in more than 20 books written by Michael Bond and illustrated by Peggy Fortnum, came to life in 1958. Bond was inspired by newsreels of child evacuees with labels around their necks sitting alone on suitcases on cold train platforms leaving London in World War 2 and the story of Paddington goes something like this. A small and lone bear from the deepest darkest Peru is sent to London by his recently widowed Aunt Lucy who has gone to live in the Home for Retired Bears in Lima. She attaches a note to his coat lapel that reads, "Please look after this Bear, thank you", hoping that someone will care for him. The Brown family take him home to 32 Windsor Gardens and decide to call him Paddington after the train station where he was found.

The small English-speaking bear wears an old brown hat, carries a tattered suitcase, sports a blue duffle jacket with large pockets and wooden buttons, and is ever so fond of marmalade. I loved Paddington's coat and wished for one just like it. My childhood home located in the Central Highlands in Victoria is cold, bone cold; complete with grey skies, lazy winds and drizzle, the cold is a constant companion for what feels like nine months or more of each year. Standing waiting for the bus after school I imagined that the chilly winter air was slowly but surely freezing me from the inside out. I fancied I could feel the cold sliding and creeping around deep down up and around my mind and body, and I always thought if I had a thick duffle coat just like Paddington's my thinking heart might find some warmth. I didn't mind if it wasn't blue, any colour would do, as long as it was a duffle coat with wooden buttons and large pockets. Most important of all though were the pockets; they needed to be big enough to fit a marmalade sandwich. Paddington's strategy for dealing with the crises that life brought his way was to always have a marmalade sandwich on hand, preferably orange marmalade. At critical moments inbetween life and death, all Paddington needed to do was reach inside his pocket and pull out his marmalade sandwich, and voilá! Said sandwich consumed and crisis averted. Paddington's pocket, large enough to hold a marmalade sandwich, was a pocket of joy. Writing critical autoethnography for me is like wearing a duffle coat, fashioned in the style of Paddington's, and reaching inside the self-same pocket to find joy. Sticky, sweet, spreadable, scruffy and always already surprising. Writing to encounter, embrace and become entangled by pockets of joy amidst the crises.

12.

I reach inside the pocket of my coat, hoping to find a much-needed metaphorical marmalade sandwich to pull me out of the trouble, which seems to have wheedled and needled its way into my thinking and wondering about critical autoethnography, to become the defining feature this chapter. Instead I find a screwed-up piece of white paper; torn and bleeding with black ink. It's a list and the handwriting mine. There is no date on it and I am one, upset that there is no sweet relief to be found only naked scraps of thinking and wondering on a page, and two, frustrated once again by my seeming inability to dutifully document said crumbs of what might just be insight-full iotas of intuition. Resisting the temptation to toss the paper in the rubbish bin, I re/turn to read—more care-fully this time—the list I have written. This list has lines about critical autoethnography on it, lines with words which seem to be categorising, coding, and concepting what critical autoethnography may or may not be.

♥ Let's start with Carolyn Ellis. Do you remember when you met her? It was 2009 at the music and autoethnography conference. She embodied the *very* researching and writing practice she came to speak about; she laughed, she cried, she sat quietly and listened, she spoke when she felt she had something to say, something that might make us all think and wonder anew. Most of all I remember her talking as an ethnographer about the centrality of the social to the self, and the self to the social. While *ethnography* may be thought of as a way of thinking about and being in the cultural world as an involved participant (Ellis, 2004, p. 26), *autoethnography* refers to "writing about the personal and its relationship to culture" (Ellis, 2004, p. 37). And much of what she has written emphasises this relationality. "Doing autoethnography", she writes, "involves a back-and-forth movement between experiencing and examining a vulnerable self and revealing the broader context of the experience" (2007, p. 14).

One scrap of writing leads to another academic remainder, a conversation sequestered and shelved away in secret.

Ruth: It is far from easy to think up interesting ways to locate oneself in one's own text (Behar, 1996, p. 13)…Since I have put myself in the ethnographic picture, readers feel they have come to know me. They have poured their own feelings into their construction of me and in that way come to identify with me, or at least their fictional images of who I am… When you write vulnerably, others respond vulnerably (1996, p. 16).

Elizabeth: I remember the first time I put myself into an ethnographic text—it was my PhD thesis in ethnomusicology. I had done everything I thought I was expected to do in a music ethnography in my discipline; introduced the performers and their culture, provided thick descriptions of song, dance and performance, specified my list of Yanyuwa musical terminology, and included detailed musical transcriptions and analyses. Yet, I knew it was not quite complete, I felt that something was missing, something important. Very close to submission I realised that the something was not a *thing* at all but a some-*one*, and it was my-self—my-self in relation. I wrote, "I am a woman, an ethnomusicologist and a member of the extended Yanyuwa family. These three aspects of my life closely intersect and one can never be free of the others. My work is at once personal and professional. The literary style I have adopted in this work is as close as I can come to portraying the people with whom I have worked and the music they make while remaining true to my sense of family obligation" (Mackinlay, 1998, p. 82). I felt bare, exposed and uncertain—my secret was out—but hiding such being-in-relation was no longer an ethico-onto-epistemological option for me.

Ruth: To write vulnerably is to open a Pandora's box (Behar, 1996, p. 19). This anthropology isn't for the soft-hearted (1996, p. 24). Clearly, vulnerability isn't for everyone. Nor should it be (1996, p. 25).

Elizabeth: I think I learnt that lesson the hard way.

She pauses as memories of being ridiculed for wearing her heart on her sleeve in the words she spoke in her academic presentations, of her work being dismissed as too emotional and not rational enough to be considered an ethnographic truth, and for being ignored because she had crossed a line in her professional and personal life.

Hélène nods: "Every woman has known the torment of getting up to speak. Her heart racing, at times entirely lost for words, ground and language slipping away—that's how daring a feat, how great a transgression it is" (Cixous, 1976, p. 880).

Elizabeth: There's nothing more frightening than feeling the floor open up and threaten to swallow you whole because of the self you've just secret-ed. When you know as soon as your foot removes itself from your mouth that you've said too much and realise just a moment too late that now the secret has escaped, it cannot be railed in, concealed or taken back.

Ruth: "I am tired of hiding, tired of misspent and knotted energies, tired of the hypocrisy, and tired of acting as though I have something to hide" (Behar, 1996, loc 161).

Dorothy: "I choose what to tell and what to conceal. I design and calculate the impact I want to have. When I sit down to make my stories I know very well that I want to take the reader by the throat, break her heart, and heal it again" (Allison, 2013, loc 2590).

Ruth: Call it sentimental, call it Victorian and nineteenth century... Ethnography, anthropology and autoethnography "that doesn't break your heart, just isn't worth doing anymore" (Behar, 1996, loc 2380).

Hélène: And that's the moment when woman's "flesh speaks true. She lays herself bare. In fact, she physically materializes what she's thinking; she signifies it with her body" (Cixous, 1976, p. 881).

Elizabeth: And in doing so, as you've so gently reminded me Hélène, "she draws her story into history" (Cixous, 1976, p. 881). At that moment of arrival, some-*thing* happens because some-*one* happens to be there with some-*bodies*—when the connectedness between the self and other, the self and the social, the self and experience which comes from vulner-ability—begins to make and becomes to move.

Virginia: These are, to my mind, moments of being. "The truth is, I get nearer feelings in writing than in walking [sic]—I think: graze the bone; enjoy the expression; have them out of me; make them a little credible to myself; I daresay suppresses something, so that after all I'm doing what amounts to confiding…[we] must make a great try for it!"(1980, pp. 239–240).

Hélène: Yes! "Because she arrives, vibrant, over and over again" (Cixous, 1976, p. 882) to write through her body with a voice that cuts through to touch you, affect you, urge you, launch you, laugh you, and love *you*.

Elizabeth sits there for a moment, somewhat overwhelmed. She picks up her pen and begins to write.

♥ The descriptor "analytic" autoethnography often comes hand in hand with discussions of what autoethnography is; I keep coming across it and yet the more I read in, around and about it. I am beginning to realise that the kind of autoethnography I seek to embody, the kind of *critical* autoethnography, is not the same as analytic autoethnography: Analytic autoethnography seems bent (and not in the Butlerian sense of the word) on distancing the writer from the work. This kind of autoeth-nography might be described as distanced observation with a fondness for generalising, an ethnographic research and writing practice that looks outward without emotion; disconnected, disembodied, depersonalised, depoliticised, the prefixes dis- and de- gather on masse. In a word then, this kind of autoethnography might be described he(art)less. This is not the kind of autoethnography I hope to write, because without heart, it is not *kind* at all. I am reminded, not for the first time, of Lather's warning that the hold that the "centre" has on the world is formidable; she is talk-ing explicitly about positivism in collusion with logic and reason, capital T truths and objectivity, and rigour and validity. It is hard not to feel despair. In some ways analytic autoethnography is clever; it makes way for the "centre" to creep and crawl its way into the margins in order to claim scientific authority while conveniently ignoring the sinister way in which such slithering and skulking slowly but surely seeks to smother the emotion, affect and vulnerability inherent within autoethnographic praxis. I think and wonder how Behar (1996, loc 365), writing over a decade ago, laments that while ethnographers and anthropologists are quite willing and able to make those whom they have observed vulnerable, about the vulnerablity of the self and matters of the heart, "we are still barely able to speak". I cannot imagine an autoethnography which is he(art)less because I think and wonder how an autoethnography without he(art) has stopped moving towards the very thing it is seeking.

♥ To be two; this seems to be a constant in autoethnographic work—self/social, inwards/outwards, back/forth, past/present—always a doubleness. Stacy Holman Jones (2005, p. 764) notes this too, that is, to engage in autoethnography is to be two and to perform a delicate balancing act between self and culture, flux and movement, story and context, fiction and fact, art and science, writer and reader. I think and wonder how "doubleness" is one of the re/turns in autoethnography and the autoethnographic work I find myself engaged in. It turns around, it turns the I/you/we around to re/turn in a process which I think now of as un-forgetting.

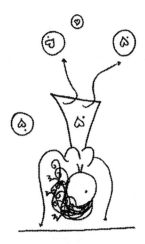

Fig. 9.1 Juggling

♥ Perhaps the trick to writing autoethnography is to be able to juggle; the word juggle in and of itself is multiple. Managing multiple things at once in a context which is precarious, assembling these multiplicities in a search to make meaning, and being able to do so in a manner which resembles the art of juggling. An im/possible ask and task perhaps and I think and wonder how being upset down might just be the best position to create a scene, tell the story, weave intricate connections, evoke experience and theory, and then ruthlessly let them all go (Holman Jones, 2005, p. 765). All of the balls that have been juggled fly into the air and I/you/we stand waiting with baited breath to see how they might fall. This is the moment when critical autoethnography becomes writing, and yet, there is always already uncertainty around what it will be. Will the writing take the form of a short story, poetry, fiction, novel, photographic or visual essay, script, personal essay, journal, fragmented and layered writing, and social science prose (Ellis, 2004, p. 38), or perhaps all of these things at once?

♥Always moving; a type of messy, uncertain, engaging, emotional, thoughtful traffic of writing which ultimately seeks to *move*; to set in motion, to motor a-way backwards and forward to tell stories. Virginia Woolf often likened writing to travelling in and through traffic, entranced and intrigued by how it feels to be swept away in perpetual motion. "What I like, or one of the things I like, about motoring", she muses, "is the sense it gives one of lighting accidentally, like a voyager who touches another planet with the tip of his toe, upon scenes which would have gone on, have always gone on, will go on, unrecorded, save for this chance glimpse. Then it seems to me that I am allowed to see the heart of the world uncovered for a moment" (p. 153). I have always loved the final words she uses here, writing to uncover the *heart* of the world. I think and wonder how close, so close, critical autoethnography seeks to move towards these moments of being that Woolf speaks so poignantly and passionately about. In much the same a-way as Woolf motoring through traffic, critical autoethnography seeks to move on; to move us all on, Turner insists; "we show our workings out, we display the process of our struggles along with the detritus left along the way as we work to move ourselves (and others) along the personal, social and political road" (2018, p. 7).

I turn over the page, expecting to find more lists and lines and words and instead I find something else; or perhaps more aptly, some-*one* else. It's "Ms Autoethnography", a character I drew some time ago to try to imagine what autoethnography might be like if she were a person; an embodied, corporeal, affective and material presence.

Fig. 9.2   Ms Autoethnography

I sit back and look at the image of Ms Autoethnography and begin to un-forget the moment of drawing her. I un-forget that in *that* particular moment, I desperately wanted to *be* the critical autoethnographer I imagined she embodied. Drawing her was a-way to bring the words and worlds I had found myself thinking and wondering and writing about as an ethnographer to escape from secret into life, a-way to draw "not the person, but the precious in that person" (Cixous, 1993, p. 96).

As the memory of her making lifts from there and then on the page to here and now, I un-forget the moment I gave her breath life; the moment

I introduced Ms Autoethnography to my academic colleagues and community.

It is 9 am and my breath creates a small cloud of condensation as I step inside the chilly wooden panelled room. I shake off the instinctive shiver which threatens to re/turn me outside as I notice the portraits of past male Deans hanging on the walls, stony faced and disapproving. Not for the first time, Virginia Woolf's (1929/2001, p. 28) thinking and wondering about the unpleasantness of being locked out of rooms dominated by the presence of white men and her conclusion that perhaps it is worse to be locked in alongside them, accompanies me. In mimicry of her, I decide to crumple up the images of Beadles walking on lush grass (1929/2001, p. 6) and dining on partridges washed down with fine wine while women like me are confined to tramp upon gravel and condemned to eat stringy beef and prunes that being here conjures; for "time flaps on the mast… and there are things I ought to do" (Woolf, 1980, p. 233). I busy myself with the busy-ness of turning on the technology I need for my presentation and it begins to buzz in anticipation. The room soon warms and fills with the humming earnestness of postgraduate students balancing the beginnings of research projects in their heads, computers and coffee in their hands, and a sure but quiet uncertainty in their hearts about what might happen next. I think and wonder how many have done the pre-workshop reading and writing I sent them.

There is nothing more theoretical or analytical than a good story
An autoethnography text-work-play-shop
Pre- text-work-play-shop readings
Ellis, C. (2004). Class one: The call of autoethnographic stories. In C. Ellis, *The ethnographic I: A methodological novel about autoethnography* (pp. 24–57). Walnut Creek, CA: AltaMira Press.
Mackinlay, E. (2009). In memory of music research: An autoethnographic, ethnomusicological and emotional response to grief, death and loss in the Aboriginal community at Borroloola, Northern Territory. In B-L. Bartleet & C. Ellis (Eds), *Musical autoethnographies: Making autoethnography sing/ making music personal* (pp. 225–244). Bowen Hills, QLD: Australian Academic Press.
Pre- text-work-play-shop writing task

Imagination (Ginny) begins another day in the office

Imagine you meet Autoethnography in person—it might be a coffee shop, in a meeting, at the library—you choose the setting.
What is he/she like? Are they male/female/other? What is the experience of meeting Autoethnography like and how do you respond as a researcher?
Remember to fire your internal critic, write as though no-one is watching and relish the opportunity to explore your voice as a writer/researcher/ story-teller. Bring your writing with you to our autoethnography text-work-play-shop.

mermaidliz21@gmail.com
Liz Mackinlay

The first slide appears on the overhead projector screen behind me; it's a definitional explanation of the origins of the term "autoethnography" and as soon as it appears I hear keys tapping and pens scribbling as members of the audience begin to dutifully take notes.

auto - ethno - graphy

personal experience + cultural experience + description and analysis

Fig. 9.3 Lecture

An introductory slide providing a basic definition of autoethnography is as traditional as I am prepared to go, for after all, shouldn't a presentation on autoethnography perform the praxis?

"There is no doubt that thinking and wondering about the word 'auto-ethno-graphy' is an important step to being and becoming in relation to this kind of research and writing practice", I say with a smile. "And now that we have the formalities out of the way, I would like to move a-way from playing by the usual rules of academic engagement in this context to make room for you think and wonder about autoethnography in an embodied way".

With a flourish, I strip away the sheet covering a small structure in the centre of the stage to reveal a dress mannequin. The sound of bodies shifting papers, portable devices and positions in seats permeates the pause this gesture creates.

Fig. 9.4 Mannequin

A woman has been waiting patiently and in secret behind the wire frame and pops her head out.

"Are you ready for me yet?"

"One moment!" I call back.

"Just reminding you…I'm waiting…naked back here. Naked, that means, no clothes!"

"I heard you!"

"I'm waiting for the flesh of experience to breathe life into and onto my bare bones!" She replies in a sing-song voice.

I place a small brown and worn suitcase in front of the dress mannequin and turn to ad/dress the audience.

"In a moment, I am going to introduce you to my friend but first, I need to give her time to dress", I add with a wink.

"Are you ready yet?" I ask her cheekily. "I hope you like what I've brought for you to wear—I went to all of your favourite fashion outlets".

The woman groans from behind the dress mannequin. "I honestly don't mind, at this point any kind of a/effective material and/or materiality will do".

"Well, here's a not-so-subtle lavender frock in heavy knit fabric. The decorative floral weave and weft show-cases a blend of elegant and exploratory poetry on the bodice. The design is made complete by plunging into a deep-water neckline and a touch of feminist lace one the sleeves and hem. It's brave, vulnerable and reveals just enough heart".

An arm appears from behind the sewing model and grabs the outfit. "Thank *you*!"

I give her a moment to put on the dress.

"Any chance of some underwear to go with that?"

I silently kick myself—I knew that she would be looking for something more intimate to wear and share but I had trouble finding lingerie which would care, feel, empathise and *do* something more.

"Sorry", I mumble. "But I do have the perfect pair of shoes!"

I hand her a pair of rebellious black leather knee length boots with a heel that is not too chunky and boring but high enough to stand out in a crowd. These are *sense*-able shoes that ground her attire firmly to the social and cultural structures of the everyday.

"Now, these are *nice*!"

"Wait until you see the hat!"

Her hat is a hand-made beanie. My Auntie Florence made it for me from homespun and dyed wool. It is pale pink in colour and I un-forget the smell of beetroot lingering in her kitchen during autumn as she prepared the wool she would use in her winter knitting. I loved this beanie the moment I saw it; everything about it screams resistance. The weave is ribbed, coarse, unconventional and a distinct challenge to what is expected in a feminine headpiece. This beanie is brave and out of place in so far as it willfully gets in the way of the cold truths of positivist thinking by keeping the wearer toasty warm.

"Mmm, I wasn't sure at first but this beanie…well this beanie is just perfect for me", the woman murmurs from behind the mannequin.

The final addition to the outfit is a small Tiffany and Co. platinum diamond encrusted heart pendant with matching hoop earrings. I know this jewellery is extravagant, but both were a gift from a friend to remind me in my darkest never to un-forget; un-forget that the he(art)ful words and worlds we write as autoethnographers are beacons of being in and through relation, being in and through hope, and being in and through change.

"Ta da!" The woman steps out from behind the dress mannequin. How do I look?"

I turn to the audience, "And without further ado, it is my pleasure and privilege to introduce you to Ms Autoethnography!"

No-one moves, no-one says anything, no-one does anything but stare. Disbelief, suspicion, and defensiveness hang uncomfortably in the air.

"Well, the *polite* thing to do would be to welcome her here", I say pointedly to my academic colleagues and community which seem to have forgotten the matter of manners.

Ms Autoethnography sighs and places her hands on her hips. She has been here and now before.

"It's OK, Liz, I know that not everyone thinks my style is appropriate. I deliberately place emphasis on re-uniting the personal with the physical, emotional, mental, relational, social and cultural dimensions of everyday life in my outfit (Ellis, 2004, p. xix). I am constantly seeking to make my autoethnography *feel* true and real *like* life which is inherently messy, entangled and contradictory. It's easy to un-forget what my clothing is attempting to do—that is, to observe the self-observing the social, so that I can come to a better understanding of the phenomena I began gazing at in the first place", Ms Autoethnography shrugs. "And that is what you see here, my body thinking and wondering and writing in a way I would like to think is at once appealing but apprehending".

I scan the crowd and sense a subtle shift; ears, eyes, minds and maybe, maybe even hearts, are beginning to open. Ms Autoethnography has noticed too, and she reads this as a moment of invitation.

"Yes, I know what you're thinking and wondering, where can I source an academic outfit just like this one?" Her voice chimes with optimism. "My answer is most simply and complexly this. Re/turn to embody those pieces of clothing-as-experience-as-life which re/present who, what and why you stand for in the words and worlds you write. I'm a fan of thrift shops—call me a second-hand woman, I don't mind—but the lives we have are those we live and being and becoming autoethnographic means re/turning the scenes from there and then to here and now so that we may write them into meaning for, with, through and to our-selves and others. Autoethnography is a method of living and re/turning meaning to life. Next time I'm heading down to my local Vinnie's, you're most welcome to join me—I think it's worth at least a visit, don't you?"

13.

"The time has come for us to close", Stacy says with a sigh and the room exhales in collective agreement. "This conference might be winding down but we, as critical autoethnographers, *we* are waking up", she snaps her fingers rhythmically and with urgency, calling us to attention, calling us to account, calling us to action.

"We are waking up to the readiness of the moment. In our work as critical autoethnographers we rehearse the world we would want and in doing so, we begin again—we re/turn in turn to do the work of creating something new and thereby build a monument to waking up".

"Life is a small gesture and so is critical autoethnography", says Anne.

References

Ahmed, S. (2010). Feminist killjoys (and other willful subjects). *The Scholar and Feminist Online, 8*(3), 1–10.

Ahmed, S. (2011). Willful parts: Problem characters or the problem of character. *New Literary History, 42*, 231–253.

Allison, D. (2013). *Skin: Talking about sex, class and literature* (Kindle ed.). New York, NY: Open Road, Integrated Media.

Arendt, H. (1983). *Men in dark times.* New York, NY: Harcourt Brace & Company.

Behar, R. (1996). *The vulnerable observer.* Boston, MA: Beacon Press.

Bochner, A., & Ellis, C. (2014). *Evocative autoethnography: Writing lives and telling stories.* New York, NY: Routledge.

Boylorn, R. (2018). Writing lesson(s). In L. Turner, N. P. Short, A. Grant, & T. E. Adams (Eds.), *International perspectives on autoethnographic research and practice* (pp. 228–233). New York, NY: Routledge.

Cixous, H. (1976). The laugh of the Medusa (K. Cohen & P. Cohen, Trans.). *Signs, 1*(4), 875–893.

Cixous, H. (1993). Without end no state of drawingness no, rather: The executioner's taking off (C. MacGillivray, Trans.). *New Literary History, 24*(1), 91–103.

Cixous, H. (1997). My Algeriance: In other words, to depart not to arrive from Algeria. *Triquarterly, 100*, 259–279.

De la Garza, S. (2014). Mindful heresy, holo-expression, and poiesis: An autoethnopgraphic response to the orthodoxies of interpersonal and cultural life. In R. Boylorn & M. Orbe (Eds.), *Critical autoethnography: Intersecting cultural identities in everyday life* (pp. 209–221). Walnut Creek, CA: Left Coast Press.

Ellis, C. (2004). *The ethnographic I.* Walnut Creek, CA: AltaMira Press.

Ellis, C. (2007). Telling stories, revealing lives: Relational ethics in research with intimate others. *Qualitative Inquiry, 13*(3), 3–29.

Holman Jones, S. (2005). Autoethnography: Making the personal political. In N. Denzin & Y. Lincoln (Eds.), *The Sage handbook of qualitative research* (3rd ed., pp. 62–793). Thousand Oaks, CA: Sage Publications.

Holman Jones, S., Adams, T. E., & Ellis, C. (2013). Introduction: Coming to know autoethnpgraphy as more than method. In S. Holman Jones, T. E. Adams, & C. Ellis (Eds.), *Handbook of autoethnography* (pp. 17–48). Walnut Creek, CA: Left Coast Press.

Mackinlay, E. (2009). In memory of music research: An autoethnographic, ethnomusicological and emotional response to grief, death and loss in the Aboriginal community at Borroloola, Northern Territory. In B. L. Bartleet & C. Ellis (Eds.), *Music autoethnographies: Making autoethnography sing/making music personal* (pp. 225–244). Bowen Hills, QLD: Australian Academic Press.

Mackinlay, E. N. (1998). *For our mother's song we sing: Yanyuwa women performers and composers of anguyulnguyul.* Unpublished doctoral thesis, University of Adelaide, Department of Music Studies.

Stewart, K. (2013). An autoethnography of what happens. In S. Holman Jones, T. E. Adams, & C. Ellis (Eds.), *Handbook of autoethnography* (pp. 659–668). Walnut Creek, CA: Left Coast Press Inc.

Turner, L. (2018). Introduction: A place to start. In L. Turner, N. P. Short, A. Grant, & T. E. Adams (Eds.), *International perspectives on autoethnographic research and practice* (pp. 228–233). New York, NY: Routledge.

Woolf, V. (1929/2001). *A room of one's own.* New York, NY: Harcourt, Brace, Jovanovich.

Woolf, V. (1980). *The diary of Virginia Woolf, Volume III: 1925–1930.* London: Hogarth Press.

10

Writing, an Ethical Conversation

*If I choose to publish books, that's my own look out. I must take the
consequences.*
Woolf (2002, p. 69)
But the balance between truth and fantasy must be careful.
Woolf ([Diary entry 22 October, 1927], 1980, p. 162)
Where, I asked myself, picking up a notebook and a pencil, is truth?
Woolf (1929/2001, p. 29)
*It was impossible to make head or tail of it, I decided…my own notebook
rioted with the wildest of contradictory jottings. It was distressing, it was
bewildering, it was humiliating. Truth had run through my fingers. Every
drop had escaped.*
Woolf (1929/2001, p. 35)

© The Author(s) 2019
E. Mackinlay, *Critical Writing for Embodied Approaches*,
https://doi.org/10.1007/978-3-030-04669-9_10

Fig. 10.1 Got ethics?

1.

Got ethics?
I whisper my enquiry quietly.
An uncomfortable silence descends upon the room like a heavy and damp woollen blanket.
Cold, clammy, and itchy.
I watch mind-as-body-as-mind positions shift in an attempt to ease the scratching.
Legs cross and uncross themselves in an attempt to settle feet that jiggle up and down in an edgy dance.
Blushing faces look downwards in an attempt to hide from the question.
If I don't look at *you*, I hear you say,
Then you won't be able to look at me.
You won't be able to see me; *really* see me.
You won't be able to look into my eyes.

You won't be able to see the secrets that are hiding truths.
You won't be able to see the truths that are hiding the answers you seek.

Got ethics?
I ask again, a little louder.
I want to make sure my question is heard.
Blank eyes stare back at me.
Avoid at all costs.
Ignorance is bliss.
Don't mention the c word.
Or the f word for the matter.
Do you even know what they are?
What goes on in the field, stays in the field.
Never mind the field not-es; they become field nots.
If nobody names it, it remains nothing.
No-body, no-thing.

Got ethics?
If no-body will answer no-thing
I decide I will ask myself.
Why is this question full of such angst?
It's angst-ridden
The question is riddled with angst, they need not even say.
The angst sits there, in and of itself, riddling away.
Once diagnosed, the question died quickly, riddled as it was with angst.
So rapidly was it riddled in fact that there was no time to answer it.
Once named as angst the question became a riddle in and of itself
Impossible to answer not right, impossible to answer not wrong.
What happens if I am either?
Can I un-forget the moment I first asked myself to answer?

2.

"Research merit and integrity, respect, beneficence and justice. These are the four ethical principles which guide our research *and* the way that we review research applications for ethical approval", I explain.

I am an invited as guest at this meeting today in my role as Chair of Ethics in the Faculty for low and negligible risk research involving humans and Deputy Chair of our University wide committee for review of high risk applications. Today I've been asked specifically to speak to the changes and initiatives we are undertaking in our Faculty in relation to the ethical approval of research to ensure that our processes are expedient, and our practice represents research excellence. The reception to my discussion so far has been, well at best, frosty. My experience as an ethics reviewer and chair of review boards over the past few years has taught me that, while I might like and want to be viewed as a guide, mentor and enabler of ethical research, the majority of my colleagues see me as the enemy, a bureaucratic enforcer of rules and regulations aimed at hindering and halting their research. What is so threatening and terrifying that sits, I think and wonder, behind the question "Got ethics?" I sigh, battle worn and weary before our discussion has even begun.

The academics sitting around the table sit and stare. Their faces are still and stony, arms are folded hard and tight across their bodies in a gesture that screams they are now in defend at all cost mode. Deep frown lines make a criss-cross patterns on their foreheads, and I fancy if I look closely enough, the markings etched there spell the word "hostile". The mood emanating from the dark suits is conservative and cold and I am conscious, so very conscious, that this is a context where I need to be care-full.

A young male academic from the School of Social Science puts up his hand.

"Look, I think I can say on behalf of everyone, we don't *need* a lecture on ethics. I…I mean *we* just need to go back to a form and a process which understands, differentiates and is considerate of what we do as Social Scientists and that our way of researching requires a different kind of ethical clearance procedure than the kind of research done in the hard sciences", he mansplains.

"I understand that the new ethical clearance form is different and requires a different approach", I begin my response care-fully. "The ethics procedures we have in place now are different in so far as not only are we engaged in an institutional ethics process, in focussing on the four ethical principles for conducting research, that process in and of itself is asking researchers to think, as much as is possible, about 'process ethics' or 'situational ethics'—the kinds of on-going ethical decision making which takes place during the 'doing' of research", I say with confidence. One of my agendas in taking up the ethics service roles of Chair is to enact a distinctly feminist ethical sense- and response-ability for embedding an attentiveness to "relational ethics" in the application, review and approval of research.

He does not look convinced. "You see, there's the problem. No-one on the ethics committee understands our *situation* and what we do in *research situations*; we do ethnography, we enter into relationships with people to collect data from them via interviews, observations and fieldwork".

I look at him incredulously; putting aside my own long engagement as an ethnographer in research, the mis-informed assumptions about who, what and why people become reviewers of ethics applications, sit on ethical review boards and the kinds of experience and expertise they bring to these roles he has just shared, is disappointingly dismissive and denigrating.

I remind myself, just in time, to be care-full before asking, "And your point is?"

"Well, we want the ethics review process to be done in House; back in our School, on our own form, reviewed by our own colleagues and friends. That way we can avoid unnecessary delays and get on with core business, the reason, may I remind you", he points his finger in my direction, "why we are all here as academics in a university—to *do* research".

"Thanks for sharing your perspective", I say as politely as I can. "However, there is no going back. We are in a change moment where we can think differently about research, differently about our relationships and response-abilities to the people we work with in and through our research, and therefore think differently about what this looks like as ethical research practice".

"So, you are trying to tell me that we have to just put up with a form which is not ethnographically friendly, to be reviewed by no-bit-no-bodies who know no-thing about ethnography with no-certainty of approval?" His face has begun to turn a deep shade of red.

"I think you and I have a different interpretation of…"

"This is the biggest crock of you know what…change for change sake, you can't seriously have just said that!" Small droplets of saliva fly from his mouth. He stands up and roughly pushes his chair away from the table, spitting his words at me like sharp bullets. "Well, you leave us with no choice—I guess we are all going to have to become *auto*-ethnographers, researching the self won't *need* ethical clearance!"

3.

An autoethnographic moment: Written by a Chair of Ethical Review and critical autoethnographer	An autoethnographic moment: Written by a Critical Autoethnographer applying for ethics
She walks away from the meeting in despair.	She walks away from the meeting in despair.
She worries about the misunderstanding applicants seem to hold about autoethnography.	She worries about the misunderstanding the Ethics Review Committee holds about autoethnography.
She knows that doing autoethnography *sounds* like an easy way to side-step Ethical Review but if she knows *anything* about autoethnography, she knows that it does not eliminate ethical concerns or the need to engage with others. Quite the contrary, it can lead to more and more complex ethical dilemmas.	She knows there is no easy way to side-step Ethical Review, particularly because, if she knows *anything* about autoethnography, you would know that it does not eliminate ethical concerns or the need to engage with others. Quite the contrary, it can lead to more and more complex ethical dilemmas.
She sighs. It concerns her that applicants do not understand the ethical complexities of doing autoethnographic research and do not account for the entanglements of self and other in their applications—after all, writing about selves always involves writing about others (Ellis, 2009) because we are *dialogic* subjects always and already in relation.	She sighs. It concerns her that she will not be able to convey the ethical complexities of doing autoethnographic research and that the Ethics Review Committee will not be able to understand the entanglements of self and other in their review of her application—after all, writing about selves always involves writing about others (Ellis, 2009) because we are *dialogic* subjects always and already in relation.
She and other members of her Ethics Review Committees are keenly aware of the need to take into consideration and respond to the dynamic research environment of autoethnography which is at once field and text, contextual and contingent, relational and reflexive (Tullis, 2013, p. 247).	She is keenly aware that autoethnography presents a dynamic research environment of which is at once field and text based, contextual and contingent, relational and reflexive (Tullis, 2013, p. 247) and feels that Ethics Review Committees need to understand this more fully.

She wishes that applicants would take more time to explain the ethical complexities of autoethnographic research, for example, the way in which informed consent will be sought and given from others.	She wishes Ethics Review Committees would take time to understand the ethical complexities of autoethnographic research, for example, the way in which informed consent will be sought and given from others. Writing about the past vs the present, the content, and how prevalent others are in the texts are good questions they might ask when reviewing (Tullis, 2013, p. 249).
And then there is the first principle of "do no harm" and questioning if the risks outweigh the benefits. She thinks and wonders that this is a central ethical question for autoethnography, particularly given that in telling the stories of self and other in-relation, both are incredibly vulnerable. Here "codes of confidentiality" (Chang, 2008, p. 68) and the "ethics of consequences" are everywhere (Tullis, 2013, p. 249) and autoethnography becomes a risky research process.	And then there is the issue of our ethical response-abilities to identifiable others, some of whom are family and friends, some may be alive, and some might have passed away (Ellis, 2009). She thinks and wonders how transparency, availability, dialogue and care are all strategies for engaging with the "ethics of consequences" that telling stories and lives in autoethnography bring into focus.
She understands that sometimes autoethnographers have difficulties in conveying *all* of this in writing in the form submitted to the Ethics Review Board.	She understands that somewhere and somehow, she will need to convey *all* of this in writing in a form to the Ethics Review Board. She knows that this is going to be difficult because autoethnographers don't think they are more ethical or have got the ethics right because of the ways we try to link the personal-political-cultural. Quite the opposite; we live with tensions, our research stories and research are *never* finished, and uncertainty is a condition that has almost become our mantle (Douglas & Carless, 2013, p. 97).
She sighs again. She is disappointed that Ethics Reviews Committees are often thought of as the arch enemy of autoethnographic researchers.	She sighs again. She is disappointed that Ethics Reviews Committees are not friends of autoethnography.
She is dismayed that many applicants appear to have little or no knowledge of the history behind why we have Ethics Review Committees.	She is dismayed that members of the Ethics Review Committee seem to have no experience of or expertise in autoethnography.

There are national guidelines and statements and regulations and legislation that the Ethical Review of research must follow; she has done the training and is fully aware of the responsibilities and obligation the University holds.

There are a myriad of documents to read and adhere to when filling out the form for Ethical Review; she has done the training.

She wishes that autoethnographic applicants would see her and her colleagues on the Ethics Review Committees as being in a position to guide or mentor through collegial conversations.

She wishes that the Chair and members of the Ethics Review Committee could play role of guide or mentor rather than guard and micro-manager.

She understands institutional ethics and ethical review to be a social movement which places extra-ordinary value on the preciousness of human life and the right each and every person has to respect and dignity, choice and agency, beneficence and justice in the research process.

She understands institutional ethics and ethical review of research to be a tick the box exercise which can never account for the extra-ordinary value of human life and the ways in which autoethnography attempts to ensure each and every person included in the stories told is given respect and dignity, choice and agency, beneficence and justice in the research process.

She worries about the fragility of Ethical Review and its capacity to continue to aid research in proceeding.

She worries about the infrangibility of Ethical Review and its capacity to impede research proceeding.

She is disturbed by applications— particularly by autoethnographers— where researchers do not show any regard for relational ethics, that is, mindful self-reflection about their role, motives, feelings and relationships to the people they are working with.

She is disturbed by the disregard that Ethical Review shows towards relational ethics in autoethnography, that is, mindful self-reflection about our role, motives, feelings and relationships to the people we are working with.

She feels strongly that Ethical Review needs to be thought of as situational, relational and a reflexive dialogue where the test is whether the Committee feels that the research is free of the corruption of power between the researcher and the researched.

She feels strongly that the Ethical Review of autoethnography needs to be assessed as situational, relational and a reflexive dialogue where the power relations between the researcher and the researched are laid bare, critiqued, challenged and sent into ruin.

She cares deeply about bringing Ethical Review rules and processes closer to making room for and accounting for the very real ethical issues that doing autoethnography presents.	She cares deeply about being able to be accountable to and for the very real ethical issues that doing autoethnography presents and is unsure whether Ethical Review rules and processes have capacity to allow for such complications.
The form in and of itself seems to be at the heart of the problem because researchers do not seem to approach it with an autoethnographic heart and mind, but rather a bureaucratic "I must tick the boxes" mindset. She resolves to revisit the form.	The form in and of itself seems to be at the heart of the problem because it does not seem to want us to respond with an autoethnographic heart and mind, and instead, it's looking for us to tick the bureaucratic boxes. She resolves to revisit the form.

4.

angst (noun).
A feeling of anxiety:
DREAD, ANGUISH.
First known use: 1887.
angst (intransitive verb).
Pause.
Intransitive; it means it's a double verb, it does two things at once.
First, it expresses something that can be done like laugh or move.
Second, it does not have a direct object receiving the action and does not require an object therefore to a express a complete thought or not.
And again then, *angst* (intransitive verb).
angst-ED; angst -ING; angstS:
To experience anxiety, apprehension, or insecurity.
First known use by me in relation to the question: 1994.

I said, I trusted you.
You never talked to me about ethics.
You never talked to me about *your* ethics.
She said, well then you can't exactly blame me, can you?
It was your mistake.
This is the last conversation I had with her that I remember.

I walked away from her office feeling at fault.
Furious. Flawed. Failed. Foolish.
She told me her way of doing business in the field was the right way.
No, she said more than that.
She said her way was the *only* way.
To go my own way, was to go away
To go a-way that was not hers.

You see, I *thought* I had done the right thing.
I had written a letter on our/her behalf.
I had the family connections, it was my role.
It was my response-ability she said.
Dear Mr McDinny.
A note on official university letterhead that said the *ethnographers* shall be arriving.
One by two by three of a kind.
Dance ethnographer, ethnomusicologist, then linguist.
We did not ask, we said we would, and we did arrive.
At the beginning of July in 1994.
The research team in the research car complete with research matter.
Funding, fieldnotes and files.
Fuelled to find.

You see, once we arrived, I *thought* was doing the right thing.
Funding, field-noting, filing: finding.
That's what I was there for after all.
Never mind the ethics.
Finding, keeping.
Mind over matter.
Got ethics?
Out of sight and out of mind.
At least at first.
And then something changed.
I found myself wrapped in the self-same
Heavy and damp woollen blanket
Scratching and itching
Asking the question.

5.

Enter Woolfian ethics. If we cast Virginia in the light of critical autoethnography—of her edging towards being an autoethnographer, *and* a critical one—ethics seems to be a silent presence in her works. In true Virginia fashion, this is a thought "tugging" (1929/2001, p. 5) at the end of the line and perhaps now is the time to cautiously haul it in. I think and wonder, is it *her* thinking and wondering about writing, and her writing in and of itself where an ethical understanding is puzzled out? Woolf's writing attempts to tell us about our experience of the world, to cut through the "cotton wool of daily life", embodied perhaps by the kind of heavy and damp woollen blanket I often find myself smothered underneath, to moments of being. She (2002, p. 85) professes that the "shock receiving capacity of emotions is what makes me a writer" and further that this sensation is followed immediately by a desire to explain it and put it into words. "It is only by putting it into words," she insists, that the experience and the emotion it holds, becomes real and whole.

There is a doubleness here that Virginia is dancing around and seeks to embrace. I think and wonder my way to the beginning of *A room of one's own* where she calls herself "I" and then immediately invites the reader to think of her as other—as "Mary Beton, Mary Seton or Mary Carmichael or by any name you please" (1929/2001, p. 5). The novel *Mrs Dalloway* (1925) is another example where, a constant hithering and thithering as Woolf might describe it, between observing a self living and loving in a social world and observing others experiencing and emotion-ing the self-same world, takes place. The chiming of the clock every hour on the hour across the span of one day, marks and divides the comings and goings in the thoughts and actions of ordinary Londoners. The main character, Clarissa Dalloway, is a keen observer of her own and the behaviour of others. She rapidly moves between watching others, watching herself, and then watching the others watching her watching. Her gaze moves backwards and forwards in fascination, in fear, in search of something which she knows she will never find and yet she persists in her desire to share the exhilaration and the terror of the present moment. The opening and closing of the curtains of the window is an example of this. She walks to the window, Clarissa parts the curtains, she looks across the way to the room opposite her, and watches the old lady climbing upstairs, "Let her climb upstairs if she wanted to", Woolf writes, "let her stop; then let her, as Clarissa had often seen her, gain her bedroom, part her curtains and disappear again into the background. Somehow one respected that-that old woman looking out the window, quite unconscious that she was being watched" (p. 126). The "privacy of the soul" that the old lady exhibits in her everyday movement was a sight that made Clarissa "want to cry" (p. 127); there is something about looking into the face of *and* as a stranger that moves her, moves her to see the other's alterity and respond without containing her. Clarissa observes the old lady once more at the very end of the novel and to her surprise, the old lady who lives across the way, stares straight back (pp. 185–186). "Could she see her?" Clarissa wonders as she watches her neighbour, a woman at once strange and familiar, close her blinds and turn out the light. As Berman (2004, p. 169) notes, Clarissa in turn, turns away from the possibility of mutual connection and the "obligation imposed by being-with".

Woolf's words in this novel, as they do in much of her writing, ebb and flow between the everyday and the imagined, between inside and outside, between public and private, between the I and the collective, and as Berman notes, "between the potentially universal and the personal... between the face of the other as stranger and the call of the ethics of intimacy" (2004, p. 159). Ahmed too suggests that Woolf "captures something" as selves/I and others/you pass each other by and just for a moment "look up at the same thing...the oddness of a connection" (2017, loc 896). Woolf was fully aware that knowing is an act of being subject in the world and being in subject-to-subject relationships; both the one and the two ways of knowing-as-being hold obligations and response-abilities and writing for Woolf was a way to make "an imaginative leap into an ethical one" (Berman, 2004, p. 165). Berman describes Woolf's writing then as an aesthetic "bridge" (p. 159) which brings the ontological, epistemological and moral into conversation with one another.

I move to put *Mrs Dalloway* back on the white book shelf next to *A room of one's own*, for now way a-way but so close. The ticking of the clock both distracts and reminds me that like Virginia herself, I "find myself again on the old driving whirlwind of writing against time" (Woolf, 1980, p. 180) and the book slips from my hand onto the floor. The pages flutter in the falling draft and it lands with the opening facing down. I pick it up care-fully and the first line catches my air, "Mrs. Dalloway said she would buy the flowers herself" (Woolf, 1929, p. 3). I read it again, "Mrs. Dalloway said she would buy the flowers herself"; and again, "Mrs. Dalloway said..." I have read this novel many times but upon this re/ turn, the ethnographic sense-abilities and ethical response-abilities of the opening sentence gently tap me on the shoulder. The narrator calls herself "Mrs. Dalloway" and we know immediately that she is a married woman of and in her own time. She "said" gives Mrs Dalloway voice as the observer of her-self and others, both real and imagined, in conversation and connection. "She would buy the flowers herself" tells us that Mrs Dalloway and Virginia Woolf as narrators-in-relation will take literal and literary response-ability for their thoughts and actions; they will attend to their obligations to act in response to others and with response-ability. In this moment of beginning, Mrs Dalloway presents us to an ethics of being-in-time, being-in-relation and being all of these through an atten-tiveness to writing—I think and wonder anew about Woolf and upon retrieving the book from the floor, begin to move her works onto the shelf which holds the words and worlds of autoethnographers.

6.

> Got ethics?
> We can pay you by the hour.
> For singing your culture.
> $25 is the going rate.
> Unless you'd prefer another payment method?
> Blankets?
> Flour?
> Tobacco?
> No problem.
> It's your preference.
> Your choice.
> Your empowerment.
> White goods it is then.
>
> Got ethics?
> I say I again, loudly.
> I wait, I watch, for an answer.

I watch empty promises waft and curl their way
High into the sky with tobacco smoke
I wait for the blankets to smother the fire
That fuels the finding, field-noting, and filing.
The research matters begin to fill the research team and the research car.
Melodies and moves.
All on tape, all on the record, all on the way
A-way to elsewhere
Out of sight, out of mind
Possible because payment has been made.

You see, once I/she/we got down to it
Down to the *real* ethnographic work
Finding, field-noting and filing culture
Culture that mattered more
That's when the question was asked
Dear Mr McDinny
Do you give your permission?
Will you give your permission?
If you say no, never mind
We can ask someone else
We will ask someone else
Because *we* have arrived
One, two, three.

7.

The woman arrives fifteen minutes late to the workshop. She enters the room noisily, pointing and pushing her way through to the centre chair in the centre of a row of chairs in the centre of the room. She makes no apology as her satchel swings and sways into the bodies of others she passes by, she is focussed solely on locating her presence in the centre of the room.

Elizabeth stops midway through her introductory and definitional slide titled, "What is autoethnography?" to acknowledge the woman's arrival. "Welcome! We've only just started, please take one of the handouts."

The woman reaches across the rows of people in front of her and snatches the printed sheets of paper from Elizabeth's hand. "Well, I'm not so sure I'm going to need this but let me say *you* are very lucky I found you. This campus is a nightmare to navigate and the map—don't get me started on the inadequacy of the directions you gave to get here", the woman says with a humph. "If I didn't know better, I could almost be fooled into thinking you were deliberately trying to mislead me!"

Elizabeth is lost for words. She has no idea who this woman is and why she has joined the workshop.

"Hmph, while we're talking about misleading, what kind of non-sense has she been spinning you about autoethnography?", the woman raises one eyebrow and turns to look at the others in the room. They too are lost for wards and sit in stunned silence.

"I can see this presentation is going to be similar to others you've given—*performative*. I do remember somewhere reading or someone telling me that she was a dancer in a former life", she says, nudging the person sitting beside her. "But seriously, is this performance of ethnography, this autoethnography, *proper* social science? *That* is the question for us to consider today".

Elizabeth has now had time to collect herself and musters up a professional response. "I was just about to get to that, and I'm glad someone brought that up. Autoethnography certainly has its critics…"

"And they can all get in line behind me!" the woman interrupts.

"Excuse me", the organiser of the workshop leans forward and taps the woman on the shoulder. "I'm wondering whether you would mind saving your comments and questions until the end? We are on a tight schedule today and I think everyone here is keen to listen to what Elizabeth has to say".

There is a pause. Every-one seems relieved that some-one was brave enough to stop the woman in her tracks and yet no-one is quite sure will happen next.

"Uh-huh, yep, I can see your point", the woman seems to be acquiescing. "While I am prepared to excuse you, I am not prepared to excuse her. I'm not quite finished with her yet. You see, whether I like it or not—and I happen to *not* like it—the self has always been present (now there's timing for you) in ethnography and the postmodern turn shifted our attention to issues of voice, power, authority and representation in the work that we do in, out and between the field. These theoretical, philosophical and methodological debates certainly laid fertile ground for the growth of autoethnography over the past 15–20 years".

"Yes," Elizabeth agrees, "autoethnography has grown up in a particular climate which insists that an understanding of others, can only begin from our own experiences as selves—the 'I' is always already there in ethnography, autoethnography fesses up, lays bare and entangles the personal and its relationship to culture".

"Now don't get me started on *that*", the woman breathes out loudly in frustration, "If the goal of social science—which you claim autoethnography to be an example of—is to study the social world; let me say that again, the *social* world and yet the focus of autoethnographic research is the self, how on earth can it be considered valid and legitimate social science? Self-absorbed naval gazing is what I'd call it! By the way, is your Head of School here?"

The woman turns and looks around the room. He is, and cautiously raises his hand. "Did you know this is what she does, gets paid a generous salary to sit in her office obsessing about herself?" Elizabeth's Head of Schools squirms uncomfortably in his chair.

"What happened to you Elizabeth? Why did you start writing like this? You used to be such a nice dutiful daughter of traditional ethnographic method. I've all read your early papers and PhD on the social and musical lives of Aboriginal women—such solid pieces of analytic research grounded in data from the field".

Elizabeth is taken aback. She suspends the moment so that she might think and wonder, takes a sip from her water glass before responding.

"Thanks for your question…umm, what did you say your name was?"

The woman wags her finger, "I didn't, and given that there has been no ethical understanding reached between us about the disclosure of my identity, I'm not sure I'm going to give it. I mean that's another thing that really pisses me off (oops, am I allowed to say that?) about autoethnographic research…it's basically unethical".

"Again, an about important question about autoethnography that we need to discuss. So perhaps if you let me continue with my presentation…"

"No", the woman's head shakes again, "No, you don't. You are not going to wriggle and worm your way out of this so easily. You know in that paper we read in preparation for this workshop that you wrote on death and dying? Did you ask your family at Burrulula if you could describe the moments of their passing and the members of their family who had passed away in such an intimate way? Did you get permission?", the woman narrows her eyes as she stares long and hard at Elizabeth; in fact, it seems to Elizabeth that the entire room now takes a slightly edgier and narrower look at her.

The woman smirks, "No, I didn't think so. And you dare to rant and rave about how autoethnography is more responsive and more responsible to the social condition and for bringing about social change. From where I stand, when you claim to do autoethnography, the only thing you are responsible for is standing on the wrong side of the fence. Because you cannot see beyond yourself, you can only focus on the powerful— you. It's the powerless to whom we should be directing our sociological gaze is ignored. Autoethnography is ethically suspicious, *that's* what it is".

Elizabeth has almost lost her patience, "I think it's my turn to disagree with you, you see from my experience…"

"A-ha! Exactly! Autoethnography is *all* your experience—there is no data and therefore no analytic mileage (Delamont, 2009, p. 58). Research is supposed to be analytic Elizabeth, not experiential, and autoethnography is noticeably lacking in analytic outcome once it starts flipping and flopping around with creativity and emotion. It abrogates our duty to go out and collect data as social scientists—we collect data and analyse, that's what we do", the woman gives a self-assured nod.

"Now hang on a minute, if you could just let me respond", Elizabeth tries to intervene.

"Oh yes—it's all about *you* in autoethnography isn't it. It's just a little too familiar, subjective and evocative for my liking. And quite simply, I/we/you as selves are not interesting enough to write about in journals, to teach about, or to expect attention from others".

"Well, you are certainly giving us plenty of attention now, so it can't be all that useless, hopeless and boring", Elizabeth mutters.

"The *important* sociological questions are not about your anguish— and most autoethnography is angst ridden autobiography devoid of any obligation to the people and cultures who share their lives with us so that we, as ethnographers, can research and write about them", the woman waves her arms around for emphasis. "There is a line when studying social phenomena that you do not cross, the line that says there is an appropriate and beneficial amount of autobiography and reflexivity in ethnographic projects (Delamont, 2009, p. 51), and an inappropriate amount. No prizes for guessing which side of the line autoethnography falls on!"

"I am not sure I would make such broad sweeping generalisations".

The woman disregards Elizabeth's comment and continues her denunciation of autoethnography, "Let me remind you, that sociologists, anthropologists, ethnomusicologists, and anyone else who engages in ethnographic work, are a privileged group. For example, qualitative sociologists are particularly lucky as our work lasts: think about those texts sociology is remembered for—the great ethnographies: *City of women* by Landes is a ripping read. Autoethnography is an abuse of that privilege. Our duty is to go out and research the classic texts of 2050 or 2090, not sit in our homes focusing on ourselves".

"I'm not sure I've said that's what we do. If you read…," Elizabeth tries to speak but her the woman's criticism is reaching fever pitch.

"I'm sorry—actually, strike that—I'm not sorry about anything I've said here. Your responses and the way you are presenting autoethnography here today is mischievous—some would say mendacious even".

Elizabeth is momentarily caught up in thinking and wondering about the etymology of the word "mendacious", a word aimed at catching the very lying quality it alludes to.

"Now that's a fairly serious kind of accusation. Would you care to elaborate?"

The woman has barely drawn breath, "You're nothing but bricoleurs—tricksters! You assert, exaggerate, speculate, improvise, and don't test out ideas! Autoethnographers are essentially lazy—yes, literally lazy and intellectually lazy. And what's more, you all think that by being 'artistic' and 'creative' you are performing science, you might want to call me a dinosaur waiting to get hit by a meteor for that statement but at least I'm not deluding myself into thinking that autoethnography as story is a more ethical practice! I mean", she scoffs and sounds a little like a horse with a bad cough, "most of you can't even write well, you're just second-rate writers and poets".

Of all the offensive things the woman has said, Elizabeth takes offense to this and goes on the offence, "Most autoethnographers I know spend a lot of time writing and crafting their work, in much the same way as a novelist would and I certainly don't think that could be called lazy. And as for…"

"Your stories—or what is it that you have started calling them? Storylines as heartlines?—they are nothing more than ethnographic lies", the woman saw the horror stricken look on Elizabeth's face and went straight for the jugular. "The only honest thing to do, is *not* to do auto-ethnography at all!"

Elizabeth is left speechless.

"Given that you seem incapable of responding in an objective way to my suggestions, I think it's time I left".

The room is quiet, so quiet that Elizabeth is sure everyone must be able to hear how fast her heart is racing as it sinks heavily to the floor.

"Very well then, I'll be going," the woman stands up from her chair and turns to address the audience. "Come on then, aren't you coming with me?"

Her invitation is met with silence.

"Suit yourselves, but remember, I could very well be one of the review-ers next time you submit an article to a Social Science journal, and mark my words, if you send anything remotely or closely autoethnographic, I will NOT be recommending publication. It's your funeral!"

Elizabeth waited until the last of the staff and students attending the workshop had left the room before sitting down heavily on the nearest chair, her breathing shallow and fast. In that moment, she felt as though she had become the embodiment of the woman as "trampled space" Cixous (1976, p. 878) speaks of, her lovely "mouth gagged with pollen" and the "wind knocked out" of her. The accusatory words hurled by the woman at her had cut right through to the raw and ragged uncertainties she held as an autoethnographer about doing autoethnography. The woman's parting condemnation of autoethnography as a dishonest way of researching and writing caused her to wince now as it played over and over in her head. That particular comment was designed to hurt, it *did* hurt, and Elizabeth's autoethnographic sense-abilities were smarting with the caustic sting it had left in its wake. Very loudly and very publicly, the woman had deemed autoethnography *and* Elizabeth as unethical.

The word unethical twisted around her thoughts uneasily; *not* ethical, *in lack of* ethics, *with-out* ethics, *in opposition* and reverse action to that which is ethical, *deprived* of ethics, *released from* ethics. It didn't matter which way Elizabeth re/turned it, she couldn't shake the dis-ease that the woman's words had set into motion. If there was no shedding it, perhaps, Elizabeth began to think and wonder, she was meant to sit with the re/turn. After all, that is one of the purposes of autoethnographic work, to make space for a "turn, a change, a reconsideration" (Holman Jones, Adams, & Ellis, 2013, p. 21) of how we think, how we do and how we be in-relation, and how we live. Elizabeth kept coming back to the woman's claim that the attention autoethnography gives to the "self" as a knowing subject in subject-to-subject relationality is in/appropriate. The more she thought and wondered about it however, Elizabeth kept coming back to Spry's (2016, p. 39) insistence that "giving an account of oneself always and already involves an account of who we are with others" and the important role critical reflexivity has to play in autoethnographic work. Being critically reflexive in autoethnography, is about being "personally accountable for one's situatedness in systems of power and privilege" (2016, p. 39) and for Spry, investing in the "politics of postionality" (Madison, 2012), is the defining methodological praxis in critical autoethnographic research, writing and performance.

The "truth" is then, Elizabeth mused, writing critical autoethnography is the only *honest* thing she knows *how* to do in this particular ethico-onto-epistemological somewhere she finds herself—it is the only interpretative move, which holds the possibility for living the material and affective discomforts of writing, researching and being-in-relation as a white settler colonial woman. Acknowledging, embracing and waking up to the cold hard ethical entanglements of this location steadied her. Elizabeth became filled with the "courage, the desire, to approach" (Cixous, 1993, p. 7) critical autoethnography as a way of learning to die, to break with the darkness of dominator culture (Cixous, 1976, p. 880) she imagined the woman represented, and follow Spry's lead to embrace the complexities of "articulating the effects of difference within a 'critical, deconstructive relationality' of an Inappropriate/d Other and an unsettled performative-I" (2016, p. 51).

8.

Got ethics?
I scream it this time.
You see, I thought I *was* doing the right thing
And then angst arrived and began its riddling
That's what it does, it riddles in other words
DREAD
Oh no, there's going to be a fight
ANGUISH
There is too much upset
APPREHENSION
No, we don't really need to, do we?
Field-note it and file it now we have found it
Really we don't, not this, not *ever* this

You see, the arguments from her came thick and fast
I did not know what thoughts to think
I waited and watched them fly by
Out from sight and into mind
It's for your own good she said.
We can save your culture she said.
We can find it, field-note it and file it she said.
For the future she said.
Whose? I asked a different question.
Mine, of course; maybe theirs.
She said they were one and the same.
I said I didn't think so.
I might have once, but not anymore.

Got ethics?
I kept asking and the angst-ing
Kept riddling away.
It was there with me as I sat with Jemima.
My kundiyarra.
Holding hands with me in the morning.

Sitting side by side late at night.
Talking life, talking love.
Becoming an/other together.
Here and there at the in-between.
In relation.
Be-cause and in-cause of difference.
So close.

Got ethics?
I kept asking and I became
Angst-ed.
Because I then saw.
Ethnography being its worst.
Fuelling the force behind the c word.
Ethnography doing its worst.
Finding and field-noting.
Ethnography knowing its worst.
Flying in, flying out.
Flying away with it all.
Filing it for the future.
I refused.

9.

Enter Cixousian ethics. I think and wonder about the direction this writing on ethics and critical autoethnography has taken. It seems fitting that I arrive to begin this ending with Cixous; her writings moved me to go a different way in my approach to, of and for the other which in and of itself moves a-way towards being and becoming all at once loving, non-appropriating, lingering in the between-ness respect of distance and ethico-onto-epistemologically non-violent. At first a gesture and then a gift, her writing a gesturing gift which there and then and here and now, guides a-way of thinking and wondering through "the lessons of calling, letting ourselves be called. The lessons of letting come, receiving" (Cixous, 1991, p. 61). Yes, I think and wonder now how Cixous called me to this calling; this way of thinking, wondering and writing difference which demands, as Klobucka suggests, a "faithful recognition of the Other's autonomous meaning" (1994, p. 42). And yet, yet—I fear that I will never be able to write a-way to the ethical relationships Cixous calls for, because after all she whispers, "whoever writes doesn't know" (Cixous, 1991, p. 134).

A "moment of collection" (Cixous, in Cixous & Calle-Gruber, 1997, p. 104) and a gathering of her words about writing and the other come to join me. Many of them re/turn from Cixous being "inter view" in *Rootprints* (1997) but also make their a-way here from the pages of *Coming to writing* (1991) and other texts; words once strange now familiar, words once familiar now stranger than ever before—words that grope around in the dark, searching for the unhoped-for, trying not to crush it: in order to un-lie (Cixous, 1991, p. 134).

She writes.

"When I begin to write, it always starts from something unexplained, mysterious and concrete. Something that happens here. I could be indifferent to these phenomena; but in fact I think these are the only important phenomena. It begins to search in me. And this questioning could be philosophical: but for me, right away it takes the poetic path. That is to say that it goes through scenes, moments, illustrations lived by myself or by others, and like all that belongs to the current of life, it crosses very many zones of our histories. I seize these moments, still trembling, moist, creased, disfigured, stammering" (Cixous, in Cixous & Calle-Gruber, 1997, p. 43).

I write.

But first, a side step, a step to the side which speaks to the heart of critical autoethnographic writing. Here it is, laid bare, the call to autoethnography; the answer to the question "Who I are?" as autoethnographer begins its own explanation of the thinking and wondering which become words. Words that manifest a moment, words in a moment of mystery, words that make material, words that meaning make, words that move, words that mourn, words that melt the world through writing. Affective and aesthetic, philosophically poetic and political these are the *kind* of words we search for in our work as critical autoethnographers.

She writes.

"The origin of the material in writing can only be myself. I is not I of course, because it is I with others, coming from the others, putting me in the other's place, giving me the other's eyes" (Cixous, in Cixous & Calle-Gruber, 1997, p. 87).

I write.

"I" is a second side step, necessary, and one which plunges into the heart of the critical autoethnographic cupboard. The heartlines of auto-ethnography play with the relationship of self to other, self to the social, self to sentiment; other to sentiment, other to social, other to self; a constant playing with and re/turning around relationships to knowing that happen at the heart of these in-betweens.

She writes.

"Difference is the differential…and that difference is a movement. It always passes, always come to pass, between the two…it passes. It surpasses us…what I know is the point of contact between two impossibilities: I will never know, you will never know. But at the same time we know that we will never know. In that instant I touch what remains your secret. I touch your secret with my body. I touch your secret with my secret and that is not exchanged. But smiling, we share the bitter and sweet taste (regret and desire mixed) of that impossibility" (Cixous, in Cixous & Calle-Gruber, 1997, pp. 52–54).

I write.

This is the writing around difference that begins to move a-way towards a different kind of ethical relationship between self and other in our work as critical autoethnographers. Writing which accepts the impossibility of knowing the other, knowing the self; writing which accepts and insists that the essence of both is secret-ed a-way so we write to find another way. A-way which un-distracts, un-deafens, un-denies, un-destroys, un-deadens and un-does the differences we write.

She writes.

"It is the living space, the betweenus, that we must take care to keep… Having the humility, the generosity, not to jump over it, not to avoid it. We must save the approach that opens and leaves space for the other" (1991, p. 62).

I write.

And here is the ethical drive that sits behind the wheel of critical auto-ethnography; the drive that directs us down a road with less traffic but one that we know we have to follow; this too is the ethical drive. Writing to leave space for the other is to let the other be *as* other; to "let alterity speak as alterity" is a Cixousian gesture replete with "acceptance, tolerance and non-comprehension" of the other (Conley, 1990, p. xi). This is the lesson of things—a lesson she learns from Clarice Lispector, at the School of Clarice; "Claricewege" (Cixous, 1991, p. 60)—sense refers to the affective materiality of things presenting them-selves as others and performing a resistance to the peak-hour rush to absorption as all-knowing; as annihilation.

She writes.

"*Clarice Lispector.* This woman, our contemporary, Brazilian (born in the Ukraine, of Jewish origin), gives us not books, but living saved from books, from narratives, repressive constructions. And through her writing-window we enter the awesome beauty of learning to read: going by way of the body, to the other side of self" (1991, p. 59).

I write.

Hélène Cixous found the writings of Clarice Lispector at a time when she was "unfindable to herself" and with the words of Lispector, Cixous engages—almost obsessively Klobucka (1994, p. 51) suggests—in an exploration of the ethical entanglements of approaching, relating to and interpreting the other. Cixous reads Lispector with the question of otherness sitting close beside her. And the question often re/turns, does Cixous appropriate in her absorption and assimilation of Lispector? I found the writings of Hélène Cixous who had since found the writings of Clarice Lispector at a time when I was entangled up and down in the self-same dilemma, the self-same questioning around positioning, privilege, power and the re/presentation of others. Her words took me by surprise and led me to secret-e my thinking, wondering and writing differently, in deference and difference to the biggest secret of all: C, C for comfort in, compliance with and complicity in C for coloniality.

She writes.

"The secret other, the other secret, the other itself…And this secret we take by surprise, we do not speak of it; we keep it. That is to say, we keep it: we do not touch it. We know for example where the other's vulnerable heart is situated; and we do not touch it, we leave it intact. This is love… Loving not knowing. Loving: not knowing" (Cixous in Cixous & Calle-Gruber, 1997, p. 17).

I write.

Bray reminds me that for Cixous, "feminine writing is an attempt to demonstrate a loving fidelity to the other, to let the other come into being within writing by remaining faithful to the essence of the other, knowing all the while that this essence cannot ever be captured or totally reproduced within writing" (2004, p. 59). I think and wonder if perhaps, critical autoethnography tries to come close, so close to, with and through the other in the self-same way. A loving relationship to, with and for the other in critical autoethnographic writing is one which seeks to step back from the thinking and writing which invades, alienates, pacifies and objectifies.

She writes.

"In these violent and lazy times, in which we do not live what we live, we are read, we are forcibly lived, far from our essential lives, we lost the gift, we no longer hear what things still want to tell us, we translate, we translate, everything is translation and reduction" (1991, p. 65).

I write.

To write critical autoethnography in a-way which is attentive to the ethics of alterity Cixous speaks of, is to push and pull a-way from such ethico-onto-epistemo-*textual* violence at every re/turn. I think and wonder that this is the struggle, the labour, the movement critical autoethnography takes response-ability and sense-ability for; always and already. And yet, yet; repeat the question?

She writes.

"How do we behave with the other?…How do we lose? How do we keep? Do we remember? Do we forget? Do we take? Do we receive?" (Cixous, 1991, p. 155).

I write.

Got ethics?

References

Ahmed, S. (2017). *Living a feminist life*. Durham: Duke University Press.

Berman, J. S. (2004). Ethical folds: Ethics, aesthetics, Woolf. *MFS Modern Fiction Studies, 50*(1), 151–172.

Bray, A. (2004). *Hélène Cixous: Writing and sexual difference*. New York, NY: Palgrave Macmillan.

Chang, H. (2008). *Autoethnography as method*. Walnut Creek, CA: Left Coast Press.

Cixous, H. (1976). The laugh of the Medusa (K. Cohen & P. Cohen, Trans.). *Signs, 1*(4), 875–893.

Cixous, H. (1991). *Coming to writing and other essays* (S. Suleiman, Ed., S. Cornell, Trans.). Cambridge, MA: Harvard University Press.

Cixous, H. (1993). *Three steps on the ladder of writing* (S. Cornell & S. Sellers, Trans.). New York, NY: Columbia University Press.

Cixous, H., & Calle-Gruber, M. (1997). *Hélène Cixous, rootprints: Memory and life writing.* London: Routledge.

Conley, V. A. (1990). Introduction. In H. Cixous (Ed.), *Reading with Clarice Lispector* (pp. vii–xviii). Minneapolis, MN: University of Minnesota Press.

Delamont, S. (2009). The only honest thing: Autoethnography, reflexivity and small crises in fieldwork. *Ethnography and Education, 4*(1), 51–63.

Douglas, K., & Carless, D. (2013). A history of autoethnographic inquiry. In S. Holman Jones, T. E. Adams, & C. Ellis (Eds.), *Handbook of autoethnography* (pp. 17–48). Walnut Creek, CA: Left Coast Press.

Ellis, C. (2004). *The ethnographic I: A methodological novel about autoethnography.* Walnut Creek, MA: AltaMira Press.

Ellis, C. (2009). Telling tales on neighbours: Ethics in two voices. *International Review of Qualitative Research, 2*, 3–28.

Holman Jones, S., Adams, T. E., & Ellis, C. (2013). Introduction: Coming to know autoethnography as more than method. In S. Holman Jones, T. E. Adams, & C. Ellis (Eds.), *Handbook of autoethnography* (pp. 17–48). Walnut Creek, CA: Left Coast Press.

Klobucka, A. (1994). Hélène Cixous and the hour of Clarice Lispector. *SubStance, 23*(1), 41–62.

Madison, S. A. (2012). *Critical autoethnography: Method, ethics, and performance* (2nd ed.). Los Angeles, CA: Sage.

Spry, T. (2016). *Autoethnography and the other: Unsettling power through utopian performatives.* London: Routledge.

Tullis, J. (2013). Self and others: Ethics in autoethnographic research. In S. Holman Jones, T. E. Adams, & C. Ellis (Eds.), *Handbook of autoethnography* (pp. 244–261). London: Routledge.

Woolf, V. (1929/2001). *A room of one's own.* London: Vintage Press.

Woolf, V. (1980). *The diary of Virginia Woolf, Volume III: 1925–1930* (A. E. Bell, Ed.). London: Hogarth Press.

Woolf, V. (2002). *Moments of being: Autobiographical writings* (J. Schulkind, Ed.). London: Pimlico, Random House.

11

Beginning Writing at the Ending; a Second Take, a Second to Take

I have a feeling it is time to finish this race…I am trying to conclude.
Suddenly, as it was page 158- and the third hour was ending, I realized that
perhaps there must be "conclusions" to my journeys, because these sheets I'm
walking across with my hand are "lectures." But there is no "conclusion" to be
found in writing.
Cixous (1993, p. 156)
Let us go to the school of writing, where we'll spend three school days
initiating ourselves in the strange science of writing, which is a science of
farewells. Of reunitings. I will begin with: This is what writing is.
Cixous (1993, p. 3)
She has told you how she reached the conclusion—the prosaic conclusion—
that it is necessary to have five hundred a year and a room with a lock on the
door if you are to try to write fiction and poetry. She has tried to lay bare the
thought and impressions that led her to think this.
Woolf (1929/2001, p. 121)
But when I began to consider the subject in this way, I soon saw that it had
one fatal drawback. I should never be able to come to a conclusion.
Woolf (1929/2001, p. 2)

© The Author(s) 2019
E. Mackinlay, *Critical Writing for Embodied Approaches*,
https://doi.org/10.1007/978-3-030-04669-9_11

1.

The telephone rings, piercing the quiet and close, so close, dead of night where few find themselves alive. I lift my word- and world-weary heart and head from the dreams that have become the front and back story to the darkness I have found myself in. There is a cold and empty space in the bed beside me and I have been tossing and turning and re/turning all night, drifting in and out of there and then, here and now; un-forgetting the past in the present and beside myself with worry. Looking at the clock I notice it is two minutes past one and silently calculate the time difference between Australia and France; yes, it must be her, her phoning me once more. The telephone shrieks again, "Hélène? How did you know to call?"

"Is this Elizabeth Mackinlay?" The female voice on the other end asks. My heart skips a beat; the accent is English-Australian, and it is not Hélène.

"Hello", my voice is thick and raspy from lack of sleep. "Who is this?"

"My name is Senior Constable Kate Frank", she says. "Do you have a moment? We need to talk".

My heart is no longer skipping, it is careening at break-neck speed to the pit of my stomach. "Yes, how can I help?"

"Is there somewhere you can talk in private?"

The silence of the night is the perfect cloak for this conversation.

"Yes, I am on my own".

"I'm afraid I have some shocking news for you", Kate pauses, gauging my response. I am struggling to breathe, I say nothing.

"I need to tell you that we arrested your husband earlier today. He is in custody at the city watch house waiting to be charged", she explains.

I try to gather the pieces of myself together, "No, that can't be right, you must have the wrong person".

"I'm sorry, I know this must come as a shock to you", Kate's voice is soft. "We have your husband in custody and he will be charged. He will appear at the Magistrates court in the morning. I think you need to be there".

I lay down and longed to never to wake, to become woke, ever again.

The telephone rings again.

"Mac?" It's my husband. "Mac? Are you there?"

My breath catches; with anxiety, fear, relief, I can't be sure. "Thank god! I've been so worried. Where are you? Are you alright?"

"I haven't got much time to talk, I'm in the watch house. They haven't charged me yet. I don't think anything will happen until Monday".

"Is it true?", my voice falters. "Is it true what they're saying?"

He pauses for a moment too long, "They are recording everything I say, don't ask me those kinds of questions".

I am reeling and confused, "The police told me you'll be in court tomorrow morning".

"Did they?" He sounds distant. "It'll be OK Mac, I'll fix it. I don't know what the police have told you but don't listen to them—and don't worry".

"Don't worry", I whisper back.

"And tell the boys I am fine—it will be fine. Tell Maxie, I'm like Andy, the character Andy Dufresne in our favourite movie *The Shawshank Redemption* (1994)", he laughs lightly and then I hear the clink of a coin as the telephone call cuts out.

I place the telephone back in the cradle.

"Who was that Mum? Was that Dad?" Max asks as he pads softly into the room.

"It was", my voice is soft and already far a-way.

"What did he say?"

"He told me to tell you it will be alright because he's Andy Dufresne", I reach forward to hold his hands. "I have no idea who that is. Does it mean anything to you?"

He shrugs, "Dunno, I've got no clue. Maybe he's saying he's been framed, maybe he's saying he'll be gone for a long while".

2.

Writing to life
A-way to
Keep breathing daily
Running out of
Love to give
Needing to rest
Lay my head
Down and out
A blue sky

Day fit for
An indigo heart
Writing keeps calling
Me to stop!
Close the book
Quick hide them
Scars that threaten
To give the
Secret a-way
I hold them
Myself to me
Reminding not to
Look back eyes
Forward always towards
Moments and movements
Fighting to flight
Becoming and being
Thinking and wondering
As it is
And may be
Writing to love
A faithful friend
Let me lay
Finally and completely
There and then
Here and now
These and those
Words and worlds
You and I
Let us descend
Together down low
Your hand in
Mine in yours
One and two
It is done

3.

This is the ending, the ending which led me to write this book-I-don't write. It is a relief to arrive here at the conclusion; for in reaching this moment, I sense have come close, so close, to drawing a close on my *arrivance* as a white-settler-colonial-woman wording the worlds of others. I have secret-ed all the secrets that sit within this story and it is time to secrete them and me a-way. Now and again I feel, in much the same way as Virginia Woolf did (1980, p. 248), other memories, ideas, plans and images of my work as an ethnographer over the past few decades forming and threatening to flood this ending, but I know if I am patient they too will move on, up and "over the horizon". I am in no mind to beg them to stay for as much as they speak a shared story of love, generosity and wisdom shared with me as a self and other that I have become in-relation, they carry with them unbearable loss, sadness, and grief. Ending this book-I-don't-write here and now was always and already a-way to conclude because: *because, I have no more words* to speak this world; my Pa's leather-bound Merriam-Webster dictionary sits closed and dusty on the hallway table; the white book shelf is empty and bereft. The words and worlds I once wrote and may have wanted to write are too heavy, two heavy handed, three heavy headed and four heavy hearted; they are *and* in requiem.

This book-I-don't write was written most often in the morning; holding hands with this time of day it mourns, these words and the worlds they write are in mourning. And yet; *yet*. At this ending, Cixous reminds me that to "begin (writing, living) we must have death…the death of day, today's death. The one that comes right up to us so suddenly we don't have time to avoid it" (1993, p. 7). The secret is that I have died a thousand million deaths in trying to find the "courage, the desire, to approach, to go to the door" (Cixous, 1993, p. 7) and write as a-way to un-forget; and yet, *yet*, I did not die. Perhaps, the words and worlds in this book-I-don't-write served me well; when both were in danger of falling a-part (Ellis, 2004, p. 33) as critical autoethnographic work, they enabled me to "write through painful, confusing, angering and uncertain experiences" (Holman Jones, Adams, & Ellis, 2013, p. 34) and laugh with great hilarity as I watched and witnessed death passed me by. "What is liberated by a straightforward and simple soul's mourning can also be life", Cixous (1993, p. 12) writes and seems to mirror my hope that this kind of work about the words and worlds of writing critical autoethnography offers something close, so close, of the self-same to others. The door to the room of one's own where death awaits us is open; to danger in writing then, as critical autoethnographers we must go in order that we may live.

4.

Tell me, did she provide a definition of critical autoethnography?
No, not a definite one, two or three.
Did she tell the truth about her auto/ethnographic work?
No, the truth was never on her agenda.
Did she include reliable data and reportable facts from the field?
No, she wrote fiction tied lightly and tightly to shared memories, experiences and understandings.
Did she cite widely and appropriately?
No, she tried her damnedest to avoid appropriation, lest she be damned.
Did she cite writers like Carolyn Ellis, Stacy Holman Jones, Robin Boylorn, Soyini Madison, and Anne Harris *enough*?
No, but she hopes that she has chosen their words wisely and with love so that she might close, so close.
Did she include a separate discussion of feminism and autoethnographic work?
No, instead she engages in a relational conversation with feminists and feminist concepts who have become her critical and autoethnographic friends.
Did she *even* use *the* f word?
No, not just the f word, those f words, all of them, in all of their finery she wrote them in homage, in awe and in solidarity.
Did she explore literature on decoloniality?
No, she thought and wondered deeply about the c word and her place in it, and im/possibilities of the d word.
Did she explain what she means by embodied approaches in explicit terms?
No, she wrote through her body implicitly and explicitly for her woman's writing must be heard.
Did she follow her original book proposal at *all*?
No, because this is the book-she-doesn't-write.

5.

And then there he was. Standing by the side of her bed, just watching, watching and waiting and wasting the moment. She woke with a fright; he was not meant to be there. She knew she was going to die. He had come for her in the dead of night to render her lifeless. She was not surprised, she too had been waiting and watching and wasting for this moment to arrive and when all was said and done, she was ready. She stared at him in the dark, both of them a shadow of what they once were and knew. Their voices were lost but their eyes knew how to find one another, and in that instant, a sure but certain recognition passed between them. He was there to annihilate and destroy her. She didn't argue or answer back; there was no point. She had been in this place so long and had lost the will to fight.

"You're wasting my time", he said as he moved towards her.

"Minutes, hours, days have passed by in this the same-same way, it's always the same", he said as he grabbed her hands and roughly pulled her up from the bed.

"There are so many things you didn't do", he said, his face so close she could taste the dis-tase for her in his mouth.

"You are done, you have no more moves to make, nothing new to say", he said as his reached for her throat.

"What is your life worth if you have wasted it?" He said as he began to strangle her.

"What I think", he said, "is that it's a life not worth much at all, a wasteful and wasted life". As she struggled to breathe she saw herself standing on the edge of a chasm ready to fall.

"Falling is one way", a-not/her whispered, "flying is another way a-way".

"Kill the false woman who is preventing the live one from breathing. Inscribed the breath of the whole woman" (Cixous, 1976, p. 880), a-not/her whispered again.

"Write and return yourself to your body, your body to yourself, a-not/her continued to whisper. The moment of your liberation has come", a-not/her whispered once more.

She heard the whisper; she felt it giving her life breath life. His voice became a dull mumble, his hands on her neck a breakable chain.

"Stop", she softly stammered.

"StoP", she said, spitting out the elocution.

"StOP!" she shouted.

"STOP!" She screamed a roar that shattered the sky and lit up the stars.

She spread her arms wide, stepped forward into the abyss; and flew. And then there she was.

6.

What astonishes me is what I do not know; it is *so* astonishing, and it leaves me speechless, without a world of words, without words to world. At the ending of this book-I-don't-write I find myself dwelling in a *kind* of Cixousian silence (Cixous, in Cixous & Calle-Gruber, 1997, p. 72); nothing more to say, nothing more to see, nothing more to write. I have turned and tossed and re/turned to throw myself backwards and forwards through memories and moments of being; a self being in moments with others, always and already with others, as a way to think and wonder who I/we are as critical autoethnographer/s. What astounds me is that I still do not know; the answer escapes me: a fear, a sorrow, a grief, an intensity, an excitement, a passion; these call me to attention and remind me that in the end, a not-knowing *kind* of critical autoethnography is perhaps the *kind* of critical autoethnography that seeks to be written.

Kind critical autoethnography; researching and writing that follows a heartline and a headtype that suggests the nature of what, how and why it might be done in that kind of a-way by that kind of people. "You know what kind", my mother-in-law would say to me with a knowing look, "*that* kind!"

Kind critical autoethnography; affectionate and affective researching and writing that turns and re/turns us to empathy, love, and compassion as an ethico-onto-epistemological sense-ability and response-ability.

Kind critical autoethnography; a willful sifting and searching for the right kind of words to kindly put the betweenus worlds as, through and with research and writing; always already in relation all of the twos in the world as one and the other, this *kind* of critical autoethnography will find a-way.

Kind critical autoethnography; a-way to write words about worlds without absorbing, acquiescing, appropriating and annihilating, but apprehending, making space in the pause inbetweenus.

Kind critical autoethnography; do I/we/you know what *kind*?

What awakens me and keeps me "woke" is the kind of critical autoethnography that insists, we are what we are not yet (after Greene, 2005) but forever on the a-way; what we "still have to discover is endless" (Cixous, in Cixous & Calle-Gruber, 1997, p. 72) and that *kind* of critical autoethnography is worth w/ri/gh/ting for.

7.

Let me list the ways.

List, n.1, a row or line.

He reads mine, I read his; our words and worlds becoming a betweenus on the page that is life.

List, v.1, meaning to prefer, to choose or to be inclined.

He stands beside me—not in front of me, not behind me but by my side—and lovingly holds my body, mind and heart as I search for and select the words which seek to come close, so close, to the "grains of truth embedded in all this mass of paper". (Woolf, 1929/2011, p. 30).

List, v.2, in nauticle parlance as to lean to one side.

When I am not sure whether to take this re/turn to worlds in words, he is there, beside me, and opens his arms so that I might lean into his love; a love that does not wish to want and own, a love that lets go as one and the two; always and already love waiting there.

List, v.3, from hylst (hearing), to harken, to hear, to list-en to.

His gifts me the words that speaks the worlds I cannot bear to say.

List, v.4, to insert in a list, as in public service, as soldiers, to en-list. List, v.4i, to enclose for combat.

This is what he does; he gently holds my face in his hands and lets me fly to, for and in love with him, in love with writing, I have arrived. I have re/turned from a-far a-way and I am ready to "to break up the 'truth' with laughter" (Cixous, 1976, p. 888).

8.

The day begins in an ordinary way.

"So, everyone still breathing?" I ask.

Max and Hamish have just joined me at the kitchen bench for breakfast. Hamish's face is still crumpled and creased from sleep, he manages a nod.

"Yes Mum," Max says softly, "Alive and well".

We ask this question of each other daily, just to make us smile, just to make sure.

"And you Mum? Are you still breathing on your own?" Max laughs.

His words are a shout out to a song called "Still breathing" by American punk rock band Green Day from their latest album *Revolution radio* (Armstrong, Dirnt, & Cool, 2016). It's number one on my playlist at the moment and when I listen to the lyrics in the second verse, "I'm like a son who was raised without a father, I'm like a mother barely keeping it together", I'm convinced Billie Joe Armstrong had us in mind when he wrote this song.

"Oh, I'm still alive," I sing a line from the song back to him in reply. "What's on the plan for today boys?"

"Our QCS (Queensland Core Skills) practice tests start today Mum. And I couldn't give a fuck!" Max takes a bite of his peanut butter on toast. He is now 17 and in Year 12, the tail end of high school, and so far, so good.

"Spanish, history, Maths and then footy training tonight", Hamish is now awake and fully present. He is at the front end of high school and the smile on his face tells me he is looking forward to a good day.

"What have you got on today Mum?" he asks.

I pause; work. So much has changed—I have changed. I am not sure showing up each day to work means anything anymore. Showing up to writing however, *that* means something.

"I'm going to work from home today I think", I give a safe answer. "I need to write like a monstrous woman if I am going to finish this book".

Max puts his plate in the sink and his arm around my shoulder, "I have faith in you Mum, you'll get it done, you always do".

"Yeah Mum", Hamish echoes his big brother and he points to the pile of books and papers spread across the dining room table, "just channel Hélène Cixous and laugh like the Medusa, that's the way you like to write!"

"Wait—what? How do you even *know* that Mishka? How do you even *know* who that woman is, what did she say her name was?" Max shakes his head incredulously.

"I", Hamish points to himself, "*I* know these things Max because I read, *and* I take notice of things people are reading". He gives Max a reproachful look well beyond his years.

"Yeah whatever Mishka moo. Gotta go Mum!" Max grabs the lunch I have made for him and heads for the door.

"Max! Max! Max!" Hamish scrambles to pack his bag. "Can I get a lift?"

"Oh what? Hurry up then, while we're still young!" Max stops, waits and walks back to the bench.

"Mum?" His voice is quiet.

"Mmm?" I murmur back, absorbed in the daily crossword which has arrived in my inbox.

"I forgot something", he says as the arms of a six foot two eyes of blue young man wrap around me. "I love you Mum".

"What's up with you two?" Hamish looks across the room and hesitates. "Is this a group hug?"

"Sure, come here Mishka", Max pulls his little brother into our embrace.

And the day begins again in a most extra-ordinary way.

References

Armstrong, B. J., Dirnt, T., & Cool, T. (2016). Still breathing [Recorded by Green Day] On *Revolution radio* [Digital download]. New York, NY: Reprise.

Cixous, H. (1976). The laugh of the Medusa (K. Cohen & P. Cohen, Trans.). *Signs, 1*(4), 875–893.

Cixous, H. (1993). *Three steps on the ladder of writing*. New York, NY: Columbia University Press.

Cixous, H., & Calle-Gruber, M. (1997). *Rootprints: Memory and life writing*. London: Routledge.

Ellis, C. (2004). *The ethnographic I*. Walnut Creek, CA: AltaMira Press.

Greene, M. (2005). *Releasing the imagination: Essays on education, the arts, and social change* (The Jossey-Bass education series). San Francisco, CA: Jossey-Bass.

Holman Jones, S., Adams, T. E., & Ellis, C. (2013). Introduction: Coming to know autoethnography as more than method. In S. Holman Jones, T. E. Adams, & C. Ellis (Eds.), *Handbook of autoethnography* (pp. 17–48). Walnut Creek, CA: Left Coast Press.

Woolf, V. (1929/2001). *A room of one's own*. London: Vintage Press.

Woolf, V. (1980). *The diary of Virginia Woolf, Volume III: 1925–1930* (A. E. Bell, Ed.). London: Hogarth Press.

Index

© The Author(s) 2019
E. Mackinlay, *Critical Writing for Embodied Approaches*,
https://Doi.org/10.1007/978-3-030-04669-9

Printed in the United States
By Bookmasters